For The
Perfecting
Of The
Saints

BOOK II
The Power Pack For Preacher Series

For The
Perfecting
Of The
Saints

BOOK II
The Power Pack For Preacher Series

Dr. Ronald Sanders PhD.

ARPress
ILLUMINATING IDEAS
EMPOWERING VOICES

Special thanks to:
King James Version of the Bible
Bible Works 5 Software
Strong's Exhausted Concordance of the Bible

We would like to thank Pastor Gardner Kealon for the use of the cover picture.
This picture was taken in Richmond, VA. during one of Pastor Kealon's tent revivals.

ARPress
45 Dan Road Suite 5
Canton MA 02021

Hotline:	1(888) 821-0229
Fax:	1(508) 545-7580

Ordering Information:

Quantity sales. Special discounts are available on quantity purchases by corporations, associations, and others. For details, contact the publisher at the address above.

Printed in the United States of America.

ISBN-13:	Softcover	979-8-89330-736-8
	eBook	979-8-89330-737-5

Library of Congress Control Number: 2024902784

For The Perfecting Of the Saints
(Book Two of Power Pack For Preachers)
Contents

Prayer for Salvation

Jesus,
Forgive my sins,
Come into my heart,
Be Lord of my life,
Change my life Lord,
Make me what you want me to be,
Give me peace and joy,
In Jesus' name, Amen.

If you believed the prayer you just prayed, then according to God's word you have gotten saved. It is up to you what you do from this point on. You can get into a good church, read your Bible and pray everyday, or you can go back to the life you just came out of. The choice is yours, but I ask you, why not give God an opportunity to truly change your lifestyle and the direction your life was headed?

For more information about this study and other books,
contact us @

Dr. Ronald Sanders PhD
Apostle
5448 Palmers Branch Dr. NE
Leland, NC 28451
910- 470- 9126 Cell
fbiconference@aol.com

Is That
You Lord?

We will study the 9 ways God deals with man. As Christians, God is always communicating with us, but do we recognize him when he is? We pray that through this study, it will become clear how God moves upon us and how to be receptive to his Spirit.

Revised by Dr. Ronald Sanders PhD on 08/07/05

Chapter I

IS THAT YOU LORD?

Revised 08/05/05 from "Is That You Lord" written in 1997 by Rev. Ronald Sanders

Have you ever asked yourself the question "Is that you Lord? This study will attempt to give better understanding of how God deals with man. God's love for us is so overwhelming and we for the most part are so clueless. I have found nine ways that God deals with man. In this study we will explain each of these manifestations of God's presence. The nine ways are:

1) The word of God
2) A small still voice
3) Impressions
4) Prophesy
5) Audible voice
6) Visions
7) Dreams
8) Revelations
9) Visitations

In asking the question "Is that you lord", there are two things to keep in mind. The word will always confirm these two things.

1) Any word or impression from God will never contradict the written word of God. It will confirm and reveal a clearer understanding of it.

Galatians. 1:

6 I marvel that ye are so soon removed from him that called you into the grace of Christ unto another **gospel**:

7 Which is not another; but there be some that trouble you, and **would pervert the gospel of Christ.**

8 But though we, or an angel from heaven, **preach any other gospel** unto you than that which we have preached unto you, **let him be accursed.**

That's pretty simple to understand. If it does not line up with the word of God, then it's not God! God said;

Numbers. 23:

19 **God** *is* **not a man**, that he should lie; neither the son of man, **that he should repent: hath he said, and shall he not do it? or hath he spoken, and shall he not make it good?**

20 Behold, I have received *commandment* to bless: and he hath blessed; and I cannot reverse it.

God doesn't have the luxury of changing his mind after he has spoken it. He cannot lie nor contradict himself. That's powerful when it comes to understanding the leading of God. Even though God's actions astound you, his words or his leading will not.

Isaiah 28:

9 Whom shall he teach knowledge? and whom shall he make to understand doctrine? *them that are weaned from the milk, and* drawn from the breasts.

10 For **precept** *must* **be upon precept**, precept upon precept; **line upon line, line** upon line; here a little, *and* there a little:

11 For with stammering lips and another tongue will he speak to this people.

12 To whom he said, This is the rest *wherewith* ye may cause the weary to rest; and this *is* the refreshing: yet they would not hear.

13 But the word of the LORD was unto them precept upon precept, precept upon precept; line upon line, line upon line; here a little, *and* there a little; that they might go, and fall backward, and be broken, and snared, and taken.

Because the word is so dependable, it will cause rest to your soul. You can rest assured that what is spoken is true.

I Thessalonians 5:
23 And the very **God of peace** sanctify you wholly; and *I pray God* **your whole spirit and soul and body be preserved blameless** unto the coming of our Lord Jesus Christ.

When God leads, it's with a peace. The word will keep you blameless and righteous before God.

2) That leads us to the second thing we can be assured of in following his lead. Not only can we rely on the truth of God and his unchanging word but we also will have a peace about what God is dealing with us about.

Hebrews 10:
15 *Whereof* the **Holy Ghost also is a witness to us**: for after that he had said before,
16 This is the covenant that I will make with them after those days, saith the Lord, I will put my laws **into their hearts, and in their minds will I write them;**
17 And their sins and iniquities will I remember no more.
18 Now where remission of these is, *there* is no more offering for sin.
19 **Having therefore,** brethren, boldness to enter into the holiest by the blood of Jesus,
20 By a new and living way, which he hath consecrated for us, through the veil, that is to say, his flesh;
21 And *having* an high priest over the house of God;
22 Let us **draw near with a true heart in full assurance of faith**, having our hearts sprinkled from an evil conscience, and our bodies washed with pure water.
23 **Let us hold fast the profession of our faith without wavering**; (for he is faithful that promised;)
Several things here we need to pay attention to. The Holy Ghost or Holy Spirit is our witness. Where you may ask, in our hearts and mind. Why? Because he wrote his laws there. Having therefore his laws in our heart because we have

received his redemption for our sins, we can live and walk in a boldness of God knowing his leading is the leading of peace.

John 14:
26 But the Comforter, *which* is **the Holy Ghost**, whom the Father will send in my name, **he shall teach you all things, and bring all things to your remembrance, whatsoever I have said unto you.**
27 Peace I leave with you, my peace I give unto you: not as the world giveth, give I unto you. Let not your heart be troubled, neither let it be afraid.

To put it simply. If it's not of peace, it's not of God!

I Corinthians 14:
33 For God is not *the* **author** of **confusion**, but of peace, as in all churches of the saints.
40 Let all things be done decently and in order.

Twice in this one chapter God impresses Paul to pen these words concerning peace. This is in the church. How much more does it apply to our personal lives?

James 3:
15 This wisdom descendeth not from above, but is earthly, sensual, devilish.
16 For **where envying and strife** is, there is confusion and every evil work.
17 But the wisdom that is from above is first pure, then peaceable, gentle, *and* easy to be intreated, full of mercy and good fruits, without partiality, and without hypocrisy.
18 And the **fruit of righteousness is sown in peace of them that make peace.**

If you think God is dealing with you and it comes in line with verse 15- 16, then you know it's not of God; but, if it comes in line with 17- 18, you know it's of God! One thing we have to understand about the leading of God is that God isn't going to beat you over the head to commune with you. Finally watch this next scripture.

Romans 8:

14 For as many as are led by the Spirit of God, they are the sons of God.

15 For ye have not received the spirit of bondage again to fear; but ye have received the Spirit of adoption, whereby we cry, Abba, Father.

16 **The Spirit itself beareth witness with our spirit,** that we are the children of God:

17 And if children, then heirs; heirs of God, and joint-heirs with Christ; if so be that we suffer with *him*, **that we may be also glorified together.**

If we are being led of the Spirit then his spirit will bear witness with us. If we walk in Christ then Christ ought also to walk in us. If such wonderful communion exists between us, then how much more should we be attentive to the Spirit of God and not to doubt so much?

I. THE WORD OF GOD

II Timothy 3:
14 But continue thou in the things which thou hast learned and hast been assured of, knowing of whom thou hast learned *them;*
15 And that from a child thou hast known the holy scriptures, which are able to make thee wise unto salvation through faith which is in Christ Jesus.
16 **All scripture *is* given by inspiration of God, and *is* profitable for doctrine, for reproof, for correction, for instruction in righteousness:**
17 **That the man of God may be perfect, throughly furnished unto all good works.**

God says continue in the things you have learned. Learned from where? The word of God. In our society today so many people doubt the legitimacy of God's word. Some say it is not for today. Some say it doesn't apply to us. Some say it is left up for interpretation of each individual. The fact is, if we are called by the name of Christ, then we ought to follow the word of Christ. Yes, we need to study in order to grasp an understanding of what the word is saying to us and how we can apply it today. That's why we have Strong's concordances so we can understand the word as it was originally given. You may ask why that is so important. Let me explain. Seventy-five years ago there was an English word that had only one meaning. That word was "pot". Today the word pot has multiple meanings. One, something to cook in. Two, something to sit by the bed to poop in. Three, something to put plants in. Four, something you smoke that is illegal. Five, something you put wood in to keep warm on construction sites. Six, something that crabs are caught in. You see what I mean? One simple word means so much. Research will reveal which one applies to our situation. It in no way compromises what the bible says, but clarifies so there is no misunderstanding. Here, look at this scripture.

II Timothy 2:
14 Of these things put *them* in remembrance, charging *them* before the Lord that they strive not about words to no profit, *but* to the subverting of the hearers.
15 **Study to shew thyself approved unto God**, a **workman** that needeth **not to be ashamed, rightly dividing the word of truth.**
16 But shun profane *and* vain babblings: for they will increase unto more ungodliness.

We are to study for revelation understanding of the word; so we won't be made ashamed. If we don't study we will just be stupid and be easily led astray by every wind of doctrine. So many who have learned something want to argue and debate the word. God said not to strive about with words. See the word of God is a fact and a concrete line in time. Our opinion of this word does not change the truth of it. The word is still the truth no matter what we think of it or interpret it. The word does not line up with us but rather we have to line up with the word.

Ephesians 4:
14 That we *henceforth* be no more children, tossed to and fro, and **carried about with every wind of doctrine, by the sleight of men,** *and* **cunning craftiness,** whereby **they lie in wait to deceive;**
15 But **speaking the truth in love**, may grow up into him in all things, which is the head, even Christ:

God is tired of his people being spiritually illiterate. The old cliché "Stupid is as stupid does" applies very well here. That's why there are so many cults in the United States. People assume so much with so little evidence. Oh, or are too lazy to research and find out the truth about the scripture.

I Timothy 4:
14 Neglect not the gift that is in thee, which was given thee by prophecy, with the laying on of the hands of the presbytery.
15 **Meditate** upon **these things**; give thyself **wholly** to them; that thy profiting may appear to all.

16 Take heed unto thyself, and unto the doctrine; continue in them: for in doing this thou shalt both save thyself, and them that hear thee.

Meditation takes time and effort. If we don't pray and ask for revelation knowledge, then we can believe a lie and be damned.

II Thessalonians 2:
9 *Even him*, whose coming is after the working of Satan with all power and signs and lying wonders,
10 And with all deceivableness of unrighteousness in them that perish; because they received not the love of the truth, that they might be saved.
11 And for this cause **God shall send them strong delusion, that they should believe a lie:**
12 **That they all might be damned who believed not the truth**, but had pleasure in unrighteousness.
13 But we are bound to give thanks always to God for you, brethren beloved of the Lord, because God hath from the beginning chosen you to salvation through **sanctification of the Spirit and belief of the truth:**

There's more at stake than just my opinion. Your soul lies in the balance. Do we agree because it feels good, or do we obey because it gives life? We either believe the word because it is written by inspiration of God or we delete or dilute the word because we don't agree. God's word will always be:

Genesis 41:
15 And Pharaoh said unto Joseph, I have dreamed a dream, and there is none that can interpret it: and I have heard say of thee, that thou canst understand a dream to interpret it.
16 And Joseph answered Pharaoh, saying, It is not in me: God shall give Pharaoh an answer of peace.
Who gives the answer of peace? That's right, God does. If the word is true then you will feel and know the answer of peace. Because:

I Corinthians 14:
33 For God is not the author of confusion, but of peace, as in all churches of the saints.

By this shall all men know that you are of God by the peace in serving him? God doesn't cause or encourage anything but peace. The word is peace!

John 5:
39 Search the scriptures; for in them ye think ye have eternal life: and they are they which testify of me.

How do you know if there is truly life in the scriptures unless you search them out? Just because you know a few scriptures from the bible, eternal life is not just given to those who can quote John 3: 16, but to them who hear it, apply it and live it. Then you have eternal life. How can he minister to us through his word if we are not willing to search the scriptures to find out the revelations God has for your life? The old cliché "If you don't stand for something, you'll fall for anything" applies well here. Why do people serve God any old way and think its all right?

Hosea 4:
4 Yet let no man strive, nor reprove another: for thy people are as they that strive with the priest.
5 Therefore shalt thou fall in the day, and the prophet also shall fall with thee in the night, and I will destroy thy mother.
6 My people are destroyed for lack of knowledge: because thou hast rejected knowledge, I will also reject thee, that thou shalt be no priest to me: seeing thou hast forgotten the law of thy God, I will also forget thy children.
7 As they were increased, so they sinned against me: therefore will I change their glory into shame.
God's word here is stern. He says he will destroy not just you, but the ability to hear from God by killing your preachers. Then to make sure your insolence won't spread, God will destroy your mom. Because we don't read and study to know God,

he said he would allow the generational curses to arise again and destroy your children and their descendants. God says he will forget you and your children. How can that be? Let's find out.

Ezekiel 18:
20 The soul that sinneth, it shall die. The son shall not bear the iniquity of the father, neither shall the father bear the iniquity of the son: the righteousness of the righteous shall be upon him, and the wickedness of the wicked shall be upon him.

21 But if the wicked will turn from all his sins that he hath committed, and keep all my statutes, and do that which is lawful and right, he shall surely live, he shall not die.

22 All his transgressions that he hath committed, they shall not be mentioned unto him: in his righteousness that he hath done he shall live.

23 Have I any pleasure at all that the wicked should die? saith the Lord God: and not that he should return from his ways, and live?

24 But when the righteous turneth away from his righteousness, and committeth iniquity, and doeth according to all the abominations that the wicked man doeth, shall he live? All his righteousness that he hath done shall not be mentioned: in his trespass that he hath trespassed, and in his sin that he hath sinned, in them shall he die.

The point I'm making is this. If you don't read and study the word of God you will backslide and fall away from God. It doesn't matter how many souls you have led to Christ or how many miracles you've done, if you walk away from God he will not even remember who you were in the day that you stand before him! How sad is that? I hope we have established the necessity of reading and studying the word of God. How can we avoid such a travesty?

Deuteronomy 4:
9 Only take heed to thyself, and keep thy soul diligently, lest thou forget the things which thine eyes have seen, and lest

they depart from thy heart all the days of thy life: but teach them thy sons, and thy sons' sons;

10 Especially the day that thou stoodest before the LORD thy God in Horeb, when the LORD said unto me, Gather me the people together, and I will make them hear my words, that they may learn to fear me all the days that they shall live upon the earth, and that they may teach their children.

We can avoid God forgetting us by taking heed and not forgetting the word of God. Then teach them to the next generations after you. You are leaving a spiritual heritage or as the bible called it "The blessing". You can't teach what you don't know. Ignorance begets superstitions and witchcraft. Back to I Timothy 4: 16. You will save yourself and them that will hear thee. Thank God!

A precedent has to be set first. That precedent is that the word of God is truth as was spit out of the mouth of God.

II Peter 1:

16 For we have not followed cunningly devised fables, when we made known unto you the power and coming of our Lord Jesus Christ, but were eyewitnesses of his majesty.

17 For he received from God the Father honour and glory, when there came such a voice to him from the excellent glory, This is my beloved Son, in whom I am well pleased.

18 And this voice which came from heaven we heard, when we were with him in the holy mount.

19 We have also a more sure word of prophecy; whereunto ye do well that ye take heed, as unto a light that shineth in a dark place, until the day dawn, and the day star arise in your hearts:

20 Knowing this first, that no prophecy of the scripture is of any private interpretation.

21 For the prophecy came not in old time by the will of man: but holy men of God spake as they were moved by the Holy Ghost.

Oops, there it is! We have stayed with the word and not deviated. We have not obeyed superstitions and religious fables. The sure word of prophecy that they heard was written down for us to know and can't be changed. God reveals his word to whosoever will hear and obey it. God moved and the men of God responded by writing down what was told them. My question to you is, why aren't you writing down what God is telling and showing you? Do you think the word of revelation he is giving you through the bible is any less important? The bible is the sure foundation that all other foundations have to be built on. The revelations of God that you receive today may still be read in a hundred years with the same anointing that you felt as you wrote it! If you don't write it, then how will they read it? I know, you want me to prove it, well ok.

I Peter 3:
15 But sanctify the Lord God in your hearts: and be ready always to give an answer to every man that asketh you a reason of the hope that is in you with meekness and fear:

2 Corinthians 3:
1 Do we begin again to commend ourselves? or need we, as some others, epistles of commendation to you, or letters of commendation from you?
2 Ye are our epistle written in our hearts, known and read of all men:
3 Forasmuch as ye are manifestly declared t o be the epistle of Christ ministered by us, written n ot with ink, but with the Spirit of the living God; not in tables of stone, but in fleshy tables of the heart.

There is so much written in your heart. God has changed your life and made the word alive. What you have seen heard and experienced is all tucked away in your spirit. So…

Habakkuk 1:
2 And the LORD answered me, and said, Write the vision, and make it plain upon tables, that he may run that readeth it.

3 For the vision is yet for an appointed time, but at the end it shall speak, and not lie: though it tarry, wait for it; because it will surely come, it will not tarry.

4 Behold, his soul which is lifted up is not upright in him: but the just shall live by his faith.

How can they see your faith? By obeying the word and write it down. Make it plain where anyone can understand. Your writings may not hit the best sellers list today, but God has an appointed time for it to change the face of Christianity, as we know it. Look at the teachings of Dr. Charles Stanley, and many others. They have changed how we think and respond to Christ forever. Do you think they started writing thinking they would change the course of religious history? Of course not, they were just obedient trusting God to be financially able to pay for the vision and desire God had set upon them. Yet today, they are great icons in the history of the church. You may be the next landmark!

By reading and studying we find another phenomenon.

I Peter 5:

9 Whom resist stedfast in the faith, knowing that the same afflictions are accomplished in your brethren that are in the world.

10 But the God of all grace, who hath called us unto his eternal glory by Christ Jesus, after that ye have suffered a while, make you perfect, stablish, strengthen, settle you.

11 To him be glory and dominion for ever and ever. Amen.

We see that others before us have fought and won the same trials that we are now experiencing. The advantage we have is, they wrote down the trials and how they won the victory. You now have a road map to go by. It wasn't by accident that the authors of the bible pinned the things they did.

Hebrews 4:

14 Seeing then that we have a great high priest, that is passed into the heavens, Jesus the Son of God, let us hold fast our profession.

15 For we have not an high priest which cannot be touched with the feeling of our infirmities; but was in all points tempted like as we are, yet without sin.

16 Let us therefore come boldly unto the throne of grace, that we may obtain mercy, and find grace to help in time of need. God knew we needed help so he sent Jesus. Jesus knew that in the mouth of two or three witnesses we would believe so he not only lived it for us but great men and women of God lived it after him showing us the way to conquer all our fears and infirmities. The word of God lives!

II. SMALL STILL VOICE

I have found that one of the hardest things to do as a Christian is to get still and quiet my mind. Yet this small still voice we will address is one of the greatest keys to hearing the voice of God. God will guide you by this small still voice more than any other way that we will discuss in this study. I have heard any number of preachers tell me that God does not speak to man. I wanted to laugh but out of respect I wouldn't. When you're so tied up and hurried with life's events, of course you won't hear God's voice? Watch this scripture.

I Kings 19:
9 And he came thither unto a cave, and lodged there; and, behold, the **word of the LORD** came to him, and he said unto him, **What doest thou here, Elijah?**
10 And he said, I have been very jealous for the LORD God of hosts: for the children of Israel have forsaken thy covenant, thrown down thine altars, and slain thy prophets with the sword; and I, *even* I only, am left; and they seek my life, to take it away.
11 And he said, Go forth, and stand upon the mount before the LORD. And, behold, the LORD passed by, and a great and strong wind rent the mountains, and brake in pieces the rocks before the LORD; but the LORD *was* not in the wind: and after the wind an earthquake; *but* the LORD was not in the earthquake:
12 And after the earthquake a fire; *but* the LORD *was* not in the fire: and after the fire a still small voice.
13 And it was *so*, when Elijah heard *it*, that he wrapped his face in his mantle, and went out, and stood in the entering in of the cave. And, behold, *there came* a **voice unto him,** and said, **What doest thou here, Elijah?**
14 **And he said**, I have been very jealous for the LORD God of hosts: because the children of Israel have forsaken thy covenant, thrown down thine altars, and slain thy prophets with the sword; and I, *even* I only, am left; and they seek my life, to take it away.

18 Yet I have left *me* seven thousand in Israel, all the knees which have not bowed unto Baal, and every mouth which hath not kissed him.

Elijah was one of the most unique prophets you'll ever read about. He had initiative. He had a confidence in God that others didn't. He saw an injustice and he fixed it. Most of the times he challenged the Gods of Baal, he did it on his own initiative. He didn't receive a word from God to go and insult their Gods. However, God always supported Elijah when he did. They had such a bond of unity that was unheard of in the Old Testament. Yet one very important aspect of Elijah was that he knew the voice of God and listened. Notice that before he went out to stand on the mount, he was communing with God and hearing God already. God just wanted to emphasize the importance of knowing the true voice of God and teaching us the same. God wasn't heard in the great noise of the wind, earthquake or even the fire. Now you would think that God would have been in the fire wouldn't you? Of course you would, me too. Even though God has ministered to man in these ways that was not the precedent God wanted to set here. So many times in our life we are looking for God to answer by fire or by fleeces and he doesn't. That leaves us bewildered and confused. Actually the whole time God was trying to speak to us in a small still voice. If God had to always speak to us as an earthquake or fire, then it would be no better than God trying to train a dog. There is always another reason that God desires to speak in a soft voice.

Proverbs 15:
1 A soft answer turneth away wrath: but grievous words stir up anger.

When God speaks in a soft voice, it enhances his peace in us. When our parents spoke loudly to us, we had great concern as to what we had done now. As long as my mom spoke in a soft voice, I knew I was in pretty good shape and I wasn't in trouble.

I Corinthians 14:
33 For God is not *the author* of confusion, but of peace, as in all churches of the saints.
40 Let all things be done decently and in order.

In a crisis situation we have found that a calm voice will get quicker results every time over a loud emotional tone. God's desire toward us is to invoke love. He would rather lead us like a small toy sail boat. Just a slight touch on one side or the other would send that boat across the pond. Ever so gentle a nudge. God is teaching us to be nudged by him. If God always spoke in an audible tone, where would the faith be? Watch this next scripture.

Acts 8:
29 Then **the Spirit said unto Philip**, Go near, and join thyself to this chariot.
30 And Philip ran thither to *him*, and heard him read the prophet Esaias, and said, Understandest thou what thou readest?
31 And he said, How can I, except some man should guide me? And he desired Philip that he would come up and sit with him.

The Spirit spoke and Philip went. When he spoke to the Ethiopian eunuch he was already trying to figure out what the prophet Isaiah was speaking. The largest fear anyone has when dealing with the spirit of God is; "Is That You Lord?" God is always confirming his directions. He will never lead you astray.

II Corinthians 10:
1 Now I Paul myself beseech you by the **meekness and gentleness of Christ, who in presence *am* base among you**, but being absent am bold toward you:
The spirit of Christ is meek and gentle. So shall his voice be. If we are following his voice in obedience, then we will have a meek and gentle voice also. How can two walk together lest they be agreed?

Matthew 11:

25 At that time Jesus answered and said, I thank thee, O Father, Lord of heaven and earth, because thou hast hid these things from the wise and prudent, and hast revealed them unto babes.

26 Even so, Father: for so it seemed good in thy sight.

27 All things are delivered unto me of my Father: and no man knoweth the Son, but the Father; neither knoweth any man the Father, save the Son, and he to whomsoever the Son will reveal *him*.

28 Come unto me, all ye that labour and are heavy laden, and I will give you rest.

29 Take my yoke upon you, and learn of me; for I am meek and **lowly** in **heart**: and ye shall find rest unto your souls.

30 For my yoke *is* easy, and my burden is light.

Doesn't he say that he will deal with us as sons and heirs of salvation? He has revealed his heart to us and will convey his heart to us just as he would a child. That means several things. First, he will speak softly. Secondly, he will do it with simplicity. Thirdly, he will impart to us his peace and liberty. That reminds me of two scriptures.

Hebrews 12:

6 For whom the Lord loveth he chasteneth, and scourgeth every son whom he receiveth.

7 **If ye endure chastening, God dealeth with you as with sons**; for what son is he whom the father chasteneth not?

14 **Follow peace with all *men*, and holiness,** without which no man shall see the Lord:

15 Looking diligently lest any man fail of the grace of God; lest any root of bitterness springing up trouble *you*, and thereby many be defiled;

He deals with us as sons because he loves us. Yet if he commands us to follow peace then how much more will he deal with us in peace?

Romans 12:

6 Having then gifts differing according to the grace that is given to us, whether prophecy, *let us prophesy* according to the proportion of faith;

7 Or ministry, let us wait on our ministering: or he that teacheth, on teaching;

8 Or he that exhorteth, on exhortation: he that giveth, **let him do it with simplicity**; he that ruleth, with diligence; he that sheweth mercy, with cheerfulness

God's word to us is not hard to understand. Neither should our word to anyone else be hard to understand.

John 14:

23 Jesus answered and said unto him, If a man love me, he will keep my words: and my Father will love him, and we will come unto him, and make our abode with him.

24 He that loveth me not keepeth not my sayings: and the word which ye hear is not mine, but the Father's which sent me.

25 These things have I spoken unto you, being *yet* present with you.

26 But the Comforter, *which is* the Holy Ghost, whom the Father will send in my name, he shall teach you all things, and bring all things to your remembrance, whatsoever I have said unto you.

Too many ministers today don't know the voice of God. Many have confessed that they have never heard the small still voice of God. Jesus starts here telling his disciples that he will speak to them. I know what you're thinking; he was talking about then while he was here in the flesh. Yet he concluded this conversation with the promise that he would not stop speaking to his people by sending the Holy Ghost to speak to us the words the Father would desire you to hear. It's not the word here that will come to remembrance, but the actual words he will speak to you during your life. Think about it? Well, how do I know that I can hear his voice?

John 10:
26 But ye believe not, because ye are not of my sheep, as I said unto you.
27 My sheep hear my voice, and I know them, and they follow me:
28 And I give unto them eternal life; and they shall never perish, neither shall any *man* pluck them out of my hand.
If we are unable to hear his voice today, it's because we are not his sheep. As long as the Father has given us eternal life and he has keeping power over us, then we can also hear his voice!

John 14:
15 If ye love me, keep my commandments.
16 And I will pray the Father, and he shall give you another Comforter, that he may abide with you for ever;
17 *Even* **the Spirit of truth**; whom the world cannot receive, because it seeth him not, neither knoweth him: but ye know him; for **he dwelleth with you,** and shall be in you.
18 I will **not leave you comfortless: I will come to you.**
19 Yet a little while, and the world seeth me no more; but ye see me: because I live, ye shall live also.
20 At that day ye shall know that I *am* in my Father, and ye in me, and I in you.
21 He that hath my commandments, and keepeth them, he it is that loveth me: and he that loveth me shall be loved of my Father, and I will love him, and will manifest myself to him.

Watch the word **manifest**.

1718 evmfani,zw emphanizo {em-fan-id'-zo}
Meaning: 1) to manifest, exhibit to view 2) to show one's self, come to view, appear, be manifest 3) to indicate, disclose, declare, make known

Christ will reveal him self to us. Let me not get ahead of myself. We can see him because he lives in us. When we look in the mirror each morning we should see Christ. The word **Christian** means;

5546 Cristiano,j Christianos {khris-tee-an-os'}
Meaning: 1) Christian, a follower of Christ

Which is a duplicator of him? So many boast that they are Christians with a joint or beer in their hands. This statement "Christian" has become a byword because we live in America. That's like saying because I live in America I'm rich. You and I know that there is nothing further from the truth. We are indeed blessed, but with the degree of starving and homeless in America, to say we are all rich is a lie. So is the word Christian America. If I am a Christian I will be unique and different from the world. I can never quite understand why people who are so in love with the devil want to try and convince us they are Christ like? They need to get a life, and that life is Christ! Enough on that subject.

III. IMPRESSIONS

Being impressed of God to go or do something is commonly misunderstood. We hope to uncover some of the mystery of being led of the spirit by impressions. As you grow in God impressions are not as obvious as when we first received Christ. When we first got saved it seemed like our heart would leap out of our chest when God impressed you to do something. As you grow in God that wondrous and mysterious feeling seems to lessen. Does that mean God is not using me through impressions? Of course not; God will continue to use impressions as a vital means of leading and guiding you through life's hurdles. So, let's get to it.

Matthew 4:
1 Then was Jesus led up of the Spirit into the wilderness to be tempted of the devil.
2 And when he had fasted forty days and forty nights, he was afterward an hungred.
3 And when the tempter came to him, he said, If thou be the Son of God, command that these stones be made bread.

First notice that the spirit of God led Christ into the wilderness. Why? For preparation. For what? Trials that were ahead. He was not led into the wilderness to be tempted, but to be in solitude to prepare. The trials he was about to face would take forty days of fasting to gain enough strength spiritually to overcome. What would have happened to Jesus if he had not been obedient to the spirit to get prepared? We may not have the plan of salvation, as we know it? This will be discussed in another teaching. Impressions are vitally important to us as Christians. Now back to John 14:

John 14:
15 If ye love me, keep my commandments.
16 And I will pray the Father, and **he shall give you another Comforter**, that he **may abide with you for ever;**

17 *Even* **the Spirit of truth**; whom the world cannot receive, because it seeth him not, neither knoweth him: but ye know him; for **he dwelleth with you, and shall be in you**.
18 I will **not leave you comfortless: I will come to you**.

I underlined comfortless. This is the impressions of God that bring comfort. He dwells with you and you will be led from the inside out.

I Corinthians 10:
13 There hath no temptation taken you but such as is common to man: but God *is* faithful, who will not suffer you to be tempted above that ye are able; but will with the temptation also make a way to escape, that ye may be able to bear *it*.

I watch so many people fall under the weight of temptations. Yet I am powerless to intervene on their behalf. Why, they will not let you. Yet the Holy Ghost of God has the advantage. He can minister from the heart of that individual.

John 16:
12 I have yet many things to say unto you, but ye cannot bear them now.
13 Howbeit when he, the Spirit of truth, is come, **he will guide you into all truth:** for he shall not speak of himself; but whatsoever he shall hear, *that* shall he speak: and **he will shew you things to come.**
14 He shall glorify me: for he shall receive of mine, and **shall shew *it* unto you**.

In my opinion, this is a powerful scripture on impressions and revelations. First he guides. How? You will feel like you need to go this way instead of the way you first thought or reasoned out. Impressions are just a thought transfer from God's heart to yours. In many testimonies this thought transfer has saved lives, transformed lives, and been the inspiration for divine appointments. My life has been saved on numerous occasions because I felt led or impressed to alter my schedule by waiting a few minutes longer or even taking a different route or approach. The reason God doesn't always deal with you on such a grand emotional scale is that emotions fail and can be rationalized. Impressions are slight movements of the spirit of God in you. Just like the sail boat we spoke of previously. It's all about faith. As Christians learn to trust your instincts. Because they got saved too! I don't want to get ahead of myself because so many of the ways God deals with man intertwine. The fact is you are getting an advance warning of things that are about to take place but haven't yet. Why do you think witches, warlocks, and fortune tellers hate you so bad? You expose them for the demoniacs they are. They operate on the preemies of fear while you operate through love.

Acts 11:

12 And the Spirit bade me go with them, nothing doubting. Moreover these six brethren accompanied me, and we entered into the man's house:

Bade Means
2036 e;pw epo {ep'-o}
Meaning: 1) to speak, say

See how closely that the small still voice and impressions are?

Acts 16:

6 Now when they had gone throughout Phrygia and the region of Galatia, and were **forbidden of the Holy Ghost** to preach the word in Asia,
7 After they were come to Mysia, they assayed to go into Bithynia: **but the Spirit suffered them not**.

Forbidden Means
2967 kwlu,w koluo {ko-loo'-o}
Meaning: 1) to hinder, prevent forbid 2) to withhold a thing from anyone 3) to deny or refuse one a thing

Suffered Means
1439 eva,w eao {eh-ah'-o}
Meaning: 1) to allow, permit, let 2) to allow one to do as he wishes, not to restrain, to let alone 3) to give up, let go, leave

The Holy Ghost withheld them. He denied them liberty or peace in traveling that way. Suffered meant that the Holy

Ghost impressed the importance upon them not to do as you wish but obey the Spirit of God. The wonder of it all is the Lord did not speak to them, just impressed it upon their hearts. They both felt it. They were in one mind and one spirit. Wow! They were learning to be led of the Spirit. Why? They did not know at that time, but the result is divine appointment. Being at a given place in a given time to do a specific thing for God.

I John 2:
25 And this is the promise that he **hath promised** us, *even* **eternal life.**
26 These *things* have I written unto you concerning **them that seduce you.**
27 But the anointing which ye have received of him abideth in you, and ye **need not that any man teach you: but as the same anointing teacheth you of all things, and is truth, and is no lie**, and even as it hath taught you, ye shall abide in him.

This is so important. One of the great functions of the Holy Ghost is that he leads and guides into truth. Seduce in the Greek means to lead astray. If the Spirit of God isn't agreeing with what you are hearing, then you can be assured it's not the Spirit of God in them that's guiding you away.

Matthew 24:
23 Then if any man shall say unto you, Lo, here *is* Christ, or there; believe *it* not.
24 For there shall arise false Christs, and false prophets, and shall shew great signs and wonders; insomuch that, **if *it* were possible, they shall deceive the very elect**.
25 Behold, I have told you before.
26 Wherefore if they shall say unto you, Behold, *he is* in the desert; go not forth: behold, he is in the secret chambers; believe *it* not.

Wow! It is not possible to deceive those who are founded in God because they are experienced in discerning the spirits. The word "If" is so important. Christ is just emphasizing the importance of knowing the Spirit and not believing every wind of doctrine that blows in.

Hebrews 5:
13 For every one that useth milk is unskilful in the word of righteousness: for he is a babe.
14 But strong meat belongeth to them that are of full age, even those who by reason of use have their senses exercised to discern both good and evil.

Ephesians 4:
13 Till we all come in the unity of the faith, and of the knowledge of the Son of God, unto a perfect man, unto the **measure of the stature of the fulness of Christ**:
14 That we *henceforth* be **no more** children, tossed to and fro, and **carried about with every wind of doctrine**, by the sleight of men, *and* cunning craftiness, whereby **they lie in wait to deceive;**
15 But speaking the truth in love, may grow up into him in all things, which is the head, *even* Christ:

The devil won't come right out and say there is no God. He won't say you shouldn't serve God. He will tell you there's no hurry you have plenty of time. He will tell you that you don't have to be so fanatical about serving God. As we grow in God and in faith we learn to trust our spirit man. Our heart if you will. As we learn to walk after the spirit and deny what the flesh wants then we are becoming mature in God. We can walk in a fullness of Christ and live above sin. That's what maturity is about. So many religious devils have told us we cannot be spiritually perfect that the church world has accepted this ridiculous lie. If it were not in our scope of abilities, then there would have been no mention of fullness of Christ or being of full age and maturity in Christ. Many will say, "I'm afraid that it wasn't God dealing with me". My question is two fold. First, what if it was? Secondly, was it your nature to think about doing this thing? Was there a peace about what you felt impressed to do? If so, then God doesn't lie! Oh yea;

Romans 10:

11 For the scripture saith, Whosoever believeth on him shall not be ashamed.

If you walk in doubt, then ashamed you will be. Obedience by faith will not make you regret or ashamed you trusted the Father of lights.

James 1:

16 Do not err, my beloved brethren.
17 **Every good gift and every perfect gift is from above**, and cometh **down from the Father of lights**, with whom is no variableness, neither shadow of turning.

Variableness or changing. God is the same today and tomorrow. If it's good and an answer of peace, then you can count on God.

Genesis 41:

15 And Pharaoh said unto Joseph, I have dreamed a dream, and *there* is none *that* can interpret it: and I have heard say of thee, that thou canst understand a dream to interpret it.
16 And Joseph answered Pharaoh, saying, *It is* not in me: **God shall give Pharaoh an answer of peace**.

It's about peace and love. That's the gospel in a nut shell. When God deals with you, you will know it's him. You can trust what you feel. As we said earlier your conscience and instincts got saved too. You will feel impressions in the middle of your chest. Yep, right where your heart is located. That's the central core of the spirit of God in you. Learn to feel and sense what is going on in that area of your body. Whether you're at peace in a circumstance or you feel troubled. Peace, love and joy will always lead you. These three attributes of God never fail. Trust them!

IV. PROPHECY

Prophecy works at several levels. You may receive prophecy from someone else or you may prophesy to yourself. Always remember this scripture concerning prophecy.

I Corinthians 14:
3 But he that prophesieth speaketh unto men to edification, and exhortation, and comfort.

Edification
3619 oivkodomh, oikodome {oy-kod-om-ay'}
Meaning: 1) **(the act of) building, building up 2)** metaph. edifying, edification 2a) the **act of one who promotes another's growth in Christian wisdom**, piety, happiness, holiness 3) a building (i.e. the thing built, edifice)
Exhortation

3874 para,klhsij paraklesis {par-ak'-lay-sis}
Meaning: 1) **a calling near**, summons, (esp. for help) 2) importation, supplication, entreaty 3) exhortation, admonition, **encouragement** 4) **consolation, comfort, solace; that which affords comfort or refreshment** 4a) thus of the Messianic salvation (so the Rabbis call the Messiah the consoler, the comforter) 5) persuasive discourse, stirring address 5a) instructive, admonitory, conciliatory, powerful hortatory discourse

Comfort
3889 paramuqi,a paramuthia {par-am-oo-thee'-ah}
Meaning: 1) any address, whether made for the purpose of persuading, or of arousing and stimulating, or of calming and consoling 1a) **consolation, comfort**

Three things that prophesy will do. Exhort, exalt, and comfort. If the prophesy you receive does not build you up, promote you in God, draw you nearer to God, encourage you, refresh you, comfort and confirm the what God is dealing with you, it's not of God!

I Corinthians 14:

6 Now, brethren, if I come unto you speaking with tongues, what shall I profit you, **except I shall speak to you either by revelation, or by knowledge, or by prophesying, or by doctrine?**

7 And even things without life giving sound, whether pipe or harp, **except they give a distinction in the sounds, how shall it be known what is piped or harped?**

8 For if the trumpet give an uncertain sound, who shall prepare himself to the battle?

9 So likewise ye, **except ye utter by the tongue words easy to be understood, how shall it be known what is spoken? for ye shall speak into the air.**

10 There are, it may be, **so many kinds of voices in the world**, and none of them *is* without signification.

11 Therefore if I know not the meaning of the voice, I shall be unto him that speaketh a barbarian, and he that speaketh *shall be* a barbarian unto me.

Prophecy builds the individual and the church. You can receive instruction and revelation knowledge thru prophecy. If I prophesy unto you and you have no idea what God is trying to say, what good is it? God will already have done or is dealing with you about doing something. Prophecy will confirm the move of God on your life. If God is not dealing with you about going over seas to a mission field and you get a prophecy to go over seas and be a missionary then this prophecy has an uncertain sound. It doesn't bear witness with your spirit. The individual prophesied out of good intentions but not from God's heart. I have seen people manipulated through so called prophetic words. God wasn't in a hundred miles of that garbage. Always remember the three rules of prophecy. You know it's amazing; I have had God to correct me in such a loving way that everyone standing by was praising God for such a wonderful word but the same word was spanking the fire out of me. It was a word of confirmation and no one knew it. God is a gentleman and is not in the business of making you look like a fool or an inbreed. Prophecy will not only confirm what is taking place in your life but will give you insight as to what the future holds on your present course. Many prophecies are for the future. Many don't come to pass for years. This is revelation knowledge of God's heart for your life and ministry. Now prophecy has yet another spectacular ability we seldom ever tap into.

I Corinthians 14:
24 But if all prophesy, and there come in *one* that believeth not, or one unlearned, he is convinced of all, he is judged of all:
25 And thus are the secrets of his heart made manifest; and so falling down on *his* face he will worship God, and report that God is in you of a truth.

The sinner can receive a prophecy and it confirms the situations of his or her life. Prophecy is a mighty tool in soul winning. God knows their heart and life where you don't. In a situation like this that person must come to grip with the decision of accepting a God who is actually viewing their life or cold heartedly refuse to surrender.

Watch the words convinced and judged.

Convinced
1651 evle,gcw elegcho {el-eng'-kho}
Meaning: 1) to convict, refute, confute 1a) generally with a suggestion of shame of the person convicted 1b) by conviction to bring to the light, to expose 2) to find fault with, correct 2a) by word 2a1) to reprehend severely, chide, admonish, reprove 2a2) to call to account, show one his fault, demand an explanation 2b) by deed 2b1) to chasten, to punish

Judged
350 avnakri,nw anakrino {an-ak-ree'-no}
Meaning: 1) examine or judge 1a) to investigate, examine, enquire into, scrutinise, sift, question 1a1) specifically in a forensic sense of a judge to hold an investigation 1a2) to interrogate, examine the accused or witnesses 1b) to judge of, estimate, determine (the excellence or defects of any person or thing

First we see these are sinners who are come into our presence. The Spirit of God does these things through revelation, knowledge and prophecy. These are not done as a tool of judgment and damnation, but the Spirit reveals to the individual the things in his heart that he may testify the God is in you of a truth. In no manner is it in context to belittle or insult anyone, even sinners. The word of prophecy is to lead to Christ or to keep one in Christ. We don't have to tell a sinner he is a drunk, he has enough sense to know that for himself. God will lift him out of the mire, not rub his face in it. To rub his face in his lifestyle is to tear down, but God will acknowledge his secrets yet exhort him and exalt him to understand there is a better way and help in time of his need. Revealing a person's sinful life is one thing, but to help them out of it and to love them the whole time is Godly. To explain this mentality of prophecy a little clearer;

1 Corinthians 13:
1 Though I speak with the tongues of men and of angels, and have not charity, I am become as sounding brass, or a tinkling cymbal.
2 And though I have *the gift of* prophecy, and understand all mysteries, and all knowledge; and though I have all faith, so that I could remove mountains, and have not charity, I am nothing.
3 And though I bestow all my goods to feed *the poor*, and though I give my body to be burned, and have not charity, it profiteth me nothing.
4 Charity suffereth long, *and* is kind; charity envieth not; charity vaunteth not itself, is not puffed up,
5 Doth not behave itself unseemly, seeketh not her own, is not easily provoked, thinketh no evil;

A portion of this scripture we seem to leave unnoticed is the part about we are willing to sacrifice ourselves to show love. Those in our society who desire to prophe-lie are not willing to put their lives at risk to condemn others. When God gives us a word that reveals the sin to a sinner, it is done in such great love and consideration that the sinner is astounded and amazed at how greatly God loves and cares for them. If you notice that 1 Cor. 13: comes before I Cor. 14: This is for a reason; if we can't get the love of God to operate properly in our lives, then we will never get the word of prophecy to operate properly in our lives. First things first. We don't jump over the love of God and go straight to mean and hateful pathetic utterances. It doesn't work that way. Prophecy is the heart of God being revealed to the heart of mankind. God is exposing himself to save his sons. So, the next time someone comes to you with a harsh and condemning word just smile and walk away...

I Thessalonians 5:
16 Rejoice evermore.
17 Pray without ceasing.
18 In every thing give thanks: for this is the will of God in Christ Jesus concerning you.
19 Quench not the Spirit.
20 Despise not prophesyings.
21 Prove all things; hold fast that which is good.

It seems that rejoicing, prayer, and freedom, the Spirit is always involved when the Lord give us a word. Prophecy comes to a group of people or to an individual.

I Timothy 1:
18 This charge I commit unto thee, son Timothy, according to the prophecies which went before on thee, that thou by them mightest war a good warfare;
19 Holding faith, and a good conscience; which some having put away concerning faith have made shipwreck:

Timothy received personal prophecies from individuals. Paul is telling Timothy to remember and hold fast to the word that God has challenged you with. We have heard so many false words that we become gun shy. God says not to turn our nose up at prophecies. Amongst the array of crack pots trying to look holy, there is a wondrous word of prophecy that is ministering life to the hearer. Don't let a few chosen frozen stop you from getting from the life changing.

I Timothy 4:
11 These things command and teach.
12 Let no man despise thy youth; but be thou an example of the believers, in word, in conversation, in charity, in spirit, in faith, in purity.
13 Till I come, give attendance to reading, to exhortation, to doctrine.
14 Neglect not the gift that is in thee, which was given thee by prophecy, with the laying on of the hands of the presbytery.
15 Meditate upon these things; give thyself wholly to them; that thy profiting may appear to all.

I love this scripture. Notice Paul is specifically speaking to the young in Christ whether in age or experience. Prophecy doesn't come with an age barrier. Don't allow old dead heads to stop up your blessing. You go out there and get you some. Some of what you may ask? Flowing of the spirit and life in you. Be the example not the exception. If you have the Holy Ghost, you can hear God's voice to prophesy. In verse thirteen you see two of the manifestations in the spirit of prophesy.

There is an issue that arises in the church world today, and that is, "I'm called of God as a prophet, I don't give easy words, I receive prophecies that are of judgment". We need to go back to I Corinthians 14: 3. It is simple yet all inclusive. Many will give you a harsh word and call it of God, yet the bible doesn't lie. Many use this scripture as a base for their hateful prophe-lies.

II Timothy 4:
1 I charge *thee* therefore before God, and the Lord Jesus Christ, who shall judge the quick and the dead at his appearing and his kingdom;
2 **Preach the word**; be instant in season, out of season; reprove, rebuke, exhort with all longsuffering and doctrine.

3 For the time will come when they will not endure sound doctrine; but after their own lusts shall they heap to themselves teachers, having itching ears;

4 And they shall turn away *their* ears from the truth, and shall be turned unto fables.

5 But watch thou in all things, endure afflictions, **do the work of an evangelist, make full proof of thy ministry.**

Watch the word of the Lord here. Nowhere does God say prophesy the word, and rebuke the people. He says preach and teach. If there is a word of reproof it will come from the pulpit in a sermon or teaching, not prophecy. We must call a bird a bird. This means, if it's a prophecy then that's all it is. It is not a rebuke from your observations. Prophecy builds up and not tears down. Let your yea be yea and your nea be nea. If you are not the pastor, then God doesn't give the right to the sheep to rebuke and scorn each other. If you are a teacher, you show the word in context as it is written and allow the Holy Ghost to convict.

V. AUDIBLE VOICE

The audible voice of God is actually heard with your ears or so it seems. I am not convinced that my natural ears hear it seeing others around me did not always hear. This does not stop the fact his voice was so loud that you turn to see who is speaking to you. His voice can be startling.

Matthew 3:
16 And Jesus, when he was baptized, went up straightway out of the water: and, lo, the heavens were opened unto him, and he saw the Spirit of God descending like a dove, and lighting upon him:
17 And **lo a voice from heaven**, saying, This is my beloved Son, in whom I am well pleased.

I'm not getting into apostolic teachings or any other doctrines. Here the fact is a voice came from heaven. An audible voice that all who were gathered at Jordan heard the voice. The voice was the voice of Jesus' father. Again this voice is heard on the behalf of Jesus in Matthew 17: 4-6.

Acts 9:
4 And he fell to the earth, and heard a voice saying unto him, Saul, Saul, why persecutest thou me?
5 And he said, Who art thou, Lord? And the Lord said, I am Jesus whom thou persecutest: *it is* hard for thee to kick against the pricks.
6 And he trembling and astonished said, Lord, what wilt thou have me to do? And the Lord *said* unto him, Arise, and go into the city, and it shall be told thee what thou must do.
7 And the men which journeyed with him stood speechless, hearing a voice, but seeing no man.

Again others heard this voice. This voice was the voice of Jesus to Paul. He actually not just hearing but also seeing Jesus. Notice in the three times thus far of hearing God's voice, it was a confirmation of ministry? In Jesus' and Paul's ministry confirmed with an audible voice of God. Interesting isn't it?

Acts 10:

13 And **there came a voice to him, Rise, Peter; kill, and eat.**
14 But **Peter said, Not so, Lord**; for I have never eaten any thing that is common or unclean.
15 **And the voice *spake* unto him again the second time**, What God hath cleansed, *that* call not thou common.
16 **This was done thrice**: and the vessel was received up again into heaven.
17 Now while Peter doubted in himself what this vision which he had seen should mean, behold, the men which were sent from Cornelius had made enquiry for Simon's house, and stood before the gate,
18 And called, and asked whether Simon, which was surnamed Peter, were lodged there.
19 While Peter thought on the vision, the Spirit said unto him, Behold, three men seek thee.
20 Arise therefore, and get thee down, and go with them, **doubting nothing: for I have sent them**.

Notice two different voices spoke to Peter here. The first time the voice of Jesus. The next time, the voice of the Holy Ghost. The Holy Ghost here is not a thing but a person. "I have sent them." The first time he heard an audible voice that he talked back to. The second time he had no audible response. He just obeyed.

Acts 7:

31 When Moses saw *it*, he wondered at the sight: and as he drew near to behold *it*, the voice of the Lord came unto him,
32 *Saying*, I *am* the God of thy fathers, the God of Abraham, and the God of Isaac, and the God of Jacob. Then Moses trembled, and durst not behold.
33 Then said the Lord to him, Put off thy shoes from thy feet: for the place where thou standest is holy ground.

God speaking with man was not just a New Testament teaching but right from the oracles of the old. I want to convey a point. That point is this, God still talks to his people. Don't be afraid. As your faith grows in God you will hear his audible voice. Don't worry; he won't make himself known just for idle chitchat. God has a point and this point maybe the turning point of your life so listen.

VI. VISIONS

There are two types of visions. Open eye and closed eye. The difference is this. Closed eye visions can come while you're resting or sleighed in the spirit. Open eye visions happen while you're eyes are open. An image flashes before your eyes. In most cases you are meditating on God or involved in ministering. You may be asking yourself what is the difference between a dream and a vision in the night. In the simplest of terms I'll try to separate them. If you have a dream in the night most of the time you will recall it in the morning. When visions come in the night and you don't write it down quickly it will leave as quickly as it came. Visions are ministered through your spirit and not the mind. Thus the mind has trouble recalling them over an extended period of time. Visions in the night are so vivid that what you see is actually taking place.

Acts 2:
17 And it shall come to pass in the last days, saith God, I will pour out of my Spirit upon all flesh: and your sons and your daughters shall prophesy, and your young men shall see visions, and your old men shall dream dreams:

The manifestations of the spirit should be a normal occurrence in our lives. It should not be an unusual manifestation but we should expect it as a normal function in our life.

1) Open Eyed Visions

Acts 2:
3 And there appeared unto them cloven tongues like as of fire, and it sat upon each of them.

They were sitting together in one place. It's amazing that at the onset of the outpouring of the Holy Ghost was witnessed by open eye visions. Open eye visions are seeing the spirit realm in our realm of understanding.

Ephesians 1:

17 That the God of our Lord Jesus Christ, the Father of glory, may give unto you the spirit of wisdom and revelation in the knowledge of him:

18 The **eyes of your understanding being enlightened; that ye may know what is the hope of his calling, and what the riches of the glory of his inheritance in the saints,**

19 And what is the exceeding greatness of his power to us-ward who believe, according to the working of his mighty power,

Acts 7:

54 When they heard these things, they were cut to the heart, and they gnashed on him with their teeth.

55 But he, **being full of the Holy Ghost, looked up stedfastly into heaven, and saw the glory of God, and Jesus standing on the right hand of God,**

56 And said, Behold, I see the heavens opened, and the Son of man standing on the right hand of God.

57 Then they cried out with a loud voice, and stopped their ears, and ran upon him with one accord,

Stephen's last experience on earth was an open eye vision. After seeing a taste of his future, the present no longer compared. He would have paid them to put him out of his misery. Open eye visions will reevaluate your relationship with the father.

Matthew 3:

16 And Jesus, when he was baptized, went up straightway out of the water: and, lo, the heavens were opened unto him, and **he saw the Spirit of God descending** like a dove, and lighting upon him:

This would have blown my mind. I wondered what exactly it looked like. I know it says like a dove but that also could be describing the way it descended from heaven. I am excited about the fact we can have open eye visions. I am fascinated with God's love toward us and what extremes he will go to, to cause us to fall more madly in love with him. As long as

we are in awe of the giver of these manifestations and not the manifestation itself, God will continuously reveal himself. When we get our eyes off the giver and on the given then pride begins to penetrate our relationship with the Father.
2) Closed Eye Visions

ACTS 9:
10 And there was a certain disciple at Damascus, named Ananias; and to him said the Lord in a vision, Ananias. And he said, Behold, I *am here*, Lord.

It doesn't say that Ananias was praying but I believe he was. In this vision there was a two way conversation going on. Most visions you will have are just an insight of things God is revealing. So we see that visions also come in two ways and two types. Open and closed eye, monolog and dialog. Monolog meaning God is showing or speaking to you alone. Dialog meaning God is showing and speaking while you can answer and converse with the spirit of God whether it is the Holy Spirit, Christ, or an angel. "God is so way cool!"

Acts 10:
A devout *man*, and one that feared God with all his house, which gave much alms to the people, and prayed to God always.
3 He saw in a vision evidently about the ninth hour of the day an angel of God coming in to him, and saying unto him, Cornelius.
4 And when he looked on him, he was afraid, and said, What is it, Lord? And he said unto him, Thy prayers and thine alms are come up for a memorial before God.

Another instance of two way conversation with the Lord. Here we are pretty sure he was in prayer while this vision happened.

Acts 10:
5 And now **send men to Joppa**, and **call for** *one* **Simon**, whose **surname is Peter**:
6 He **lodgeth with one Simon a tanner,** whose **house is by the sea side**: **he shall tell** thee what thou oughtest to do.

7 And when the angel which spake unto Cornelius was departed, **he called two** of his household servants, and **a devout soldier** of them that waited on him continually;

Will you look at the specifics of this vision? The angel told him how many to send, being three which in itself is very significant. Told him what city, what street, where the house was located, who was the owner of the house, and what the owner's name was. Then he told him who is visitor was. Not only his ministry name, but his birth name which most people wasn't even aware of.

Acts 10:
10 And he became very hungry, and would have eaten: but while they made ready, **he fell into a trance**,
11 And saw heaven opened, and a certain vessel descending unto him, as it had been a great sheet knit at the four corners, and let down to the earth:

A trance is a state of meditation on God that you are not even aware of the outside world. It's just you and God. Many will fall into a trance when sleighed in the Spirit. Some trances can close out the natural world to such a degree that even the human body is excluded from the trance. In simple terms, the human body either goes into a comatose state or even stops functioning. That's right; your spirit leaves your body just like you're dead. In many cases the body's blood pressure and pulse cease. Its so bazaar, I have watched people speak in tongues while there was no pulse or heart beat. Some just stop breathing all together. In a trance you are closer to God than you are to the world! "I like it like that!" As long as we trust God in this stasis, he will allow us to continue. Yet if we become afraid our spirit will rest back into our body. So don't be afraid!!!!!

We spoke about the significance of the three men that Cornelius sent to Peter. If you study the life of Peter, you will find that God always confirmed things in three's with Peter. Peter has just been designated an overseer over the churches and he had to understand that the word was for more than just the Jewish nation. That's why the Lord told him to doubt nothing for he had sent these men. Peter was not preaching to the gentiles and God wanted to change that. We know that Paul became the overseer to the gentiles, but Peter had to know for himself it would be of God. Paul spent most of his time in the Spirit. His desire was to stay so close to God that the natural realm seemed fictitious.

II Corinthians 12:
1 It is not expedient for me doubtless to glory. I will come to visions and revelations of the Lord.

If Paul placed more emphasis on the visions and revelations of God, than he did on his reputation, then we would be wise be adhere to Paul's priority here.

II Corinthians 12:
2 I knew a man in Christ above fourteen years ago, **(whether in the body, I cannot tell; or whether out of the body, I cannot tell: God knoweth;) such an one caught up to the third heaven.**
3 And I knew such a man, **(whether in the body, or out of the body, I cannot tell: God knoweth;)**
4 How that he **was caught up into paradise**, and **heard** unspeakable words, which it is not lawful for a man to utter.
5 **Of such an one will I glory: yet of myself I will not glory**, but in mine infirmities.
6 For though I would desire to glory, I shall not be a fool; **for** I will say the truth: but *now* I forbear, **lest any man should think of me above** that which **he seeth me *to be***, or *that* he heareth of me.
7 And **lest I should be exalted above measure through the abundance of the revelations**, there was given to me a thorn in the flesh, the messenger of Satan to buffet me, lest I should be exalted above measure.

Could it be that the reason he starts this chapter with the statement that Paul would come to visions and revelations of the Lord is that this experience has transformed his life? He begins talking about a third party knowing this man and ends confessing that he was the man. He desired to emphasis the change that took place also changed his relationship with God forever. He would come to visions, will you, it may just transform your life also?

II Corinthians 10:

4 (For the weapons of our warfare *are* **not carnal, but mighty through God** to the **pulling down of strong holds;)**

5 **Casting down imaginations**, and every high thing that exalteth itself against the knowledge of God, and **bringing into captivity every thought** to the obedience of Christ;

6 And having in a readiness to revenge all disobedience, when your obedience is fulfilled.

7 **Do ye look on things after the outward appearance?** If any man trust to himself that he is Christ's, let him of himself **think this again**, that, as he *is* Christ's, even so *are* we Christ's.

8 For though I should boast somewhat more of our authority, which **the Lord hath given us for edification, and not for your destruction, I should not be ashamed:**

9 **That I may not seem as if I would terrify you by letters.**

10 For *his* letters, say they, *are* weighty and powerful; but *his* bodily presence *is* weak, and *his* speech contemptible.

11 Let such an one think this, that, such as we are in word by letters when we are absent, such will we be also in deed when we are present.

12 For we dare not make ourselves of the number, or compare ourselves with some that commend themselves: but they measuring themselves by themselves, and comparing themselves among themselves, are not wise.

13 But **we will not boast of things without *our* measure, but according to the measure of the rule which God hath distributed to us, a measure to reach even unto you.**

14 For we **stretch not ourselves beyond *our measure***, as though we reached not unto you: for we are **come as far as to you also in *preaching* the gospel** of Christ:

15 **Not boasting of things without *our measure***, *that is*, of other men's labours; but having hope, **when your faith is increased, that we shall be enlarged by you according to our rule abundantly**,

In verse seven we see a key to understanding the spirit realm. Do we rely too much on the outward evidence or do we trust the Spirit? Spiritual warfare is a reality no matter how hard we try and deny it. Paul danced around several subjects and in depth spiritual warfare is one of them. He is afraid we are not spiritually in tune with God enough to handle the whole truth at once. He limited the information he gave here to the church at Corinth because they had already testified that his letters were difficult to grasp. The word weighty is used here, meaning there was so much information to process, and we need time. Paul says that as their faith is increased they would be able to grasp the depth he is trying to convey to them. At this time however, he would limit how much he would reveal at once. In two short chapters he will unleash on them his experience with Paradise and Heaven, with as much tact and finesse as he could. Paul's excitement to finally be able to tell someone of the events God has exposed him to be probably overwhelming. Just as Paul, there are so many things we want to tell others, but realizing that these are not yet ready for it, is a pill too hard to swallow. It is in my mind that every believer has experienced God in the same manner as I have, yet in all this, we find so many who have not, and my explaining and testifying to others of it would hinder their walk with God and diminish my testimony among them. Wisdom is the principle thing, and is necessary to hold a restrain on how much we indulge in testifying of at once. When we yield ourselves totally to God, it is amazing the depth of visions we can encounter.

Matthew 14:
22 And straightway **Jesus constrained his disciples to get into a ship**, and **to go before him unto the other side, while he sent the multitudes away**.
23 And when he had sent the multitudes away, he went up into a mountain apart to **pray: and when the evening was come, he was there alone**.
24 But the ship was now in the **midst of the sea**, tossed withwaves: for the wind was contrary.
25 And in the fourth watch of the night **Jesus went unto them, walking on the sea**.

28 And Peter answered him and said, Lord, if it be thou, **bid me come** unto thee on the water.

29 And he said, Come. And when Peter was come down out of the ship, he walked on the water, to go to Jesus.

30 But when he saw the wind boisterous, he was afraid; and beginning to sink, he cried, saying, Lord, save me.

31 And immediately Jesus stretched forth his hand, and caught him, and said unto him, O thou of little faith, wherefore didst thou doubt?

32 And **when they were come into the ship, the wind ceased**.

Paul left no doubt to his intent in the spirit. I want to see the spirit realm. I want to know what my Father is up to. Most of all I want to be a participant of it. Watch the next scriptures and think about it. It will make you week at the knees and set you on your fanny.

I love this event so much. I don't even care about the thorn in the flesh. You can fanaticize and argue all day what his thorn in the flesh is. The fact is you are missing the most important message Paul is conveying. You don't have any such thorn in your flesh; so don't even lose any sleep over it. 7 times he speaks of himself or uses the word "I". He was so caught up in the spirit with visions and revelations he wasn't sure he was in his body or not! The pure fact is he was translated into heaven and saw things you and I may never see and hear. This vision and trance left his body behind. Here is the kicker. This was a constant problem with him. You ask what problem am I speaking of. This problem; he spent so much time in the spirit he could no longer tell when he was in the natural realm! He was so consumed with the nature and spirit of God; he was living closer to God than to the earth. He had the abilities of Adam. He could come into the presence of God freely. His fleshly desires had died. That sounds awesome doesn't it? That's a wonderful problem to have! God saw it however as a problem, not on his part but on Paul's. Paul's ministry was to bring us to a place of victory and empower us with the knowledge to turn the world upside down. Yet, how can Paul associate with our daily battles and trials when he no longer had them? His thorn in the flesh was sent by God from Satan, probably a prince of Satan to causing Paul to know the difference between the natural and supernatural. Paul for the first time in a long time actually had a trial of faith. Paul's thorn in the flesh was simply a reminder that there was a natural realm around him. The thorn hurt because he had stopped caring about the natural because of the stupendous earth-shattering daily events in the spirit realm. Can you image staying so close to God that you had trouble understanding what hunger, fatigue, loneliness, pain, or sorrow was? Paul's thorn didn't have to be physical; it only had to separate the natural from the spiritual. This separation would have caused such great longing that any such possible thorn you could image in your mind had no comparison. Paul had to continue writing to us to get us there. If God had not caused a separation between himself and Paul, Paul would also have been raptured just like Elijah. We would have suffered untold damage from a lack of his marvelous writings. Paul still had a job to do. No doubt this not only broke the heart of Paul as we see, but I'm sure God's heart was shattered because he had to place a narrow distance between them.

Visions are a gateway to God. Maybe you can understand why Satan tries so hard to get you to doubt what God is trying so desperately to show you? This doubt will keep you in the limited space of the natural realm. Faith is the glue that binds you to the spirit realm. Paul tried ever so delicately to give you a glimpse into this no holds bared realm of power. He found himself downplaying what he really wanted to say in fear that his knowledge of God would cause you to stumble.

This letter to us is scary. Paul wants so badly to open his mouth and make known so much of the mystery of the power of God in us but he realizes that we are not in a place to receive his manifold revelations. He continuously speaks of not speaking about the measure. He had to come to realize where mankind was as a whole and not give too much information at once. He says when your faith is increased you can begin to gather from the four corners of his writings and God will make known this power that Paul so badly wanted to write to you but kept hid in so many places in his writings. Verses 4- 5 tell us where the limitations of faith lie, in our minds. We have to bring into captivity what we think about the world around us and think like God. Let go of your imagination and try walking in God's. Verse seven says think again about what we call reality. We talk so much about one wonderful day we will be able to walk on water, right? What if we're thinking wrong? What if it doesn't have to be a wonderful day just any old day will do just fine. The water or gravity isn't the problem, we are! We look at water as being fluid and we'll sink, what if it's not? Jesus had already purposed when he sent his disciples away how he would meet them. He knew he was going for a walk about. The water or weather was not a factor only his faith.

Put two and two together. Jesus sent the multitudes away and went to a mountain to pray. They were already in the middle of the sea. Jesus just came walking. The wind just stopped blowing. Jesus asks Peter at what point or place did your faith waiver. Peter was looking at what he was hearing. Our weapons are not carnal but mighty. The weapons are not to fight the enemy with but to conquer our imaginations. Satan really isn't our enemy, we are! This instruction of Paul and Jesus is trying to get us to a place of comprehension. Listen, our downfall is our faith. We just can't get past ourselves or the world around us!!

You won't be sorry you trusted God. However bazaar it may seem God is wondrous.

It is vital that we pay attention to visions of God. There is significance to what God is showing. Jeremiah saw the boiling pot. He also saw which way the stem of it was pointing.

Romans 11:
29 For the **gifts** and **calling** of God *are* without repentance.

We must realize that however insignificant we think something is, if it is from God then it is not insignificant. God blesses us with gifts and callings upon our lives for a reason. In

Jeremiah's case, what he saw was simple yet profound and would change the course of a nation. Are you ready to change the course of a nation by a seemingly simple vision?

Jeremiah 1:
13 And the word of the LORD came unto me the second time, saying, What seest thou? And I said, I see a seething pot; and the face thereof is toward the north.
14 Then the LORD said unto me, Out of the north an evil shall break forth upon all the inhabitants of the land.

It is crucial that we pay attention and not doubt that which God is doing in our lives. If Jeremiah had not paid attention to details here, then all these evils would have come upon this nation by surprise, and guess who the people would have blamed first, God. When you are warned and you repent not, then when the enemy comes in like a flood and you are unprepared, you come to the understanding that God tried to warn me first, yet I would not repent. God still gets blamed, but them who blame God know who's fault it truly was, there's.

VII. DREAMS

You will have two types of dreams. The ones you remember when God awakes you and those that are just outside of your grasp to remember. Both are significant. The ones you remember are for your edification, exaltation, and comfort now. The ones that just slip away are of future events for confirmation and guidance. When these events are happening, the dream will come back in full view. You will recognize people, places and events that you were not previously aware of. You can even know what words are to be spoken before the speaker thinks of it. "Now doesn't that just pump your wheels up?"

Genesis 41:
7 And the seven thin ears devoured the seven rank and full ears. And Pharaoh awoke, and, behold, *it was* a dream.
8 And it came to pass in the morning that his spirit was troubled; and he sent and called for all the magicians of Egypt, and all the wise men thereof: and Pharaoh told them his dream; but *there was* none that could interpret them unto Pharaoh.

The pharaoh realized this was not just an average dream. His spirit was troubled at the thought of this dream that lingered. This dream obviously was a wake up call for the pharaoh. This dream brings Joseph to the place of anointing that God had intended. Pharaoh benefited by saving a nation and Joseph benefited by being placed in leadership God had years before promised he would be by dreams.

Matthew 27:
19 When he was set down on the judgment seat, his wife sent unto him, saying, Have thou nothing to do with that just man: for I have suffered many things this day in a dream because of him.

Again God warns or confirms his will by dreams. Pilate was in a predicament. He was caught between defending Jesus and avoiding a revolution. Jesus was going to die, but it did not have to be at Pilate's hand. He passed judgment on to the Jews.

Matthew 1:

19 Then Joseph her husband, being a just *man*, and not willing to make her a public example, was minded to put her away privily.

20 But while he thought on these things, behold, the angel of the Lord appeared unto him in a dream, saying, Joseph, thou son of David, fear not to take unto thee Mary thy wife: for that which is conceived in her is of the Holy Ghost.

Joseph was led and received confirmation of what his heart was trying to tell him by an angel in his dream.

Matthew 1:

24 Then Joseph being raised from sleep did as the angel of the Lord had bidden him, and took unto him his wife:

25 And knew her not till she had brought forth her firstborn son: and he called his name JESUS.

Not only did he marry her because of instructions given in a dream but also he did not make love with her until after Jesus was born. Mary was still a virgin when she gave birth to Jesus. Joseph believed God with all his heart and he would be led much of his life by these mysterious dreams.

Matthew 2:

19 But when Herod was dead, behold, an angel of the Lord appeareth in a dream to Joseph in Egypt,

20 Saying, Arise, and take the young child and his mother, and go into the land of Israel: for they are dead which sought the young child's life.

Joseph's dreams saved his and his family's life on more than one occasion. We could learn from Joseph. No matter how God decides to commune with us, we should listen. In the Old Testament God dealt with man in dreams that were at best riddles to see the understanding unfold at some later point in life. In the New Testament, we see God dealing in dreams plainly and not in dark speeches.

Numbers 12:

6 And he said, Hear now my words: If there be a prophet among you, *I* the LORD will **make myself known unto him in a vision, and will speak unto him in a dream**.

7 My servant Moses *is* not so, who *is* faithful in all mine house.

8 With him will I speak mouth to mouth, even apparently, and **not in dark speeches**; and the similitude of the LORD shall he behold: wherefore then were ye not afraid to speak against my servant Moses?

Moses was the exception to the rule and not the rule. Everyone else had to try to figure out what God was really saying. Therefore, in the New Testament we see a new transformation in God revealing himself. If you wonder why the answer is simple, it's called salvation.

VIII. REVELATIONS

As a general rule, we tend to think of revelations as just from the word of God, which is correct, but do not stop there. Revelations comes also out of your spirit man seeing it is saved also. Many times, you will have questions in life and not answers. After seeking God, sometimes it seems as if there is no answer, but wait, the answer is on the way. If God does not speak an answer to you quickly, it may be due to a revelation God is going to give. Many times I have gone to bed with questions and as soon as my eyes opened in the morning, it was as if my eyelids activated understanding. God had instilled the understanding of my questions in my sleep, and when I awoke, I understood clearly. This revelation knowledge of God goes as deep as to the gift of the Spirit in God gives the word of knowledge about someone and what they are going thru. Revelations in the simplest of terms is the understanding of God made known to us.

Matthew 13:
10 And the disciples came, and said unto him, Why speakest thou unto them in parables?
11 He answered and said unto them, Because **it is given unto you to know the mysteries of the kingdom of heaven, but to them it is not given**.
12 For whosoever hath, to him shall be given, and he shall have more abundance: but whosoever hath not, from him shall be taken away even that he hath.
13 Therefore **speak I to them in parables**: because they seeing see not; and hearing they hear not, neither do they understand.
14 And in them is fulfilled the prophecy of Esaias, which saith, By hearing ye shall hear, and shall not understand; and seeing ye shall see, and shall not perceive:

Jesus wants to allow you to see his heart. To sinners he cannot reveal himself in such an intimacy. Let us read on because if you turned in your bible you will have questions.

15 For this people's heart is waxed gross, and *their* ears are dull of hearing, and *their* eyes they have closed; lest at any time they should see with *their* eyes, and hear with *their* ears, and should understand with their heart, and should be converted, and I should heal them.

16 But blessed *are* your eyes, for they see: and your ears, for they hear.

17 For verily I say unto you, That many prophets and righteous *men* have desired to see *those things* which ye see, and have not seen *them*; and to hear *those things* which ye hear, and have not heard *them*.

You might say that being converted would be a great thing. If that were what Jesus was trying to say it indeed would be? You have to know what the word "understand" means.

4920 suni,hmi suniemi {soon-ee'-ay-mee}

Meaning: 1) to set or bring together 1a) **in a hostile sense, of combatants 2) to put (as it were) the perception with the thing perceived** 2a) to set or join together in the mind 2a1) i.e. to understand: the man of understanding 2a2) idiom for: a good and upright man (having the knowledge of those things which pertain to salvation)

Let's explain it in the scriptures.

Genesis 6:

4 There were giants in the earth in those days; and also after that, **when the sons of God came in unto the daughters of men**, and they bare *children* to them, the same *became* mighty men which *were* of old, men of renown.

5 And God saw that the wickedness of man *was* great in the earth, and *that* every **imagination of the thoughts of his heart *was* only evil continually**.

6 **And it repented the LORD** that he had made man on the earth, and **it grieved him** at his heart.

7 And the LORD said, **I will destroy man whom I have created** from the face of the earth; both man, and beast, and the creeping thing, and the fowls of the air; for it repenteth me that I have made them.

"I brought you into this world and I will take you out!" This was God's mentality. If the world fully understood God and his word then they would twist and distort the word more than they try to now. God is protecting himself as well as you. If man were allowed to mess up the word any more than he has, God would break his promise and annihilate every breathing moving thing on the face of the earth! God cannot lie or violate his promise so he closed the eyes of the world's understanding to the majesty of himself. Matt. 13: 11 allow us to see whom the understanding of the word is for. It is for those who are saved and walking in covenant with Christ. See the world desires to do the following.

Romans 1:
21 Because that, when they knew God, they glorified *him* not as God, neither were thankful; but **became vain in their imaginations**, and their foolish **heart was darkened**.
22 Professing themselves to be wise, they **became fools**,
23 And changed the glory of the uncorruptible God into **an image** made like to corruptible man, and to birds, and fourfooted beasts, and creeping things.
24 Wherefore **God also gave them up to uncleanness through the lusts of their own hearts**, to dishonour their own bodies between themselves:
25 **Who** changed the truth of God into a lie, and **worshipped and served the creature more than the Creator**, who is blessed for ever. Amen.
26 **For this cause God gave them up unto vile affections**: for even their women did change the natural use into that which is against nature:
27 And likewise also the men, leaving the natural use of the woman, burned in their lust one toward another; men with men working that which is unseemly, and receiving in themselves that recompence of their error which was meet.
28 And even as **they did not like to retain God in *their* knowledge, God gave them over to a reprobate mind**, to do those things which are not convenient.

II Thessalonians 2:

10 And with all deceivableness of unrighteousness in them that perish; **because they received not the love of the truth, that they might be saved**.

11 And for this cause **God shall send them strong delusion, that they should believe a lie:**

12 **That they all might be damned who believed not the truth**, but had pleasure in unrighteousness.

Do you see a pattern of why the world can only grasp the saving grace of Christ and not the revelation of who God really is and how powerful man could be if Christ walked in them? Humankind worships things that were made more than God who made them. In translation made little Gods. The old cliché "too much knowledge can be a deadly thing" is so true. That is why the world will never know the nine ways God deals with man. Their ignorance is our strength. You as a newly born Christian of 3 minutes understand more about the word of God than a foolish sinner who has been studying the bible for years! You can feel what they can only read about.

II Corinthians 6:

14 Be ye not unequally yoked together with unbelievers: for what fellowship hath righteousness with unrighteousness? and what communion hath light with darkness?

15 And what concord hath Christ with Belial? or what part hath he that believeth with an infidel?

16 And what agreement hath the temple of God with idols? for ye are the temple of the living God; as God hath said, I will dwell in them, and walk in *them*; and I will be their God, and they shall be my people.

17 Wherefore come out from among them, and be ye separate, saith the Lord, and touch not the unclean *thing*; and I will receive you,

18 And will be a Father unto you, and ye shall be my sons and daughters, saith the Lord Almighty.

We will walk according to what we are subjected to. You cannot think like the world and be in Christ. You cannot kiss the devil on the cheek and expect God to kiss you on yours. If you are hanging out with the world then you do not have to worry about having Godly dreams. You will be too busy having the world's dreams and fulfilling your lust. Why would God give you dreams or any other manifestation of the Spirit if you were lying with the dogs? That's right I said the dogs!

Matthew 7:
6 Give not that which is holy unto the dogs, neither cast ye your pearls before swine, lest they trample them under their feet, and turn again and rend you.

James 4:
4 Ye adulterers and adulteresses, know ye not that the **friendship of the world is enmity with God? whosoever therefore will be a friend of the world is the enemy of God**.

Romans 8:
6 For to be carnally minded *is* death; but to be spiritually minded *is* life and peace.
7 Because the **carnal mind** *is* **enmity against God**: for it is not subject to the law of God, neither indeed can be.
8 So then they that are **in the flesh cannot please God**.

The world cannot understand what you see as a Christian. Thus they will mock you and make fun of you for what you believe. They will stop you from leading others to the Lord. God cannot reveal himself knowing that you will carry it to the world and they will trample the heart of God under their feet. God would have to open up a can of "Good luck on your own" on their head. God desires fellowship and wants to talk with you. Will you hinder him?

Ephesians 1:
8 Wherein he hath abounded toward us in all wisdom and prudence;
9 Having made known unto us the mystery of his will, according to his good pleasure which he hath purposed in himself:

17 That the God of our Lord Jesus Christ, the Father of glory, may give unto you the spirit of wisdom and revelation in the knowledge of him:

18 The eyes of your understanding being enlightened; that ye may know what is the hope of his calling, and what the riches of the glory of his inheritance in the saints,

19 And what *is* the exceeding greatness of his power to us-ward who believe, according to the working of his mighty power,

He has made known unto us the mystery of his will. He has opened our spiritual eyes to fully understand God. It is his good pleasure to reveal all he has in store for you and the earth.

John 14:

16 And I will pray the Father, and he shall give you another Comforter, that he may abide with you for ever;

17 *Even* the Spirit of truth; whom the world cannot receive, because it seeth him not, neither knoweth him: but ye know him; for he dwelleth with you, and shall be in you.

26 But the Comforter, *which* is the Holy Ghost, whom the Father will send in my name, he shall teach you all things, and bring all things to your remembrance, whatsoever I have said unto you.

Revelations of God come to those who desire to be taught. To them who are willing to believe what they are hearing form God. Revelation comes because of being in constant communion with the Father. In God, you cannot forget anything. He will bring his word, which he has spoken, written, impressed or shown back to our remembrance. He will also bring back dreams and visions just at the right time when we need them. Prophecies that have been spoken will sound like a trumpet in our spirit man at whatever time it is needed. The question was asked in church last night, "How many of you have photographic memory"? I raised my hand. What is so strange about that is I have difficulty with my short-term memory. That does not matter because when I need to know something about God he just ups and tells me. I probably do not have enough sense to figure out how the wringing of the nose brings forth blood. Proverbs 30: 33 but that's ok too, because if I need to know God tells me so. How do you like that? I walk in revelation knowledge and I even know future events so there…

Hebrews 5:
12 For when for the time ye ought to be teachers, ye have need that one teach you again which *be* the first principles of the oracles of God; and are become such as have need of milk, and not of strong meat.
13 For every one that useth milk *is* unskilful in the word of righteousness: for he is a babe.
14 But strong meat belongeth to them that are of full age, *even* those who by reason of use have their senses exercised to discern both good and evil.

There are two levels of revelation knowledge.
1) The level of milk
2) The level of meat.

If you are unskillful in the life of Christ then revelation knowledge will not exceed your level of growth. It is just like prophecy. You cannot prophesy above your level of faith.

Romans 12:
6 Having then gifts differing according to the grace that is given to us, whether prophecy, **let us prophesy** according **to the proportion of faith**;

Some people ask me how you get so much out of the bible. They read and cannot see all that I see. I am going to tell you the secret to revelation knowledge of the word so listen closely. When I read, the word there seems to always be a scripture that just sounds weird or words are out of place in it. I have learned that another version does not help because God had something right in that spot just for me. I will ask the Lord why he had it written like that and what is he trying to say to me? I will re-read, just sit, and meditate on those combined verses one at a time. All of a sudden, I will get an understanding of his love letter. I can read between the lines. I have nothing against other versions of the bible but I do like the King James Version because it is written with such unorthodox sentence formations. Other versions reword it to make it understandable and that is fine too. Depth is not on the surface. The best meat is under the bone structure, just like a pig. The tenderloin is the sweetest and juiciest of all the meat and well worth digging for. Allow me to give an example of revelation knowledge God has set me on fire with?

Daniel 3:

15 Now if ye be ready that at what time ye hear the sound of the cornet, flute, harp, sackbut, psaltery, and dulcimer, and all kinds of music, ye fall down and worship the image which I have made; *well*: but if ye worship not, ye shall be cast the same hour into the midst of a burning fiery furnace; and who is that God that shall deliver you out of my hands?

16 Shadrach, Meshach, and Abednego, answered and said to the king, O Nebuchadnezzar, **we *are* not careful to answer thee in this matter.**

17 **If it be *so,*** our God whom we serve is able to deliver us from the burning fiery furnace, and he will deliver us out of thine hand, O king.

18 But if not, be it known unto thee, O king, that we will not serve thy Gods, nor worship the golden image which thou hast set up.

19 Then was **Nebuchadnezzar full of fury, and the form of his visage was changed** against Shadrach, Meshach, and Abednego: *therefore* he spake, and commanded that they should **heat the furnace one seven times more than it was wont to be heated**.

20 And he commanded **the most mighty men that *were* in his army to bind** Shadrach, Meshach, and Abednego, and to cast them into the burning fiery furnace.

21 Then **these men were bound in their coats, their hosen, and their hats, and their *other* garments, and were cast into the midst of the burning fiery furnace**.

We have heard this story since we were babies. I was having myself a time one day just reading away. When I noticed the two commas that are enlarged here. These seven words just seemed to stand out. As I questioned God while praying, God spoke to me these simple words. "If it be so what?" "But if not what"? I know what you are saying I do not get it. Do not feel bad I didn't at first either. Notice the other parts of the verses I have highlighted, see anything strange? Let me categorize it for you.

1) Nebuchadnezzar became furious at their response. Why?

2) His complexion changed, he turned purple from rage.

3) He commanded that the furnace be dangerously overheated seven times the normal temperature.

4) He ordered the most skilled and honored soldiers to bind them up.

5) They were not stripped to expose their nakedness as mockery.

6) Their clothes were left on because it made great fuel for the fire.

7) These war heroes threw the Hebrew boys into the fire.

8) They had to lift them up and actually toss them into the middle or hottest part of the furnace. Seeing pushing them in would result in them falling into the edge, which was not where the coals were.

9) What point was Nebuchadnezzar trying to make in response to their quick precise answer to the king?

Remember the seven words. If it be so and but if not? He is revelation knowledge at work. If it were so that you do throw us into the fire be it known unto you king we will not burn or be harmed! You do not have the power because our God will absolutely deliver us from your little fire! However, if not, meaning if you do not throw us into the fire we will under no circumstances worship you, your God, and any other than our God! These young boys issued a challenge to the king and dared him to try to kill them. However, if not was the double dare to the king? King do not have pity on us, we will not burn! As a concrete result of their faith in the almighty God a whole nation was converted back to God. Now how do you like that for revelation knowledge? I'm so in love with God oh yes I am!!!!

Now back to our study. In our zeal for God we have to be careful how we interact with other Christians. Your faith may be at a place that no one else is.

Romans 14:

15 But if thy brother be grieved with *thy* meat, now walkest thou not charitably. Destroy not him with thy meat, for whom Christ died.

16 Let not then your good be evil spoken of:

We have to be easy on those who just do not have the faith that we have. Paul so greatly longed to unleash God on us but he realizes that we were not there yet. Therefore, he left breadcrumbs for us to follow. People tell me often of revelations God has just given them. They are so excited. I refuse to tell them that God also showed the same thing to me some thirty-nine years ago. Why because it would discourage and break their spirit. I rejoice with them and ask them all about what God has shown them just as if it was new to me too. I rejoice at watching them get so exuberantly excited about this manifestation of God in their life. I want everyone else I meet to see the Lord as I do but I have to realize I did not get here overnight either.

I Corinthians 2:

7 But we speak the wisdom of God in a mystery, *even* the hidden *wisdom*, which God ordained before the world unto our glory:

8 Which none of the princes of this world knew: for had they known it, they would not have crucified the Lord of glory.

9 But as it is written, Eye hath not seen, nor ear heard, neither have entered into the heart of man, the things which God hath prepared for them that love him.

10 But God hath revealed *them* unto us by his Spirit: for the Spirit searcheth all things, yea, the deep things of God.

I love knowing a secret no one else knows. We have many secrets the world cannot know. God keeps us in suspense as to what he wants to do next. As we read and understand the revelations of God, he unfolds more of himself and reveals who we really are in him.

Romans 11:
29 For the gifts and calling of God *are* without repentance.
33 O the depth of the riches both of the wisdom and knowledge of God! how unsearchable *are* his judgments, and his ways past finding out!
34 For who hath known the mind of the Lord? or who hath been his counsellor?
35 Or who hath first given to him, and it shall be recompensed unto him again?
36 For of him, and through him, and to him, *are* all things: to whom be glory for ever. Amen.

If you receive something from God you will not regret you received it. Many people will say they felt led of God to give this to you but in all reality, it was not God. They will hold that gift over your head as advantage to sway your loyalties their way. If God gave it to you, it has no strings or catches attached. You will not regret his gifts. The callings of God are the same. If God has revealed, gifted you, or called you into something you will not be ashamed or sorry. When God drops revelations into your spirit, you won't be embarrassed when you share it. When God calls you to occupy or operate in a gift there are no regrets. His desire is to constantly commune with you and reveal more of himself to you.

II Corinthians 3:
2 Ye are our epistle written in our hearts, known and read of all men:

The word of God is still being written. We hold in such awe and reverence the bible which was written two thousand years ago but fail to realize that the amen in revelation was not the amen for the conclusion of our epistles. God was not limited to just writing the 66 books but is still being added to. You are the next bible to be read. You are receiving from God the same revelation anointing that Paul wrote under. His revelations to you are as important as God's revelations to Paul the apostle. Never ever, underestimate the revelation God gives to you. It will change your life and all those who will hear you!

Genesis 11:

6 And the LORD said, Behold, the people *is* one, and they have all one language; and this they begin to do: and **now nothing will be restrained from them, which they have imagined to do**.

If it applies to the world around us who walk in confusion how much more will it apply to the righteous of God? The whole point of impressions, his small still voice, revelations, prophesy, audible voice of Christ, dreams and visions is to undo the heavy yokes that this life has inflicted so you can imagine great things in God. That your faith would rise to the level needed to fulfill God in you. Watch the level and precision of faith here.

Joshua 10:

12 Then spake Joshua to the LORD in the day when the LORD delivered up the Amorites before the children of Israel, and he said in the sight of Israel, **Sun, stand** thou still upon Gibeon; and thou, Moon, in the valley of Ajalon.

13 And the sun stood still, and the moon stayed, until the people had avenged themselves upon their enemies. *Is* not this written in the book of Jasher? So the sun stood still in the midst of heaven, and hasted not to go down about a whole day.

14 And there was no day like that before it or after it, that the LORD hearkened unto the voice of a man: for the LORD fought for Israel.

Joshua knew that once nightfall came the enemy would flee into the night. The enemy was abiding their time so they could flee. Can you imagine how they felt when the sun refused to move? All hope in the enemy was gone. They knew that there was a God fighting for Israel. Joshua refused to believe that the sun could do anything but obey. God listened to the voice of a man because God was with him and was pleased with Joshua's decision.

IX. VISITATIONS

If you watch the New Testament you will find more visitations of angels than in the Old Testament. The fact is that angel visitations are a New Testament manifestation and a part of our lives. As we expect the supernatural, we will see it. We cannot be in awe of these things but in awe of the God who ordained these things.

Hebrews 1:
14 Are they not all ministering spirits, sent forth to minister for them who shall be heirs of salvation?

Angels are ministers unto us. They are sent by God and empowered by God. The fact is the angel that has guarded and presented your needs to God is a friend of yours. You have seen him in the natural at some point in your life. If God opened your eyes at this moment, you would recognize him.

Matthew 18:
10 Take heed that ye despise not one of these little ones; for I say unto you, That in heaven their angels do always behold the face of my Father which is in heaven.

Notice the word angels meaning more than one! Now watch this.

Mark 9:
42 And whosoever shall offend one of *these* little ones that believe in me, it is better for him that a **millstone** were hanged about his neck, and he were cast into the sea.
Not only will the angels of God gang up on you but also God will turn his back on you for offending his children. I know we are talking about visitations but I want you to be glad in the day of your visitation.

Proverbs 6:
9 How long wilt thou sleep, **O sluggard?** when wilt thou arise out of thy sleep?
10 *Yet* a little sleep, a little slumber, a little folding of the hands to sleep:

11 So shall thy **poverty come** as one that travelleth, and thy want as an armed man.

12 A **naughty person**, a wicked man, **walketh with a froward mouth**.

13 He winketh with his eyes, he speaketh with his feet, he teacheth with his fingers;

14 Frowardness *is* in his heart**, he deviseth mischief continually; he soweth discord**.

15 Therefore shall **his calamity come suddenly**; suddenly shall he be broken without remedy.

16 **These six** things **doth the LORD hate**: yea**, seven** are **an abomination unto him:**

17 A **proud look**, a **lying** tongue, and **hands that shed innocent blood**,

18 An **heart that deviseth wicked imaginations, feet that be swift in running to mischief**,

19 A **false witness** *that* speaketh lies, **and he that soweth discord among brethren**.

God utterly despises anyone who sows discord in the house of the Lord. Always up in someone's business and stirring up strife and lies. Oh yea, those who always want to tell it like it is. That's who God is speaking of. Therefore, when they have a visitation from the Lord it will not be pretty. However for the rest of us God's ministering spirits will be a time of refreshing.

Daniel 10:

4 And in the four and twentieth day of the first month, as I was by the side of the great river, which *is* Hiddekel;

5 Then I lifted up mine eyes, and looked, and behold a certain man clothed in linen, whose loins *were* girded with fine gold of Uphaz:

6 His body also was like the beryl (YELLOW JASPER), and his face as the appearance of lightning, and his eyes as lamps of fire, and his arms and his feet like in colour to polished brass, and the voice of his words like the voice of a multitude.

7 And I Daniel alone saw the vision: for the men that were with me saw not the vision; but a great quaking fell upon them, so that they fled to hide themselves.

8 Therefore I was left alone, and saw this great vision, and **there remained no strength in me: for my comeliness was turned in me into corruption, and I retained no strength**.

9 Yet heard I the voice of his words: and when I heard the voice of his words, then was I in a deep sleep on my face, and my face toward the ground.

10 And, behold, **an hand touched me, which set me *upon* my knees and upon the palms of my hands**.

11 And he said unto me, O Daniel, a man greatly beloved, understand the words that I speak unto thee, and stand upright: for unto thee am I now sent. And when he had spoken this word unto me, I stood trembling.

12 Then said he unto me, Fear not, Daniel: for from the first day that thou didst set thine heart to understand, and to chasten thyself before thy God, thy words were heard, and I am come for thy words.

13 But the prince of the kingdom of Persia withstood me one and twenty days: but, lo, Michael, one of the chief princes, came to help me; and I remained there with the kings of Persia.

14 Now I am come to make thee understand what shall befall thy people in the latter days: for yet the vision is for *many* days.

15 And when he had spoken such words unto me, I set my face toward the ground, and I became dumb

This was Daniel's encounter with this particular angel. He was sleighed in the spirit. He did not have enough strength to stand on his own. Does that sound familiar? The answer for Daniel was so important that God sent an angel with the answer. The answer would influence Daniel and Israel. Watch what else happened to Daniel?

16 And, behold, ***one* like the similitude of the sons of men touched my lips:** then I opened my mouth, and spake, and said unto him that stood before me, O my lord, by the vision

my sorrows are turned upon me, **and I have retained no strength**.

17 For how can the servant of this my lord talk with this my lord? for as for me, straightway **there remained no strength in me, neither is there breath left in me**.

18 Then there **came again and touched me** *one* **like the appearance of a man, and he strengthened me**,

19 And said, O man greatly beloved, fear not: peace be unto thee, be strong, yea, *be* strong. And when he had spoken unto me, I was strengthened, and said, Let my lord speak; for thou hast strengthened me.

This is a different angel. He looked just like a human. Notice that angels not only can speak to us but also interact with us. Daniel was touched three times by an angel. Each time his strength left. The anointing was so magnificent that our little puny bodies just cannot handle it. Isn't that so wonderful? Yet the angel calmed Daniel and revived new strength in him.

Matthew 4:

10 Then saith Jesus unto him, Get thee hence, Satan: for it is written, Thou shalt worship the Lord thy God, and him only shalt thou serve.

11 Then the devil leaveth him, and, behold, angels came and ministered unto him.

Jesus had also fasted and was in a battle. Jesus was so drained from his encounter with Satan that angels were dispatched to strengthen him. There are more angel encounters in the New Testament than the old. I want to re-emphasis the fact that angels are a part of the new church of Christ. Manifestations of the Spirit should be common place in our lives if you can catch the vision of how much God really loves you.

Acts 5:

18 And laid their hands on the apostles, and put them in the common prison.

19 But the angel of the Lord by night opened the prison doors, and brought them forth, and said,

20 Go, stand and speak in the temple to the people all the words of this life.

21 And when they heard *that*, they entered into the temple early in the morning, and taught. But the high priest came, and they that were with him, and called the council together, and all the senate of the children of Israel, and sent to the prison to have them brought.

22 But when the officers came, and found them not in the prison, they returned, and told,

23 Saying, The prison truly found we shut with all safety, and the keepers standing without before the doors: but when we had opened, we found no man within.

25 Then came one and told them, saying, Behold, the men whom ye put in prison are standing in the temple, and teaching the people.

26 Then went the captain with the officers, and brought them without violence: for they feared the people, lest they should have been stoned.

29 Then Peter and the *other* apostles answered and said, We ought to obey God rather than men.

This is so wild. Peter and his team were cast into prison. When the angel came, they were freed without having to unlock the doors to the prison, the angel did it for them. The guards were still standing outside the doors, guarding the prisoners that were in the church preaching.

Acts 12:

6 And when Herod would have brought him forth, the same night Peter was sleeping between two soldiers, bound with two chains: and the keepers before the door kept the prison.

7 And, behold, the angel of the Lord came upon *him*, and a light shined in the prison: and he smote Peter on the side, and raised him up, saying, Arise up quickly. And his chains fell off from *his* hands.

8 And the angel said unto him, Gird thyself, and bind on thy sandals. And so he did. And he saith unto him, Cast thy garment about thee, and follow me.

9 And he went out, and followed him; and wist not that it was true which was done by the angel; but thought he saw a vision. Here Peter was going to die the next day but he was sleeping soundly. By the way, so were the guards watching him? The angel woke Peter but the guards could not wake. Peter was so amazed he thought he was having a vision in his sleep. Guess what? It was the real thing. He did not even realize it was real until the angel left. He was in somewhat of a stunned status. Something about getting kicked in the side you ought to be awake.

21 And upon a set day Herod, arrayed in royal apparel, sat upon his throne, and made an oration unto them.
22 And the people gave a shout, *saying, It* is the voice of a God, and not of a man.
23 And immediately the angel of the Lord smote him, because he gave not God the glory: and he was eaten of worms, and gave up the ghost.
24 But the word of God grew and multiplied.

Here Herod had run his course. He had challenged God for the last time. He had lifted himself above God. He had already killed some of the disciples so he thought of himself as mightier than God and having more power over the Christians. He was wrong. Notice that each time an angel appeared that the word of God grew and the disciples were filled with new power and boldness. An angel occurrence will not be without incident. Angels do not just show up for any reason. They are here for business.

Acts 27:
22 And now I exhort you to be of good cheer: for there shall be no loss of *any man's* life among you, but of the ship.
23 For there stood by me this night the angel of God, whose I am, and whom I serve,
24 Saying, Fear not, Paul; thou must be brought before Caesar: and, lo, God hath given thee all them that sail with thee.

Paul had an angel encounter in a time that everyone else was in a panic. The peace that Paul was walking in gave him the ability to keep his mind secure in Christ thus resulting in an angel encounter. God had a divine appointment that God reminded Paul of by this angel. Thus, Paul knew that no harm could come to him and since the anointing was rich on his life, God would save all those with him for Paul's sake. That is awesome.

II Corinthians 11:
4 And no marvel; for Satan himself is transformed into an angel of light.
15 Therefore *it is* no great thing if his ministers also be transformed as the ministers of righteousness; whose end shall be according to their works.

If God has the real thing, Satan has the imitation. We do have to know the spirit of God. If an angel, a vision, or any other manifestation comes to you and you do not feel a peace about it, do not trust it. The peace of God will always confirm his Spirit.

Philippians 4:
4 Rejoice in the Lord alway: *and* again I say, Rejoice.
5 Let your moderation be known unto all men. The Lord *is* at hand.
6 Be careful for nothing; but in every thing by prayer and supplication with thanksgiving let your requests be made known unto God.
7 And **the peace of God, which passeth all understanding, shall keep your hearts and minds through Christ Jesus**.
8 Finally, brethren, whatsoever things *are* true, whatsoever things *are* honest, whatsoever things *are* just, whatsoever things *are* pure, whatsoever things *are* lovely, whatsoever things *are* of good report; if there be any virtue, and if *there be* any praise, think on these things.

God will confirm his word to you by peace! Angel encounters can be a fearful thing but they will minister peace unto you and his word will be as sweet water nourishing your soul!

Galatians 1:

6 I marvel that ye are so soon removed from him that called you into the grace of Christ unto another gospel:

7 Which is not another; but there be some that trouble you, and would pervert the gospel of Christ.

8 But though we, or an angel from heaven, preach any other gospel unto you than that which we have preached unto you, let him be accursed.

9 As we said before, so say I now again, If any *man* preach any other gospel unto you than that ye have received, let him be accursed.

Just because they can preach a good word or a supernatural manifestation occurs doesn't mean its God. We have to;

1 John 4:

1 Beloved, **believe not every spirit, but try the spirits whether they are of God**: because many false prophets are gone out into the world.

2 Hereby know ye the Spirit of God: Every spirit that confesseth that Jesus Christ is come in the flesh is of God:

3 And every spirit that confesseth not that Jesus Christ is come in the flesh is not of God: and this is that *spirit* of antichrist, whereof ye have heard that it should come; and even now already is it in the world.

4 Ye are of God, little children, and have overcome them: because greater is he that is in you, than he that is in the world.

Here it is. We cannot walk around with blinders on. We are just like Daniel in chapter ten. We are in warfare. The devil desires to sift you like Peter. The anointing and walking in his glory is just stupendous. The more of God's anointing you desire the more it will cost. Many come to a place of anointing and fall in love all over with Jesus but when they realize what the cost will be and what must be sacrificed for Christ they step back again into their comfort zone. One of the key factors in knowing whether it is the spirit of God is this next scripture.

II Timothy 4:
2 Preach the word; be instant in season, out of season; reprove, rebuke, exhort with all longsuffering and doctrine.
3 For the time will come when they will not endure sound doctrine; but after their own lusts shall they heap to themselves teachers, having **itching ears**;
4 And they shall turn away *their* ears from the truth, and **shall be turned unto fables**.
5 But watch thou in all things, endure afflictions, do the work of an evangelist, make full proof of thy ministry.

In days gone by the church has instigated a religious practice of "If it sounds good say it." It is nice to please people, but when it is in direct contradiction to the word, we are not allowed to just make up something. I have been raised under many religious fallacies. Many of these fallacies were concerning dress and life style. It was a sin to drink coffee or tea. It was a sin to cook on Sunday because it was the Sabbath. We were placed under such bondage that we were afraid of missing heaven. When we prayed at night, we would ask God to forgive us of sins that we did not know we committed. The problem with that is I was living under a spirit of fear and not faith. Sin is willful and not accidental.

Now back to our study.

Luke 16:
22 And it came to pass, that the beggar died, and **was carried by the angels into Abraham's bosom**: the rich man also died, and was buried;
23 And in hell he lift up his eyes, being in torments, and seeth Abraham afar off, and Lazarus in his bosom.

Matthew 28:
20 Teaching them to observe all things whatsoever I have commanded you: and, lo, **I am with you alway,** *even* **unto the end of the world. Amen**.

Isn't it wonderful? When we finally get the opportunity to be with the Lord we will be secured and escorted by angels, that way there's no possibility of getting lost. The rich man evidently fell through the grave into hell seeing there was no one there to escort him. If you do not ever have an angel encounter here on this earth make sure you will have one when you fall asleep.

In conclusion, we need to start trusting God when we are conducting our daily lives. God has so many ways of ministering to you on a daily basis that unless we are conscientious of his spirit we may miss such sweet communion. When we rise up in the morning, we need to be asking the Father how he desires to commune with us that day. We know it is easier to hear and see from God when we are in church but the real test is if we are willing to inject God into every other part of our lives. If we do then he can actually show us how to do our jobs and live our lives with greater precision and gracefulness. The main thing is not to doubt what God is showing and speaking to you.

Add-on For Is That You Lord

VII. Dreams Page 33

DREAMS OF KNOWLEDGE (FLEEING DREAMS)

This is dealing with dreams that cannot be remembered in the morning, yet were given of God. There is a nagging feeling just at the edge of your unconscious mind but just out of reach of your conscience recollection.

Daniel 2:
1 And in the second year of the reign of Nebuchadnezzar, Nebuchadnezzar dreamed dreams, wherewith his spirit was troubled, and his sleep brake from him.
2 Then the king commanded to call the magicians, and the astrologers, and the sorcerers, and the Chaldeans, for to shew the king his dreams. So they came and stood before the king.
3 And the king said unto them, I have dreamed a dream, and my spirit was troubled to know the dream.

4 Then spake the Chaldeans to the king in Syriack, O king, live for ever: tell thy servants the dream, and we will shew the interpretation.

5 The king answered and said to the Chaldeans, The thing is gone from me: if ye will not make known unto me the dream, with the interpretation thereof, ye shall be cut in pieces, and your houses shall be made a dunghill. {cut...: Chaldee made pieces}

6 But if ye shew the dream, and the interpretation thereof, ye shall receive of me gifts and rewards and great honour: therefore shew me the dream, and the interpretation thereof. {rewards: or, fee}

7 They answered again and said, Let the king tell his servants the dream, and we will shew the interpretation of it.

8 The king answered and said, I know of certainty that ye would gain the time, because ye see the thing is gone from me. {gain: Chaldee buy}

9 But if ye will not make known unto me the **dream**, *there is but* one decree for you: for ye have prepared lying and corrupt words to speak before me, till the time be changed: therefore tell me the dream, and I shall know that ye can shew me the interpretation thereof.

10 The Chaldeans answered before the king, and said, *There is* not a man upon the earth that can shew the king's matter: therefore there is no king, lord, nor ruler, *that* asked such things at any magician, or astrologer, or Chaldean.

11 And it is a rare thing that the king requireth, and there is none other that can shew it before the king, except the Gods, whose dwelling is not with flesh.

12 For this cause the king was angry and very furious, and commanded to destroy all the wise *men* of Babylon.

13 And the decree went forth that the wise *men* should be slain; and they sought Daniel and his fellows to be slain.

14 Then Daniel answered with counsel and wisdom to Arioch the captain of the king's guard, which was gone forth to slay the wise *men* of Babylon: {answered...: Chaldee returned}

{captain...: or, chief marshal: Chaldee chief of the executioners, or, slaughtermen}

15 He answered and said to Arioch the king's captain, Why is the decree *so* hasty from the king? Then Arioch made the thing known to Daniel.

16 Then Daniel went in, and desired of the king that he would give him time, and that he would shew the king the interpretation.

17 Then Daniel went to his house, and made the thing known to Hananiah, Mishael, and Azariah, his companions:

18 That they would desire mercies of the God of heaven concerning this secret; that Daniel and his fellows should not perish with the rest of the wise *men* of Babylon. {of the God: Chaldee from before God} {that Daniel...: or, that they should not destroy Daniel, etc}

19 Then was the secret revealed unto Daniel in a night vision. Then Daniel blessed the God of heaven.

20 Daniel answered and said, Blessed be the name of God for ever and ever: for wisdom and might are his:

21 And he changeth the times and the seasons: he removeth kings, and setteth up kings: he giveth wisdom unto the wise, and knowledge to them that know understanding:

22 He revealeth the deep and secret things: he knoweth what *is* in the darkness, and the light dwelleth with him.

23 I thank thee, and praise thee, O thou God of my fathers, who hast given me wisdom and might, and hast made known unto me now what we desired of thee: for thou hast *now* made known unto us the king's matter.

This story is so profound because of a simple dream. The king was so troubled over this dream but was unable to recall it. He just knew it was an urgency to understand why he dreamed this dream.

Notice two things here. One was that the men of God ordained of God were about to be slain for the sake of unrighteous prophets. Secondly, if God had wanted this dream revealed to the king he would have understood it immediately.

29 As for thee, O king, thy thoughts came *into thy mind* upon thy bed, what should come to pass hereafter: and he that revealeth secrets maketh known to thee what shall come to pass. {came: Chaldee came up}

Daniel confirms that this dream was not for now. He also lets the king know that the only reason he understands this dream today is so that he may know that there is a God in heaven who knows even your thoughts. As you read on in Daniel you will see that this dream causes great troubles in the lives of these four prophets of God. The king is lifted up in pride and builds this great statue in his dream demanding everyone in his kingdom to worship it. There is an appointed time for these types of dreams. Being impatient will cause your relationship with Christ to be hindered.

Many times God will give us dreams that will give us confirmation as to where we are to be at a particular time. When we are at our divine ordered place, we will begin to see the dream come back to our remembrance. As we see the events unfold, we know two major things. One that we have the power to change the course of events that are unfolding. Two, we know that God has pre-ordained us to be in that particular spot at that particular time. We will know what people are about to say before they even know. The thing about Godly dreams is the realization of the period in which it is to transpire. Nebuchadnezzar took this dream and run with it. The downfall was that he saw himself as a God and thought that God was setting him in that place. It is just like someone who wants a reason for pride to arise in his or her lives. Some dreams are given to us just for us and no one else. Interpreting dreams takes wisdom and patience.

Chapter II

ANGELS UNAWARES

Have you ever had an encounter with angels? Would you like to? My endeavor is to try and build your faith. The fact is the New Testament Church is founded on angelic encounters.

Written By Dr. Ronald Sanders PhD
© By the Library of Congress 2006

ANGELS UNAWARES
9/23/97

Matthew 25: 34- 40,
Then shall the king say unto them on his right hand, come, ye blessed of my father, inherit the kingdom prepared for you from the **foundation of the world:**
For I was an hungered, and ye gave me meat: I was thirsty, and ye gave me drink: I was a stranger, and ye took me in:
Naked, and ye clothed me: I was sick, and ye visited me: I was in prison, and ye came unto me.
Then shall the righteous answer him, saying, Lord, when saw we thee an hungered, and fed thee? Or thirsty, and gave thee drink? When saw we thee a stranger, and took thee in? Or naked, and clothed thee?
Or when saw we thee sick or in prison, and came unto thee?
And the king shall answer and say unto them, verily I say unto thee, inasmuch as ye have done it unto the least of these my brethren, ye have done unto me.

Notice several things.
#1 - Jesus called us the blessed of my father. That means God has taken notice of us, and has spent time watching us. It is a wonderful feeling to know that I am blessed of God. I may not be special to anyone here on earth, but I am special to God. Many times by the way I act or the unfaithfulness to God, I wonder if God even knows I exist.
#2- Notice what Jesus said about the kingdom that was created since the foundation of the earth? Not since Adam and Eve, but before them the kingdom of God was waiting for us. He has a special place prepared for you and me.
#3- The king said that we are his brethren. That's like going to a king on this earth, he knows us by name, and we are special enough that he would stop those things of such importance just to listen to us. He has told all those in his kingdom to bless me, whatever I have needed of, to see that I had it. The king will answer that same thing on that day. Those that bless

the children of God, will be standing on the right hand of God, when he judges and separates the goats and the sheep in the church. The distinction between goats and sheep are whether we give unto our brethren in love. If we do it, out of obligation, to get leverage over someone, or do it grudgingly, if we do any of these, then we will be standing with the goats.

In this study, we will try to show that we are not alone, but God is present, and there are angels around us, to minister to us. Let me tell you three true stories.

In 1983, there was a young man in our church felt the call of God for ministry. I told him he needed to go to Ashland, VA. to the Calvary Pentecostal campground. This would be one of the most powerful influences upon his ministry. We stayed four days. The first day we were there, we met a Filipino minister. We had the honor of spending three days with him. We went to service together, ate together, and learned what he knew in God. He wore a large rice hat. I told the Lord, I would like to get me one of those hats. We felt so much of the love of God when we were around him. It seemed easier to be consumed in God's presence when he was around. On the third evening he told us he wanted us to come up to his room, he had something he wanted to show us. We agreed, and went up stairs over the lunchroom to a narrow hall. He unlocked a door to his room. He reached under the bed and got out a piece of large construction paper. It was rolled up with a piece of yarn holding it together. He showed us dates and places where God had done miracles and healings all over the world in his ministry. I looked at them, and remember saying to myself, that I had seen the same in our own ministry God had blessed us with. To see God use someone as himself in such a wonderful way, I rejoiced greatly with him. It made me think that maybe I need to start writing down what God was doing in me. He carefully tied his paper back up, and slid it under his bed. He reminded us that he was leaving early the next day. We were sorrowful to hear those words. He told us that we needed to support a work in the Philippines. He gave us the address, and unfortunately, I lost it! However, it began a hunger in my heart to go to the Philippines. The next day we looked for him, and he was gone. We went to his room and there was no answer. I went to the office and asked if my friend was still there. She replied that she had no record of that individual being there then. I told her what room he was in, and she, with a strange look on her face, told me that no one had stayed in **that** room. I left the office in puzzlement. We worshipped and praised God that day, before leaving. When I arrived at home, I asked my wife about that room. (My wife had lived on the campground), and why the receptionist would say what she did. My wife's eyes got very wide and surprised. She replied," the reason no one stays in that room, it is one of the rooms reserved for **angels**!!!!!!!" **I had spent three wonderful days with an angelic host, who instilled a desire for mission work in my spirit. My heart bursts every time I think about God's love for me, to allow me to be in the presence of an angel for three days!** I began to understand that God has watched my life, and cares about me.

Around 1984, I was employed at ************ Diesel co., in NC. I was a security guard. One night as I was working third shift, I began to make my rounds inside of the plant that was under construction. Below is a layout of the building.

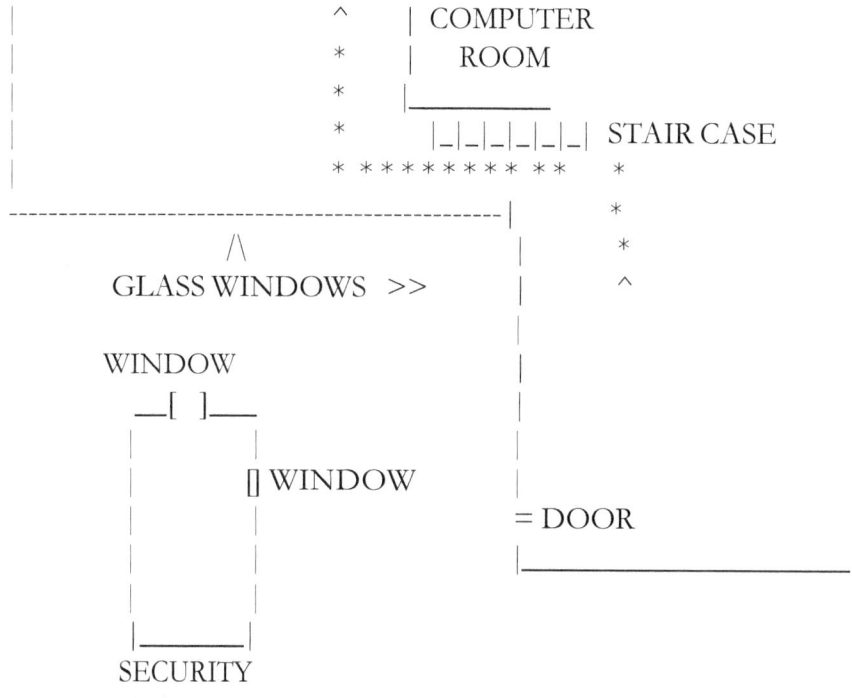

Across the front of the building is glass on two walls. From the security trailer, the lieutenant on the job could see anyone as they were walking in front of either wall. I was walking in the direction of the arrows and asterisks, going by the stairs of the computer room. When I came to that corner, I felt such an awesome presence of God, so I began to magnify the Lord for his wonderful presence. The lieutenant what man? He again answered and said, the man that passed you just as you were turning the corner. Out of curiosity, I asked why he asked. He replied that he watched him come around the row of windows, and as he came to the door, he disappeared. I could tell at this point, he was a little puzzled. I asked the lt. what this man looked like. He replied, that he was about 5' 10", medium build, brown hair, had blue jeans on, and a plaid shirt. Needless to say, I was about to go ballistic with this news. I tried to calmly answer the lt. what he had just saw. I told him, that, "Oh, it was just an angel"! He then asked me again what I said. I told him I had not seen anyone in that area. That it was just an angel. I did not want him to have a heart attack on the job. Seeing he did not quite believe in such wondrous things! Needless to say, he watched me very closely after that. I do not know if he ever figured out if I was completely sane or not. After that earth shaking news, about a couple of months later, he helped me find another job, I wonder why? The only real thing that upset me was that I did not see him, but only felt his presence. Oh well, I don't know if I could have handled it myself.

In 1982, I was leaving White's Supermarket, and a young man came up to me, and said to me, I am hungry, and I will work for food. That does not sound so strange. I told him that I did not have any money, which was the truth. I told him I could feed him. We went to the house, and I asked him to make himself comfortable. I went into the refrigerator and fixed everything I could get my hands on. He ate buffet that day, and that was before buffet was popular. After eating, we sat and talked, and then my wife came home. She asked if he wanted something else to eat, he replied, no thank you, I'm full, he got up, thanked us, asked again if there was any work we needed him to do, and we said no. Here is the strange part of this story. When he walked out of the door, we watched him cross the yard, we looked at each other, and we looked back at him. He was gone! The reason we looked at each other, we both felt such a strange stirring in our hearts. He did not have time enough to get to the street, much less cross it. I have often wondered if I had the privilege of feeding an angel. It has happened to many people before. Since that time, we have seen times we did not know where our next meal was coming from, and someone would call or come by with food. I wonder.

Luke 24: 13- 18, 29- 32,
And, behold, two of them went that same day to a village called Emmaus, which was Jerusalem about threescore furlongs.
And they talked together of all these things which had happened.
And it came to pass, that, while they communed together and reasoned, Jesus himself drew near, and went with them.
But their eyes were holden that they should not know him.
And he said unto them, and what manner of communications that ye have one to another, as ye walk, and are sad?
And the one of them, whose name was Cleopas, answering said unto him, art thou only a stranger in Jerusalem, and hast not known the things which are come to pass there in these days?
But they constrained him, saying, abide with us: for it is toward evening, and the day is far spent. And he went in to tarry with them.
And it came to pass, as they sat at meat with them, he took bread, blessed it, brake it, and gave it to them.
And their eyes were opened, and they knew him; and he vanished out of their sight.
And they said one to another, did not our heart burn within us, while he talked with us by the way, while he opened to us the scriptures?
 Wow! Could you imagine walking with Jesus himself? Could you imagine spending an evening with Jesus? They did not know it was Jesus. What if they had treated him differently?

Would they have had the opportunity to know him, to wash his feet, as the custom of the Jews toward the visitor? Can you imagine washing Jesus' feet? What an honor. Every time we wash each other's feet, we should wash them as if we are. This event shows us that just because they knew what Jesus looked like, that the knowledge of him is a spiritual revelation. The thousands of Jews saw him, but did not see the Son of God. Another example of this wondrous revelation knowledge is:

John 8: 56- 59,
Your father Abraham rejoiced to see my day: and he saw it, and was glad.
Then said the Jews unto him, thou art not yet fifty years old, and hast thou seen Abraham?
Jesus said unto them, verily, verily, I say unto you, before Abraham was, I am.
Then took they up stones to cast at him: but Jesus **hid himself**, and went out of the temple, **going through the midst** of them, and so passed by.

Here, we see an example of Jesus talking about the day in which Abraham and himself fellowshipped. The great part of this story, other than the fact he lets us know it was he who spent the day with Abraham, and not just an angel; when the Jews wanted to stone Jesus to death, he just caused the eyes of their understanding not to be enlightened. As we have already discussed, the knowledge of who Jesus is, comes by revelation and not observation. He walked right through the crowd. They did not even recognize him. They had already picked up boulders to stone him, but could not find him. To them, there was the Son of God unawares, just as there are angels around us unawares.

Hebrews 13: 1- 2,
Let brotherly love continue.
Be not forgetful to entertain strangers: for thereby some have entertained angels unawares.

Do you desire to have angels at your table? Entertain strangers, extend a hand to those you do not know.

Genesis 18: 1- 5, 8, 17- 19, 21- 22,
And the Lord appeared unto him in the plains of Mamre: and he sat in the tent door in the heat of the day;
And he lifted up his eyes and looked, and, lo, three men stood by him: and when he saw them, he ran to meet them from the tent door, and bowed himself forward to the ground.
And said, my Lord, if I have found favour in thy sight, pass not away, I pray thee, from thy servant:
Let a little water, I pray you, be fetched, and wash your feet, and rest yourselves under the tree:
And he took butter, and milk, and the calf which he had dressed, and set it before them: and he stood by them under the tree, and they did eat.
And the lord said, shall I hide from Abraham that thing which I do:

Seeing that Abraham shall surely become a great and mighty nation, and all the nations of the earth shall be blessed in him?
For I know that he will command his children and his household after him, and they shall keep the way of the Lord, to do justice and judgement; that the Lord may bring upon Abraham that which he hath spoken of him.
I will go down now, and see whether they have done altogether according to the cry of it, which is come up unto me; and if not, I will know.
And the men turned their faces from thence, and went toward Sodom: but Abraham stood yet before the Lord.

Abraham had the honor of washing Jesus' feet, feeding him the best he had to offer. Only after the angels got to Sodom were they called angels. Before, when they were at Abraham's house, they were called men. They were not angels of judgment at Abraham's house, but when they left, they judged all that they saw and heard. When you have found favour in God's eyes and heart, then the angelic beings around you are there to minister and fellowship, not to judge. In verse

21, Jesus said he was going to Sodom, but in verse 22, Abraham stood in front of Jesus, and Jesus stopped to answer Abraham's questions. Could you imagine standing in the way of what Jesus intended to do? Jesus had told Abraham that he would not even hold back his plans from revealing them to Abraham. Can you get excited about God's desire to share with us his plans for man? Abraham had one major concern, and that was his nephew Lot, whom he had taken under his wing. Jesus had made up his mind to destroy the cities of Sodom and Gomorrah. Jesus knew what Abraham was trying in a subtle way of asking him. In chapter 19: 29, God knew that he was concerned about Lot. God would not spare the city for four souls, but he did bring those four souls out before God sent his judgment on it. God remembered Abraham. God remembers your prayer requests too.

Genesis 19: 1- 2, 4- 5, 11, 29,
1 And there came two angels to Sodom at even; and Lot sat in the gate of Sodom: and Lot seeing them rose up to meet *them*; and he bowed himself with his face toward the ground;
2 And he said, Behold now, my lords, turn in, I pray you, into your servant's house, and tarry all night, and wash your feet, and ye shall rise up early, and go on your ways. And they said, Nay; but we will abide in the street all night.
4 But before they lay down, the men of the city, *even* the men of Sodom, compassed the house round, both old and young, all the people from every quarter:
 5 And they called unto Lot, and said unto him, Where *are* the men which came in to thee this night? bring them out unto us, that we may know them.
11 And they smote the men that were at the door of the house with blindness, both small and great: so that they wearied themselves to find the door.
29 And it came to pass, when God destroyed the cities of the plain, that God remembered Abraham, and sent Lot out of the midst of the overthrow, when he overthrew the cities in the which Lot dwelt.

The bible does not say it, but I feel like Lot entertained many strangers that came into those cities. He did this as hospitality and protection. He knew what would happen if these two men were to stay in the streets at night, the men of the city would have raped them. If you notice this story, it was only after the angel smote the homosexual men with blindness, that they revealed themselves to Lot. Lot entertained angels unawares. He was only trying to protect them. If he had of known it, he would not have offered his two virgin daughters to these homos. This gesture would have been an embarrassment to Lot, which the men of the city were an embarrassment enough. Notice three things

#1- in verse 8, he had two virgin daughters, who had not been married.

#2- in verse 14, he has other daughters who were married, to men of Sodom, who would not hearken to Lot's voice of the oncoming destruction.

#3- in verse 26, lot's wife looked back. Many have believed that her heart was still in the city, and all the sin and pollution thereof. Let me throw this one in. Her married daughters were still in the city. Which would she love the most, her daughters, her life, or the Lord's commandments? This is medicine to think on. The only other option available, is that the two daughters that went out of the cities were married, but were virgins, because of homosexual husbands? So take your choice. The key word is in verse 15, the angels said, ' ... And thy two daughters, which are here;" Showing that they were with Lot, and leaves the option that there were other daughters, which were not there. This explains the sons in law.

#4- I wonder how many children that lot had. Abraham stopped at ten souls. Could it be that he had three more children that were married in Sodom. Thus, would equal ten souls? Just a thought;

It would indeed be a strange feeling to know that your guests were not only angels, but have come to destroy the city. Not knowing whether you were to die with them. Thank God, for those who stood before the Lord, and found favour in God's eyes.

Joshua 5: 13- 15,
13 And it came to pass, when Joshua was by Jericho, that he lifted up his eyes and looked, and, behold, there stood a man over against him with his sword drawn in his hand: and Joshua went unto him, and said unto him, *Art* thou for us, or for our adversaries?
14 And he said, Nay; but as captain of the host of the LORD am I now come. And Joshua fell on his face to the earth, and did worship, and said unto him, What saith my lord unto his servant? {captain: or, prince}
15 And the captain of the LORD'S host said unto Joshua, Loose thy shoe from off thy foot; for the place whereon thou standest *is* holy. And Joshua did so.

Joshua saw a man, where Lot saw two. Neither one of these were known as angels. It was later revealed that they were angelic host. If Lot had not had the desire for hospitality as he did, what would have happened to him and his family? If Joshua had not went up to a man who had a sword in his hand, what would have happened? Joshua shows great boldness. Joshua did not know if he was an assassin, an enemy or what. He found out, he was the captain over the Lord's army. Not just an angel, but also a big bad sin kicking angel. The angel who defends Israel is Michael. Either this was Michael or one of his captains.
The thing we have to understand is that our understanding has to be fruitful to receive revelation of God.

Ephesians 1: 17- 19,
17 That the God of our Lord Jesus Christ, the Father of glory, may give unto you the spirit of wisdom and revelation in the knowledge of him: {in...: or, for the acknowledgement}
18 The eyes of your understanding being enlightened; that ye may know what is the hope of his calling, and what the riches of the glory of his inheritance in the saints,

19 And what is the exceeding greatness of his power to us-ward who believe, according to the working of his mighty power, {his mighty power: Gr. the might of his power}

We need to pray for the spirit of revelation for understanding of God's word. Just reading the word is not enough, we need to understand the depth of the word. Mysteries are for those who are not spiritually enlightened. Sinners cannot comprehend the depth of the word, seeing it is spiritually discerned.

Matthew 13: 11,
He answered and said unto them, because it is given unto you to know the mysteries of the kingdom of heaven, but to them it is not given.

Jesus said it was for us to understand the mysteries of the bible. I have heard that it is not for us to understand the entire bible. This is contrary to what the scripture said.

Let us look at what the angelic host does on our behalf.

Matthew 18: 10,
10 Take heed that ye despise not one of these little ones; for I say unto you, That in heaven their angels do always behold the face of my Father which is in heaven.

Here we see two things. One that there are angels assigned to our welfare, presenting our needs and petitions to the Father. In addition, we see that there is more than one angel assigned to us. The word angels, means more than one.

Hebrews 1: 13- 14,
13 But to which of the angels said he at any time, Sit on my right hand, until I make thine enemies thy footstool?
14 Are they not all ministering spirits, sent forth to minister for them who shall be heirs of salvation?

We see time and again that God has sent angels to mankind. Either to minister, declare what saith the Lord, to stand beside us, bring comfort, and strength. Angels are not outdated, because God is not outdated. God is dependable, and he never changes according to his word. Thus there are angels around us, whether the Lord opens our eyes to see them, is not important. The main thing is that they are there. If we saw many angels, we would have a tendency to exalt them, and place them above God. This is not their purpose. With each example of angelic visitations in the bible, we find that they will say two things.

1- Be not afraid.

2- Worship me not.

II Kings 6: 16-19, there is an account of angels appearing to assure the hearts of God's anointed, Elisha and his servant.

In closing, while holding prayer meetings in Kinston, NC, in 1996, I had an unusual experience. I was standing and praising God in a service where the power of God was awesome. I felt someone behind me, and could see the shadow of him over me. I felt his hands as he placed them on both of my shoulders. I opened my eyes as I looked up and over my head, I could see a figure of an individual at least a foot taller than myself. I could see him look down at me with a pleasant smile. As I closed my eyes, I was not afraid because it was a feeling of being near someone I knew very well. It was as if I had known this person all my life.

I have spoken to this man at other times in my life. I realized I had just seen an angel. I saw him more in the spirit than in the natural. It was a face I knew and recognized. You know how that we think that our imagination has run wild, I just enjoyed the presence of this angel without giving him much more thought. I still could feel his hands on my shoulders, a warm and gentle touch for such a large powerful looking individual. After I had taught that day, a lady came up after service and asked me if I knew that there was a big angel standing behind me as I was praising God. She stated that as I was facing a large picture in Sis. Cannon's living room, this angel appeared and placed his hands on my shoulders. I told her I saw him. I was stunned that someone else saw him too! God just wanted me to know that which I saw was real. That angelic being was a very familiar face and presence. He was a friend whom I had known for much of my life. What I saw was not as clearly seen as you are, he was there, and I knew what he looked like, but it was more revelation knowledge than eye recognition. I guess it is a little strange, but it was the most secure feeling I have ever known. It was like the extension of God's arms around me. Two other times I have felt this wonderful security while in services. Each time someone else saw what I felt. Only that one time did I actually recognize his facial features. The other times he was just there.

In 1982, while I was in security work at ****** - ********** tobacco co., I worked night shift as sergeant. I worked at the church during the day, and was very tired at night. At times, fatigue was so great, I asked the Holy Ghost to allow me to sleep for fifteen minutes, so I could go on. I would fall into a deep sleep, and fifteen minutes later, I would hear a strong, loud, loving voice call my name, and a loud knock at the side window. I would wake out of a deep sleep and immediately look at my time clock. Fifteen minutes had passed. There have been several times I would get out of the car I was resting in, and run around the car to see who was calling my name, knowing all the time it was the Lord's voice. I was parked in the middle of an open area of about five acres. The knock at the side glass was so loud, it sounded a little like thunder in the middle of the night. Since that time, years later, I can be in a sound sleep, and all it takes to awake me, is someone to call my name. I love God so much. It is not the appearances of angels or the voice of the Lord; it's just knowing that God loves me that much. I miss hearing that beloved voice waking me when it is time to get up. It is again time to arise and awake to his lovely voice!

If you cannot believe God for such supernatural things, then you will not be aware that it ever happened. God will only reveal himself to them who are expecting the supernatural, and are flowing in that same realm. You become thankful of his manifestations, but more enthused over the God who did it. In later years, I have received everything I have desired.

The entire things God has blessed me with; the excitement has been over how and when God blessed me with it. God has a flare all his own. He wants you to know it was he and that he loves you so much. Angelic appearances are wondrous, but I look for the sweet heart of God who sent them. I am not caught up in the angels ministering, but the ministering God.

Colossians 2: 18,
18 Let no man beguile you of your reward in a voluntary humility and worshipping of angels, intruding into those things which he hath not seen, vainly puffed up by his fleshly mind, {beguile...: or, judge against you} {in a...: Gr. being a voluntary in humility}

Romans 1: 25,
25 Who changed the truth of God into a lie, and worshipped and served the creature more than the Creator, who is blessed for ever. Amen. {more: or, rather}
Here we see a problem in our society today. People spend more time worshipping things created by God, than the God of creation. Religions are devised just to worship angels, and dead people. People call a way of life, in which they worship man, and his ability to satisfy. Humility comes from the heart, and not an outward presentation. Just like worshipping angels. They are messengers and ministers to the heirs of salvation.

Hebrews 1: 13- 14,
13 But to which of the angels said he at any time, Sit on my right hand, until I make thine enemies thy footstool?
14 Are they not all ministering spirits, sent forth to minister for them who shall be heirs of salvation?

They are God's ministers. If we see them, it is because God allows them to be seen, to build our faith in an eternal God, not in the angels themselves. Expect miracles and the wondrous supernatural. Do not get caught up in seeing angels, but in the God of them!

In 1998 about 5:00 am I was headed to church to pick up the pastor's son's car to carry a guy to Raleigh for court. I was traveling about 60 mph and all of a sudden I thought I saw a horse run out of the woods to the shoulder of the road. At second glance, this horse had at least 8 points on his rack. This deer stepped out in front of my car, having no time to slow my vehicle I centered him in the middle of my grill to limit the possibility of flipping my car. When I struck the deer, he buckled my hood, broke my bumper, forced my radiator onto the motor block, and broke my battery and alternator bracket. Both headlights were crushed and the signal lights were knocked to either side of the car. In that terrifying instant I saw these antlers headed for my windshield, specifically where I was sitting. In another instant, I would be dead from the antlers piecing my body. At that exact moment, I saw with my eyes two hands, palms facing toward the deer that came down in front of my windshield scooping up the deer and flipping with his fingers, the deer over my car and landing 20 feet or more behind my car. I could see the knuckles on the backs of his hands as the fingers rolled upward to impel this deer from my line of sight. I looked down at my speed odometer and I was still traveling at 55 miles per hour. I realize that my car was still cranked and my parking lights were still working in the dark. I turned my caution flashers on and was able to see into the darkness without headlights. I arrived at the pastor's house in Leland, NC. I got out of my car, went into the parsonage without saying a word. I was asked by the pastor how I was doing, all I could say was I am blessed, and God is so good. I left with the pastor's son's car and proceeded to Raleigh as if it were a normal day, walking in the blessings of God. When I came back to Leland, my pastor asked me if I had seen my car. That was one of those blue-collar questions. I looked at it, the hair still in the grill; the hood was buckled 18 inches above the fenders. The fenders on each side was buckled some. As I gave my testimony, they stood in amazement, as did I. They asked how you could be so calm this morning after all these events. If you had seen two hands come between you and an enormous deer, not much else that could happen could be any more shocking. The storm had passed and the Master of my storm had held my reins and steadied my course. Jesus had saved my life yet another time! Approximately 12 inches from my windshield was a tear in my fender right by the hood. The tear was 3 inches long where the antler had punctured through the car's steal. I could run three fingers into the hole and not be tight. I was 12 inches from death when the Lord rescued me. 12 inches! Now my dilemma is, was it an angel or was it Jesus' hands I saw? I don't know, but one thing I do know, I was once a dead man, but now I am alive!

II Chronicles 5:
13 It came even to pass, as the trumpeters and singers *were* **as one**, to **make one sound to be heard in praising and thanking the LORD**; and when they **lifted up** *their* **voice** with the trumpets and cymbals and instruments of music, and praised the LORD, *saying*, For *he is* good; for his mercy *endureth* for ever: that **then the house was filled with a cloud**, *even* the house of the LORD;
14 So that the priests could not stand to minister by reason of the cloud: for the glory of the LORD had filled the house of God.

When we are in a unity of the Spirit that the praises sound as one voice, the glory will fill the house and the cloud of anointing will permeate every being in the house. The fog of the glory will fill the house. Wow!

In 2007 I was videoing a revival for a pastor friend in Jacksonville, NC. God had gloriously moved during this week of services. We had witnessed many healings, Holy Ghost infillings and salvation. The Lord had given many prophetic words during these meetings. About mid-week I began to notice a couple who were missionaries to Ecuador, I think. They both were not the typical missionaries. They were quiet and possessed a great amount of love. One evening the woman evangelic called them up to pray for them. I was asked to come and minister over them. The Lord had a word of prophecy for them, but another minister stepped up and spoke a word of encouragement over them, so I stepped aside. Something kept drawing me to them and the anointing on their lives. Two days later, I had the opportunity to minister over them again. As I did, the Lord gave them the word of prophecy he had for them. The strange thing about it, first, I kept my camera recording. Secondly, as I was prophesying over them, I felt two people come by me, and I sensed that they stood on either side of them, seeing my eyes were still closed. As I was prophesying, I began to sob like a baby, which seldom happens to me. I knew what I felt; it was two angels standing beside them. I kept prophesying until God was through. I barely had enough strength to make it back to my camera. I sat down with this overwhelming presence of God in the sanctuary. When they got up off the floor, they proceeded back to their seats. The glory on them was so overwhelming, needless to say the service ended up in the realms of the miraculous! As we adjourned to the kitchen for food, they came and sit in front of me. They talked in their normal calm sweet tones. The more they talked the more trouble I had keeping back the tears. I finally could not hold it and I excused myself to go to the sanctuary to pray. I told myself there was no way possible with the presence so strong on them that the camera missed the presence of those angels. Therefore, I reviewed the DVD to where I was prophesying and sure enough you could see two images on either side of them. It was strange because only minutes after I went into the sanctuary others began to filter back in to see what I was doing. In a couple of minutes, I had a crowd around my monitor looking at the presence of angels. Where they were standing light was being distorted. When they moved the colors of people's clothing became disoriented. It looked as if the colors were running out from their clothes. You could see when they arrived and when they moved away. I will never forget the presence of such a heavy anointing.

One thing we have to realize is that angels are a normal part of our lives. Sometimes they are felt and at other times, they are behind the scenes. Where the people's voices are as one sound in praising and thanking God, angels will be in the midst!

Another aspect of angels, we indeed need to speak of, is this; are the angels subject to us, for us to command them? This is a sensitive subject seeing so many are teaching that the angels are now subject to us.

Hebrews 2:
1 Therefore we ought to give the more earnest heed to the things which we have heard, lest at any time we should let *them* slip.
2 For if the word spoken by angels was stedfast, and every transgression and disobedience received a just recompence of reward;
3 How shall we escape, if we neglect so great salvation; which at the first began to be spoken by the Lord, and was confirmed unto us by them that heard *him*;
4 God also bearing *them* witness, both with signs and wonders, and with divers miracles, and gifts of the Holy Ghost, according to his own will?
5 For **unto the angels hath he not put in subjection the world to come, whereof we speak**.
6 But one in a certain place testified, saying, **What is man**, that thou art mindful of him? or the son of man, t**hat thou visitest him?**
7 **Thou madest him a little lower than the angels**; thou crownedst him with glory and honour, and **didst set him over the works of thy hands**:
8 **Thou hast put all things in subjection under his feet**. For in that he put all in subjection under him, **he left nothing *that is* not put under him. But now we see not yet all things put under him.**

At first glance, we could say that all things are under our feet, including angels, but the last of verse eight tells us that now we see that not all things are placed under man's feet. Until the dispensation of Jesus, we never thought that angels could be. When we read scriptures like:

I Corinthians 6:
2 Do ye not know that the saints shall judge the world? and if the world shall be judged by you, are ye unworthy to judge the smallest matters?
3 Know ye not that we shall **judge angels**? how much more things that pertain to this life?

With this scripture in mind, we can translate it into; if we are to judge angels, then we must have the ability to control angels. This however is not what this scripture is saying. At the White Throne Judgment, we will also be with Christ who Judges Satan's fallen angels and experience them being cast down into the lake of fire. This does not take place now, but judging matters concerning saints with saints does. We are seeing two entirely different subjects being expressed at two different times. We are not yet in a spiritual place to command them into hell, who are made a little higher than us, but as the bride of Christ we will. We are waiting with all creation to be glorified and united as his bride. In Hebrews 2: 7- 8, it would appear to be that we have control of angels, until we define the last eleven words, so let us do so now.

"But now we see not yet all things put under him".
But
1161 de, de {deh}
Meaning: 1) but, moreover, and, etc.

Now
3568 nu/n nun {noon}
Meaning: 1) at this time, the present, now

We See
3708 o`ra,w horao {hor-ah'-o}

Meaning: 1) to see with the eyes 2) to see with the mind, to perceive, know 3) to see, i.e. become acquainted with by experience, to experience 4) to see, to look to 4a) to take heed, beware 4b) to care for, pay heed to 5) I was seen, showed myself, appeared

Not Yet
3768 ou;pw oupo {oo'-po}
Meaning: 1) not yet

All Things
3956 pa/j pas {pas}
Meaning: 1) individually 1a) each, every, any, all, the whole, everyone, all things, everything 2) collectively 2a) some of all types

Put Under
5293 u`pota,ssw hupotasso {hoop-ot-as'-so}
Meaning: 1) to arrange under, to subordinate 2) to subject, put in subjection 3) to subject one's self, obey 4) to submit to one's control 5) to yield to one's admonition or advice 6) to obey, be subject Him

846 auvto,j autos {ow-tos'}
Meaning: 1) himself, herself, themselves, itself 2) he, she, it 3) the same
Now, let us place these definitions in the order in which they fall to understand this portion of the verse.
moreover
at this time, the present, now
to see with the mind, to perceive, know
become acquainted with by experience, to experience
to care for, pay heed to
not yet
each, every, any, all, the whole, everyone, all things, everything
collectively
some of all types
to arrange under, to subordinate
to subject, put in subjection

to submit to one's control
to yield to one's admonition or advice
himself, herself, themselves, itself

With all these additives to the verse, we see that not now, do we have control of all things. Some things and types are not yet under our control, yet they at some point in the future, will be. The scripture also shows that we at this point cannot perceive or even understand how to subordinate angels under our control. Could it be, that while we are yet in this fleshly confinement, God could not trust this flesh to control things of such great magnitude as his angels, yet he has allowed us this control;

Luke 10:
17 And the seventy returned again with joy, saying, Lord, even the devils are subject unto us through thy name.
20 Notwithstanding in this rejoice not, that the spirits are subject unto you; but rather rejoice, because your names are written in heaven.

Devils
1140 daimo,nion daimonion {dahee-mon'-ee-on}
Meaning: 1) the divine power, deity, divinity 2) **a spirit, a being inferior to God, superior to men 3) evil spirits or the messengers and ministers of the devil**

Spirits
4151 pneu/ma pneuma {pnyoo'-mah}
Meaning: 1) a movement of air (a gentle blast 1a) of the wind, hence the wind itself 1b) breath of nostrils or mouth 2) the spirit, i.e. the vital principal by which the body is animated 2a) the rational spirit, the power by which the human being feels, thinks, decides 2b) the soul 3) **a spirit, i.e. a simple essence, devoid of all or at least all grosser matter, and possessed of the power of knowing, desiring, deciding, and acting** 3a) a life giving spirit 3b) a human soul that has left the body 3c) **a spirit higher than man but lower than God, i.e. an angel 3c1) used of demons, or evil spirits,**

who were conceived as inhabiting the bodies of men 3c2) the spiritual nature of Christ, higher than the highest angels and equal to God, the divine nature of Christ 4) of God 4a) God's power and agency distinguishable in thought from his essence in itself considered 4a1) manifest in the course of affairs 4a2) **by its influence upon the souls productive in the theocratic body (the church) of all the higher spiritual gifts and blessings** 4a3) the third person of the trinity, the God the Holy Spirit 5) the disposition or influence which fills and governs the soul of any one 5a) the efficient source of any power, affection, emotion, desire, etc.

In verse 20, was Jesus making a correction to the disciples' comments? The disciples said the devils were subject to them, and Jesus says rejoice not the spirits are subject to you. Could it be, that these are two entirely different classes of demonic activity? We know there are different classes of angels, then so why wouldn't there also be different classes of demons?

Ephesians 6:
10 Finally, my brethren, be strong in the Lord, and in the power of his might.
11 Put on the whole armour of God, that ye may be able to stand against the wiles of the devil.
12 For we wrestle not against flesh and blood, but against **principalities**, against **powers**, against the **rulers of the darkness of this world**, against **spiritual wickedness** in high *places*.
13 Wherefore take unto you the whole armour of God, that ye may be able to withstand in the evil day, and having done all, to stand.

Wickedness
4189 ponhri,a poneria {pon-ay-ree'-ah}
Meaning: 1) depravity, iniquity, wickedness 2) malice 3) evil purposes and desires

High Places
2032 evpoura,nioj epouranios {ep-oo-ran'-ee-os}
Meaning: 1) existing in heaven 1a) **things that take place in heaven** 1b) the heavenly regions 1b1) heaven itself, the abode of God and angels 1b2**) the lower heavens, of the stars** 1b3) the heavens, of the clouds 1c) the heavenly temple or sanctuary 2) of heavenly origin or nature

Here in this scripture we see power given to us to overcome and control Satan's kingdom, of which are
principalities
powers
rulers of the darkness of this world
spiritual wickedness in high places
When adding Luke 10: 20 we can add these variations of demonic activities to the things we can control.
demons
evil spirits
who were conceived as inhabiting the bodies of men
These are the active realms of Satan's activity. We have control of these realms over Satan's kingdom.

Isaiah 14:
15 Yet thou shalt be brought down to hell, to the sides of the pit.
 16 They that see thee shall narrowly look upon thee, *and* consider thee, *saying*, *Is* this the man that made the earth to tremble, that did shake kingdoms;
 17 *That* made the world as a wilderness, and destroyed the cities thereof; *that* opened not the house of his prisoners?
18 All the kings of the nations, even all of them, lie in glory, every one in his own house.
 19 But thou art cast out of thy grave like an abominable branch, and as the raiment of those that are slain, thrust through with a sword, that go down to the stones of the pit; as a carcase trodden under feet.

These were cast out of heaven to the sides of the pit, which is the outer crust dividing the earth from the pit inside. These are cast down and are under our feet, seeing God gave us control of all that is upon the earth, symbolizing under our feet. This of course took place in Adam's day, and in the day of the second Adam.

I Corinthians 15:
22 For as in **Adam** all die, even so in Christ shall all be made alive.
23 But every man in his own order: Christ the firstfruits; afterward they that are Christ's at his coming.
24 Then *cometh* the end, when he shall have delivered up the kingdom to God, even the Father; when he shall have put down all rule and all authority and power.
25 For he must reign, till he hath put all enemies under his feet.
26 The last enemy *that* shall be destroyed *is* death.
44 It is sown a natural body; it is raised a spiritual body. There is a natural body, and there is a spiritual body.
45 And so it is written, The first man **Adam** was made a living soul; the last **Adam** *was made* a quickening spirit.
46 Howbeit that was not first which is spiritual, but that which is natural; and afterward that which is spiritual.

There are stages of man's development. First he was a living soul, and he fell. Second Jesus a living soul became a quickening spirit. Thirdly, we become a spiritual being after that Jesus Christ has raised us by his Spirit. Now can Luke 10: and Ephesians 6: take place in us. We must first be quickened, and then we can have power over that which we have through Christ conquered. When we become one with Jesus in marriage, then all other things we will conquer, and we will also reign over them. As we overcome, he gives us power over those things conquered. We have not yet apprehended the resurrection of the dead, seeing we still live. Thus this power also lays in waiting for us to overtake.

Our prayers affect what takes place in the spirit realm. It is our prayers that effect God's reaction on our behalf. In our imagination, we need angels to accomplish everything for us, but it is necessary? We have to realize that much of what we say has power of its own, and needs not angel intervention. As an inferiority complex we feel the need for angels to perform for us, when we have the power to minister as the Holy Ghost leads.

Chapter III

THE MINISTRY OF GREAT LOVE & THE SECOND STEP ANOINTINNG

This study is a result of something Jesus spoke to me at about 3:00 am standard time in Ochos Rios, Jamaica. We had just finished our missionary journey and we as a group were resting for two days before the grueling journey back to the United States. I had noticed all the people that had given their lives to Jesus that week, and I couldn't help but wonder, "Lord how many actually got saved?" During that week the Lord had allowed me to run back into some of the people that had gotten saved. The testimony was that they felt so different and happy. One of them the night before had gotten saved at the Pineapple Motel. He was a security guard whose rounds were at the pool area where I had been counseling with people the night before. He accepted Jesus into his heart at about 2:00 am and at 6:00 am he was telling everyone he saw how that this fat guy had prayed with him and he felt so happy inside. People were knocking on my door telling me of his testimony. The joy I felt was overwhelming. So the last night I was out at the pool alone when the Lord spoke the words, "Second Step Anointing". I immediately told the Lord there was no such phrase in the Bible. He didn't respond. I told the Lord, if there is such a thing, and then prove it. Over the next few weeks, I started to type this study on my manual typewriter. God began to unfold layers of the Bible I had never really seen before. I saw the anointing in a different light from that wonderful night, an anointing that transcends time and space; an anointing that defies the laws of nature. This is a scanned copy of what was written on my type writer, so the spacing may appear odd, but it's ok. I want you to get this explosive realm of faith. Many of my studies since that time have incorporated into it parts of this study.

I John 4: 16-18,
And we have known and believed the love that God hath to us. God is love, and he that dwelleth in love dwelleth in God, and God in him.
Herein is our love made perfect, that we may have boldness in the day of judgment: because as he is, so are we in this world.
There is no fear in love: but perfect love casteth out fear. because fear hath torment. He that feareth is not made perfect in love.

Have you ever wondered what Jesus felt while he was here walking among us? This study is dedicated to understanding what it took Jesus to minister under such great anointing as he did. The opening statement is seemingly an innocent one. We have all memorized John 3: 16, and we know it is meaning in our lives. The next phrase begins to tell us about the very nature of God himself, and thus reveal the nature of Christ also. When we look up love, we of course find the word "Agape". Which means affection or benevolence a love feast; (feast of) charity. When we look at this type of love, we see it is all the love we can stand, or embrace.

Isaiah 55: 11,
So shall my word be that goeth forth out of my mouth: it shall not return unto me void, but it shall accomplish that which I please, and it shall prosper in the thing whereunto I sent it.

Notice the next verse in Is. 55: 12- 13,

Isaiah 55. 12-13,
For ye shall go out with joy, and be led forth with peace: and the mountains and the hills shall break forth before you with singing, and all the trees of the field shall clap their hands.
Instead of the thorn shall come up the fir tree, and instead of the briar shall come up the myrtle tree; and it shall be to the Lord for a name, for an everlasting sign that shall not be cut off.

Because the word of the Lord does not go out void, but accomplishes what God desires, we shall go out with joy and peace. If the results of what God says brings forth joy and peace both in the earth, think of what will happen in us if we learn to be like God! Why is the anointing limited in our lives? We have not learned how to operate in this love of the Father. If you have a child that is careless, you will not entrust him with a sharp knife, would you? Why? You would be afraid of him harming himself as well as others. God has made our mouths a vital tool in accomplishing his will in the earth. The only way God will allow us to be used, is if we can walk in his love and stay there! If our mouths flare off like our tempers, then God will put restraints on how much anointing comes out of our lips. In Is. 55; God said that when briars are planted, it will come up as the fir tree, and the myrtle. If we grasp exactly what God is saying here, it will blow your mind.

Genesis 3: 17-19,
And unto Adam he said, Because thou hast harkened unto the voice of thy wife, and hast eaten of the tree, of which I commanded thee, saying, Thou shalt not eat of it; cursed is the ground for thy sake; in sorrow shalt thou eat of it all the days of thy life;
Thorns also and thistles shall it bring forth to thee; and thou shalt eat the herb of the field;
In the sweat of thy face thou shalt eat bread, till thou return unto the ground; for out of it wast thou taken: for dust thou art, and unto dust shalt thou return.

I do not know if you caught it or not, but God is saying that if we obey and follow the commandments of the Lord, he is undoing the curse upon humanity that was pronounced in Gen. 3: 17- 19. God had said that when you plant, that you will reap thorns and thistles with your crops, but here he is saying the very opposite. Instead of the briars and thorns, your seed would be productive again. The land itself will prosper for thee. If we add the three scriptures together, we find that because of the word of the Lord not going forth void, but accomplishing what God desires, then all these blessing shall come on us! Thus, adding I John 4: 16- 17, when we walk in the perfect love of God, it places the power of God in our lips to cause productivity instead of death. As with anything that God gives, there is a condition to receiving it. This is the purpose of this study. To walk and flow in' the great heart felt love of God. Many say that you can not stay in the spirit all the time, but according to I John 4:, we can, and should! When we allow ourselves to walk in the God kind of love, then we are always open to the Spirit of God to lead and guide us. How can we know that we are walking in that perfect love of God? If we have boldness toward God, and we walk in it that means whatever our need is for that day that we have such confidence in God that we know that he is going to answer. It brings new light to the scripture;

I John 5: 13-15,

These things have I written unto you that believe on the name of the Son of God; that ye may know that ye have eternal life, and that ye may believe on the name of the Son of God.
And this is the confidence that we have in him, that, if we ask anything according to his will, he heareth us:
And if we know that he hear us, whatsoever we ask, we know that we have the petitions we desire of him.

Since the reoccurring theme for I John is the love of God, this brings us into a light that we may have overlooked for many years. That not only confidence in God is enough, but there has to be the love of God radiating from your being. That in his love, we find all our petitions answered. I do not know about you, but there have been things I have asked the Lord about, that seemingly there has been no action on the part of God about it. Could I have failed in walking into his glory and seeking him being engulfed by his love? Since we know that John's aspirations for his life was simply to fall deeper in love with Jesus, we know that all he writes to us is engulfed by this all inspiring love. For us to receive what John has given us, we must first fall as madly in love with our Saviour as

John did. You may say that is hard, if not impossible to do, but we have to realize that God is not a respecter of persons. Literally, what John is saying, is that if we also walk in this all consuming love, that whatsoever we ask of the Father, he will give it. We must realize also that in this great love, we will not desire to ask anything outside of the will of God.

How many times have you asked God about something as a result of fear? We may not be afraid of asking, or doubting what we are asking, but sometimes we ask God things as a direct result of our fears. If we did not walk in fear of someone or something, think of how many prayers would not even need to be prayed. Ex: the weatherman says a tornado or severe weather is headed your way, and you begin to pray because the wind is boisterous outside. Many of us would loose sleep because of the wind and storm. Many would tarry all night in prayer for our safety. What would Jesus have done?

Mark 4; 37-41,
And there arose a great storm of wind, and the waves beat into the ship, so that it was now full.
And he was in the hinder part of the ship, asleep on a pillow; and they awake him, and say unto him, Master, carest thou not that we perish?
And he arose, and rebuked the wind, and said unto the sea, peace, be still. And the wind ceased, and there was a great calm.
And he said unto them, Why are ye so fearful? how is it that ye have no faith? And they feared exceedingly, and said one to another, What manner of man is this, that even the wind and sea obey him?

Jesus would have went to sleep. He was not worried about the storm, or its effect on the ship. The ship had plenty of water in it. The bible says it was full. The storm was at full force and the ship was overtaken by the waves. Think of what it would take to have such a peace? Jesus and his disciples were out on the sea, no land in sight, not enough men there to drink all the water up, looked obvious that they would drown. Not to Jesus, just made him sleep better. We just have to come to grips with the fact that God loves us enough to take care of us.

John 13; 35,
By this shall all men know ye are my disciples, if ye have love one toward another.

How will the world know we are Christians? Because of our love for each other. The first question that comes to mind is, how much love is Jesus talking about? Let us answer this question with two scriptures.

Romans 5: 7,
For scarcely for a righteous man will one die: yet peradventure for a good man some would even dare to die.

Proverbs 17: 17,
A friend loveth at all times, and a brother is born for adversity.

John 15: 13-15,
Greater love hath no man than this that a man lay down his life for his friends.
ye are my friends, if ye do whatsoever I command you.
Henceforth I call you not servants: for the servant knoweth not what his lord doeth: but I have called you friends; for all things that I have heard of my Father I have made known unto you.

So I gave you three scriptures. You know how good the word is, it is hard to just eat two! Notice, a re-occurring theme here; in the first scripture, that for a righteous man a person would not desire to die. When people start talking about loving at all times, you lose many people's interest. Many people thrive on confrontations, thus, they will never know the power and anointing God has set aside for us. How would you like to be called the friend of God?

Ezekiel 33: 11,
And the Lord spake unto Moses face to face, as a man speaketh unto his friend. And he turneth again unto the camp:

but his servant Joshua, the son of Nun, a young man, departed not out of the tabernacle.

Moses loved the people God had chosen so much, that on different occasions he asked God to kill him also if he had to show vengeance against the children of Israel. Moses was God's friend! How would you like to be known as God's friend? We have to have the same kind of love Jesus and Moses had for all peoples. When we walk in God's love, then the scriptures will be fulfilled in us.

Matthew 5: 14-16,
Ye are the light of the world. A city that is set on a hill can not be hid. Neither do men light a candle and put it under a bushel, but on a candlestick: and it giveth light to all that are in the house.
Let your light so shine before men, that they may see your good works, and glorify your Father which is in heaven.

So shine. So implies a word of severe importance. Putting emphasis on the amount of light they see. They should not only see that we are Christians, but that we walk under such an anointing, that they will either draw closer to, or run, very fast from. We should never be mediocre. Many times, we run up against those types of Christians that just rub us the wrong way. It is not because of any thing that they have done, but there is just something so different about the anointing on them, that causes us to be under conviction when we are around them.

II Corinthians 5; 20,
Now then we are ambassadors for Christ; as though God did beseech you by us; we pray you in Christ's stead, be ye reconciled to God.

Now accordingly or certainly we are a senior or acting as a representative for the sake of Jesus, as in that manner the supreme divinity did invite, invoke you through us; we beg or petition you in Christ's stead, be ye changed mutually and to compound a difference to God. (Greek translation)

We are representing Jesus, as ordained by God. Paul said that God used them to get a message to us. Paul is pleading with us to be changed in the image of God. We may ask, what is wrong with us now? Maybe nothing, but how does God see us in the light of himself? We are just like most of the Christians living in Paul's day. He is exhorting us to go deeper in God. If each of us is ambassadors of Christ, his representatives:

John 14; 14- 15,
If ye ask anything in my name, I will do it. If ye love me, keep my commandments.

II. MINISTERING IN LOVE

Ephesians 4: 1-3, 11, 15
I therefore the prisoner of the Lord beseech you that ye walk worthy of the vocation wherewith ye are called.
With all lowliness and meekness, with longsuffering forbearing one another in love,
Endeavoring to keep the unity of the Spirit in the bond of peace. And he gave some, apostles; and some, prophets; and some, evangelists; and some, pastors and teachers;
 But speaking the truth in love, may grow up into him in all things, which is the head, even Christ;
 This chapter starts and ends with the importance of God's supernatural love dominating our lives. When God calls us to be his servants, he calls us to different calling and anointing. We are to fulfill that which God has equipped us to do. As we know, vocation is also our job or work. When we say yes to Christ, then we also say yes to the job he has ordained us to do. In verse two, God says with lowliness and meekness, and in verse 32, he ends with kindness, tenderness, and forgiveness. We will only be as successful in God, as the amount of God's love that flows through us. On a car, you have an oil stick to check the depth of oil, whether sufficient to cause proper and smoothness of operation. Our oil stick

measurer is the word of God, and it registers the amount of God's agape love needed for smooth operation in the Spirit and miracles. So, if God has placed a calling on your life, and we know he has, then fill up on his love, and race foreword.

Romans 13: 10
Love worketh no evil to his neighbor: therefore love is the fulfilling of the law.

Romans 12; 20-21,
Therefore if thine enemy hunger, feed him; if he thirst, give him drink: For in so doing thou shalt heap coals of fire on his head. Be not overcome of evil, but overcome evil with good.

One of the wonderful things about flowing in the love of God, you don't have to sit and reason out whether or not you are asking according to his will, because when we flow in this love, we are not asking anything that will exalt yourself above others or to cause them harm, thus God will answer and do as we pray of him.

What kind of results happens when we allow ourselves in every situation to flow in this love? It will take them by storm.

John 18: 6,
As soon as he had said unto them, I am he, they went backwards, and fell to the ground.

Jesus did not overcome them with great words, or great anointing, but great love. He loved enough to replace a lost ear back on the high priest's servant's ear. Jesus knew he was going to die at the same hands that stood before him. They would, in only a few hours, murder him! Jesus was not so much in the spirit that he did not feel death creeping up on him. A major part of his prayer was, help me to yield to what I must do. Jesus did not want to die! He felt the sting of death, which is why he descended into hell to take victory of death for us, that we might never feel the sting and torment of death like the one he did!

Revelation 1: 18,
I am he that liveth, and was dead; and, behold, I am alive forevermore, Amen'; and have the keys of hell and of death.

Jesus took the keys to hell and death. No longer do we have to fear. When we allow ourselves to walk in the perfect love of God, what keys do we possess for others? There are torments that trouble the people of God, and God has given to us the power to overcome and bring the victory for our brothers. No wonder Paul mocks death and hell.

I Corinthians 15; 55-56,
O death, where is thy sting? O grave, where is thy victory? The sting of death is sin; and the strength of sin is the law,

In John 15;13, Jesus tells his disciples that no greater love hath a man than this, that a man lay down his life for his friends. When we hear these words again in the light of what Jesus did for us, we know that to walk in the same anointing Jesus did, that each time we minister to others, we have to have such compassion and concern for them that our life is nothing compared to their needs. We must be willing to not only die for them, but also live for them and their needs to be met. Our heart must hurt so much and long so strongly to see God meet their needs that we would take their pain for them!

III. THE LOOK OF LOVE

Matthew 23; 37,
O Jerusalem, Jerusalem, thou that killeth the prophets, and stonest them which are sent unto thee, how often would I have gathered thy children together, even as a hen gathereth her chickens under her wings, and ye would not!

Jesus saw them to whom God had sent him unto. He felt the anguish of their misery, but they would not allow Jesus to help them.
He saw what God saw, and felt the compassion that God had for them. He mourned, not for himself, but for those who were blinded by the God of this world.

II Corinthians 4: 3-4,
But if the gospel be hid, it is hid to them that are lost; In whom the God of this world hath blinded the minds of them which believe not, lest the light of the glorious gospel of Christ, who is the image of God, should shine unto them.

Jesus was that light, and now he shines through us. It is our duty as rescued children to share this light with the world.

Matthew 7; 35-38,
And Jesus went about all the cities and villages teaching in the synagogues, and preaching the gospel of the kingdom, and healing every sickness and every disease among the people.

Could you imagine the physical strength it would take to evangelize the way Jesus did. He, many times said he had compassion on them.

Mark 8: 2-3,
I have compassion on the multitude, because they have now been with me three days, and have nothing to eat:
And if I send them away fasting to their own houses, they will faint by the way: for divers of them came from afar,
This is of course the miracle of the fishes and loaves. 4, 000 were fed. Notice three major things here in Jesus' ministry.

1/ the great compassion of Jesus. How he cared for each individual person's welfare. They will faint by the way. He loved greatly, those to whom he ministered to.

2/ The miracle of the multiplication of the loaves and fishes. Out of great compassion for the people, a miracle developed. Do I think it would have happened if he did not have that great love for them? No, I believe that the great God kind of love for them is what caused the great miraculous power of God to manifest itself.

3/How long, had the great crowd been assembled, hearing the teachings of Jesus? Three days! They would not even leave to go and find food for themselves or their families. They were literally spell bound by the power packed teaching of Christ. They forgot the weakness in their bodies just so they could hear every word that Jesus spoke! Wow! How many ministers or teachers of the gospel today can hold a great crowd of people in such a state of anticipation as Jesus did? Few! People can sense whether you love them, and are genuinely concerned for their lives,

IV. THE ANOINTING OF LOVE

Romans 8: 1,
There is therefore now no condemnation to them who are in Christ Jesus, who walk not after the flesh, but after the Spirit. When we are in Jesus' love, we forget all our past, and forget who we are, engulfed by his love.

Mark 6: 33- 35,
And the people saw them departing, and many knew him, and ran afoot thither out of all the cities, and out went them, and came together unto him. And Jesus, when he came out, saw much people, and was moved with compassion toward them, because they were as sheep having no shepherd: and he began to teach them many things.
And when the day was far spent, his disciples came unto him, and said, This is a desert place, and now the time is far passed:

Jesus was trying to get his disciples alone so that they might refresh themselves, seeing they were tired, but the crowds of people were so hungry for God, that they saw no rest. Jesus was moved with great compassion toward the people.
Next, we will show you how and what effect this great love had on people.

Luke 7: 37- 38,
And, behold, a woman in the city, which was a sinner, when she knew that Jesus sat at meat in the Pharisee's house, brought an alabaster box of ointment,
And stood at his feet behind him weeping, and began to wash his feet with tears, and did wipe them with the hairs of her head, and kissed his feet, and anointed them with the ointment.

Matthew 15: 25- 28,
Then came she and worshipped him, Saying, Lord, help me.
But he answered and said, It is not meet to take the children's bread, and to cast it to dogs.

And she said, Truth Lord: Yet the dogs eat of the crumbs which fall from the Master's table.

Then Jesus answered and said unto her, O woman, great is thy faith: be it unto thee as thou wilt. And her daughter was made whole from that very hour.

Two illustrations here. One felt so much of Jesus' love, she was willing to stand-alone, be embarrassed just to show her love for Jesus. All she wanted is for his love to cover her, and make her feel complete. She may have come in as a sinner, but she left as one of the children of the king. In the next illustration, a woman needed a miracle for her child, as the other illustration, she didn't care what embarrassment it would cause, or what she had to do, she was willing. I can only imagine the love this woman felt as Jesus spoke to her. His words may have sounded hard or bias, but love swept over her, and at any cost, she desired it to engulf her too. Willing to have whatever Jesus would give unto her, she placed herself in Jesus' hands, and at his mercy to do with as he pleased. One thing about humility, you cannot be embarrassed. Embarrassment happens when pride is a factor, thus, Jesus could have said anything to this woman, and would not have swayed her desire for the master. So much love radiated from Christ, that people were willing to lay down their lives to be embarrassed by this love!

V. HOW CAN I HAVE THIS ANOINTING?

First, you must know it hurts. Is. 58: says that you draw out your soul, and you open up yourself to be hurt by others. Those that you show love to, not always will return it back. Some will trample it under foot.

Hebrews 4: 15-16
For we have not an high priest which cannot be touched with the feeling of our
 infirmities: but was in all points tempted like as we are, yet without sin.
Let us therefore come boldly before the throne of grace, that we may
obtain mercy, and find grace to help in time of need.

His love. We also, as Christ, must feel the infirmities of those in need. Let us consider ourselves, lest we also be tempted. Notice the words, "let us therefore come". Because we feel the infirmities of the week, the hurting, those in need, then we will come boldly before God on their behalf. We can then understand what Moses felt when God desired to destroy the children of Israel for their sins. Moses felt the infirmities and sorrows of the people.

Romans 1: 11,
For I long to see you, that I might impart unto you some spiritual gift, to the end that ye may be established.

The word long means; to yearn, to dote upon, intensely crave possession, (lawfully or wrongly); to be excessively or foolishly fond.
Paul, desiring so badly to be with the church at Rome, ached in his body and heart to be a part of them to such a point as to grieve being parted from them.

Matthew 16: 25,
For whosoever will save his life shall lose it: and whosoever shall lose his life for my name sake shall find it.

This scripture does not specifically mean in death. Just the fact that completes fulfillment comes when your life is no longer important to yourself. To find true life, and contentment, it comes in laying down your ambitions and seeking after the heart of God, losing tract of importance in your personal life.

Another example of this is;

Acts 4: 32,
And the multitude of them that believed were of one heart and of one soul: neither said any of them that ought of the things which he possessed was his own but they had all things common.

Each of these was willing to give away all that they had worked for all their lives. Many did. Look at the great throngs of people who stood in line not to receive the possessions, but to partake of this great anointing.
We have seen two simple things we have to do to walk in this great love.
1 / love until it hurts.
2/ find fulfillment in the fulfilling of other's needs, not in self fulfillment.

PART II OF MINISTRY OF GREAT LOVE

"WHAT IS THE "NEXT STEP ANOINTING"?

You may ask, what is the next step anointing?

I asked myself that also, when the Lord spoke it to me. I was always under the impression that the anointing was the anointing, and there were no levels. I was sitting and meditating on a mission trip to Jamaica, when the Lord dropped this phrase on me. I spent the next three months preparing a study on this next step anointing. I knew that there was some¬thing else I had to understand before I could fully comprehend the scope of what Jesus was saying. When the Lord gave me the study on "The Ministry of Great Love," it floored me. I thought I was showing love, but after that study, I understand that, to flow in such an anointing, as he desires, then we have to be perfected in his perfect love. That does not mean we are always perfect at showing love, but that we are continuously conscience of his great love moving and operating in us.

The Lord showed us what that anointing will do. When we came near those that were demon possessed, they became enraged. They reminded me of a dog that stood a foot tall, barking loudly and violently, but doing very little else. When we walked down the streets, demoniacs would charge toward us, yelling profanities. At first, I thought it was because all whites in Jamaica were missionaries, but the Lord pointed out the cruise line ship that was anchored at the bauxite plant. It was then that I realized he knew who we were. That anointing of God transcended color, or nationality, seeing they were not attacking the tourists. He felt the anointing convicting him of sin. All during this particular trip, we saw the same occurrence of demons demonstrating their power. What was so great, we were not afraid, but rather found it amusing. Then we felt an awe of compassion for these trapped individuals. The Lord dealt with me, that my next visit would be to minister to the ones who were trapped by demonic spirits. My time of play was over, the Lord showed me it was time to go to work and dethrone Satan!

Matthew 8: 28- 29,
And when he was come to the other side into the country of the Gergesenes, there met him two possessed with devils, coming out of the tombs exceeding fierce, so that no man might pass by that way.
And behold, they cried out, saying, What have we to do with thee, Jesus, thou Son of God? art thou come hither to torment us before the time?

The amazing thing is that Jesus did not go to them, they came to Jesus. When we walk in the next step anointing, the demons will know when you come into their town or country. Think of the anointing that could loose demons in an entire town, just by going there under the direction of the Holy Ghost? This end time revival that we have the privilege of starting, will be with such intensity, that demons will be on the run when God sends you into city. If the devil can cause us to fear, then we have no power over him, but when we walk in the boldness of God, that even when this happens, it will not move us from the power of the almighty.

Mark 9: 18, 20, 26,
And wheresoever he taketh him, he teareth him, and he foameth, and gnasheth with his teeth, and pineth away; and I spake to thy disciples that they should cast him out; and they could not.
And they brought him unto him; and when he saw him, straightway the spirit tare him; and he fell on the ground, and wallowed foaming.
And the spirit cried, and rent him sore, and came out of him; and he was as one dead; insomuch that many said, He is dead.
All during Jesus' ministry, we see the same happening. The anointing on Jesus' life caused the devils around him to fear what Jesus may do to them.

Acts 3: 4- 5,
And Peter, fastening his eyes upon him, with John, said, Look on us. And he gave heed unto them, expecting to receive something of them.

When we walk in that great anointing, people see us, and expect to receive. It is like unto a candy store. When a person sees a candy store, when they enter in, they are looking for candy, not appliances. When that anointing abides in us, people are looking to receive what you have.

Acts 5: 14- 16,
And believers were the more added to the Lord, multitudes both men and women.)
Insomuch that they brought forth the sick into the streets and laid them on beds and couches, that at least the shadow of Peter passing by might overshadow some of them.
There came also a multitude out of the cities round about unto Jerusalem, bringing sick folks, and them which were vexed with unclean spirits;
and they were healed everyone.

We have used this example many times before, but do we really grasp what actually happened here? Such an anointing radiated off the disciples that people's faith arose when in their presence. If we were to pray for someone now, we would have to build up their faith before we could see God heal them, but these saw such an anointing in their lives, that their faith became contagious. How would you, when people saw you, see such faith arise in them that they were coming up to you asking for God to heal them. If you walk into mom's kitchen, you could smell the aroma of mom's food, taste the savory food, and handle the freshness and softness of it. When the anointing permeates our very pores, people will want to become so intoxicated with the presence of God they feel, that faith will come alive in them, and miracles will happen in our ministries without us having to lay hands on them or even pray for them. This is the type of anointing that the disciples had upon them. When they walked into a room, the demons and infirmities walked out! Did you catch the word multitudes? When was the last time we saw multitudes drawn just by the spirit of the almighty? No publicity, no big name evangelist, just the anointing.

We have already discussed the great anointing of love that Jesus walked in. We know how that Jesus had such compassion on the people, and how that the power of God flows through that love. When we see the needs of others more than the need to be approved, then we will also walk in Jesus' shoes."

Luke 9: 49- 50, 55 - 56,

While he yet spake, there cometh one from the ruler of the synagogue's house, saying to him, Thy daughter is dead, trouble not the Master.

But when Jesus heard it, he answered him, saying, Fear not: believe only, and she shall be made whole.

And her spirit came again, and she arose straightway: and he commanded to give her meat.

And her parents were astonished: but he charged them that they should tell no one what he had done.

Can you imagine asking someone not to tell what God has done in your life? Yet Jesus on several occasions asked people to do that, why? When one person receives something of the Lord, others also would desire the same thing. If the word got out that Jesus healed even the dead, how many would flock to Jesus to have their loved ones raised again? In doing of good, Jesus' ministry could have been reduced to the state of being a witch or necromancer. In that which Jesus did, there was always a crowd ready to stone him, trying to find accusation to kill him. Others, yet, would have such a fear of someone who could raise the dead, that they would not come to receive what God had for them. In either case, the controversy over Jesus would have dramatically increased. This anointing has not just started with Jesus, but is seen all through the word of God. In Moses' day, the Red Sea parted, water came from a rock, ax handle floated for Joshua, fire came down out of heaven for Elijah, the anointing on the bones of Elisha raised a soldier back to life, and 300 men of Gideon killed all the armies of the enemy. All through the bible, we see this great anointing of God that passed all reasoning and understanding. This anointing defies the laws of nature, gravity, common sense, and even human understanding. The best scripture I know to describe this great anointing is;

I Corinthians 1: 24- 29,
24 But unto them which are called, both Jews and Greeks, Christ the power of God, and the wisdom of God.
 25 Because the foolishness of God is wiser than men; and the weakness of God is stronger than men.
 26 For ye see your calling, brethren, how that not many wise men after the flesh, not many mighty, not many noble, *are called*:
27 But God hath chosen the foolish things of the world to confound the wise; and God hath chosen the weak things of the world to confound the things which are mighty;
28 And base things of the world, and things which are despised, hath God chosen, *yea*, and things which are not, to bring to nought things that are:
29 That no flesh should glory in his presence.

In essence, this second step anointing starts when we walk in the perfect love of God, desiring that our brother become whole in every way, no matter how or what it cost us and when we have the Jesus kind of compassion on the people. Then, allowing God to do how ever or whatever he desires in us to fulfill the need of those in need. Stop limiting God in doing what you can, and start desiring God to meet the needs of all the people at once. It is not the anointing of God in us that counts, but the anointing released unto the people that does. They can take that anointing, apply to their own wounds, and minister that healing needed. You bring in that release of anointing to the people, but they actually use it for themselves. You just build them up in the Lord, and make it possible for them to use what God has already supplied.

When you are in your daily lives, think continually about the ministry of love, and allow it to flow out of you, and it will. Just simply love and enjoy what you have in your soul. God said, "It's alright to have fun in my presence, and you can laugh if you want to. The anointing will do the rest. Remember, it is not what you can do, but what God is doing to multitudes through you. You will still minister to individuals as you already are, but be aware that that ministry of love is affecting all those around you, causing the next step anointing to become alive in you. Jesus always told us to preach the gospel to the entire world, not just one at a time, but effecting multitudes! Do not be afraid to ask a crowd you are in, whether at work, church, or on the streets they all want to receive Jesus into their hearts, you may be surprised to see multitudes say yes. It is an awesome feeling to find numbers of people at once saying yes to Jesus. Why only affect one, when you can affect all? God sends us divine appointments every day that we minister to just one, but God has divine appointments to minister too many at once also. Do not miss the opportunity to minister as Jesus leads you, whether to one or to a thousand and one. We have to be like the disciples, be willing to go to minister to one in the desert place, and watch God minister to the city of azotes also. The city of azotes was waiting to be won by Philip, but Jesus wanted him to minister to one eunuch first, before winning the city of azotes.

Luke 22:

60 And Peter said, Man, I know not what thou sayest. And immediately, while he yet spake, the cock crew.
61 And the Lord turned, and looked upon Peter. And Peter remembered the word of the Lord, how he had said unto him, Before the cock crow, thou shalt deny me thrice.
62 And Peter went out, and wept bitterly.
63 And the men that held Jesus mocked him, and smote him.
64 And when they had blindfolded him, they struck him on the face, and asked him, saying, Prophesy, who is it that smote thee?

I want to show you something here. Jesus in all that he was going through knew the time that his prophecy happened in Peter's life. With all the turmoil surrounding Jesus, he stopped and just simply looked at Peter. This one look caused Peter to run out of the high priest's house weeping bitterly. What kind of look could it have been, a look of disgust or one of disappointment? No, I think it was one of such dying love that Peter could see it in his eyes. If you will, the look of anointing was imparted into Peter's heart. See this second step anointing even can be transferred through sight. Just as Peter did at the gate called beautiful ministering to a lame man. This type of anointing will transcend all logic and reason. That is why those who are not Christians or not walking in the Spirit, have any comprehension of what you are referring to. Let us look back at Mark's gospel.

Mark 4:

38 And he was in the hinder part of the ship, asleep on a pillow: and they awake him, and say unto him, Master, carest thou not that we perish?

39 And he arose, and rebuked the wind, and said unto the sea, Peace, be still. And the wind ceased, and there was a great calm.

40 And he said unto them, Why are ye so fearful? how is it that ye have no faith?

41 And they feared exceedingly, and said one to another, What manner of man is this, that even the wind and the sea obey him?

Mark 5:

1 And they came over unto the other side of the sea, into the country of the Gadarenes.

2 And when he was come out of the ship, immediately there met him out of the tombs a man with an unclean spirit,

3 Who had his dwelling among the tombs; and no man could bind him, no, not with chains:

4 Because that he had been often bound with fetters and chains, and the chains had been plucked asunder by him, and the fetters broken in pieces: neither could any man tame him.

5 And always, night and day, he was in the mountains, and in the tombs, crying, and cutting himself with stones.

6 But when he saw Jesus afar off, he ran and worshipped him,

7 And cried with a loud voice, and said, What have I to do with thee, Jesus, thou Son of the most high God? I adjure thee by God, that thou torment me not.

8 For he said unto him, Come out of the man, thou unclean spirit.

9 And he asked him, What is thy name? And he answered, saying, My name is Legion (6828 demons): for we are many.

10 And he besought him much that he would not send them away out of the country.

11 Now there was there nigh unto the mountains a great herd of swine feeding.

12 And all the devils besought him, saying, Send us into the swine, that we may enter into them.

13 And forthwith Jesus gave them leave. And the unclean spirits went out, and entered into the swine: and the herd ran violently down a steep place into the sea, (they were about two thousand;) and were choked in the sea.

14 And they that fed the swine fled, and told it in the city, and in the country. And they went out to see what it was that was done.

15 And they come to Jesus, and see him that was possessed with the devil, and had the legion (6828 demons), sitting, and clothed, and in his right mind: and they were afraid.

16 And they that saw it told them how it befell to him that was possessed with the devil, and also concerning the swine.

17 And they began to pray him to depart out of their coasts.

18 And when he was come into the ship, he that had been possessed with the devil prayed him that he might be with him.

19 Howbeit Jesus suffered him not, but saith unto him, Go home to thy friends, and tell them how great things the Lord hath done for thee, and hath had compassion on thee.

Luke 8:

35 Then they went out to see what was done; and came to Jesus, and found the man, out of whom the devils were departed, sitting at the feet of Jesus, clothed, and in his right mind: and they were afraid.

This account of demon possession in this man or men, depending on which gospel you are reading. The demons came to Jesus and not the other way around. The reason I backed up to chapter four is because it lays groundwork that gives insight to the anointing. Jesus had just commanded peace upon a raging sea and it obeyed his command that it stood still. The disciples were still reeling from the phenomenon that even that which has held mankind bound, being nature itself, no longer had power over us. Here we see the demon possessed coming to greet Jesus. Now watch this power of the next step anointing. God told me that "Love is love". It took me a while to understand it but it makes perfect sense. If we love, we love completely or not at all. We think we have variables of love but we don't. I know all of you bible scholars are going over the "Phileo, Ahab, Ahabah, Rayah and Agapao" love, that's not relevant here. The one kind that is, is the "Agapao" love of God. When we close off our agapao love for others then we close off the agapao love for God. I said all that to say this, that Jesus so loved that he didn't even hate the devil. How many of you will so love that you would allow demons to re-enter other people after you have cast them out? The first thing on our minds would be to cast them into abyss where they were afraid they were doomed. This next step anointing knows no boundaries. We have to cast the devil out of whosoever is possessed but we can't hate. I have heard it said so many times "I don't hate the sinner yet I hate the sin". How about this cliché, "I have to love you but I don't have to like you". Jesus knew that no swine or pig would allow a demon to enter their bodies. Jesus knew that these demons would be loosed back on society to find another willing vessel. His magnitude of love would not allow him to dam anyone or anything to an eternity without hope. Wow, watch this scripture and it will make better sense to you.

Luke 9:
52 And sent messengers before his face: and they went, and entered into a village of the Samaritans, to make ready for him.
53 And they did not receive him, because his face was as though he would go to Jerusalem.
54 And when his disciples James and John saw this, they said, Lord, wilt thou that we command fire to come down from heaven, and consume them, even as Elias did?
55 But he turned, and rebuked them, and said, Ye know not what manner of spirit ye are of.
56 For the Son of man is not come to destroy men's lives, but to save them. And they went to another village.

But Elijah would have Lord? Jesus just left and did nothing. Just as he did when they were mocking and scourging him at his mocked trial. Ye know not what spirit ye are of. That is powerful.

I John 4:
15 Whosoever shall confess that Jesus is the Son of God, God dwelleth in him, and he in God.
16 And we have known and believed the love that God hath to us. God is love; and he that dwelleth in love dwelleth in God, and God in him.
17 Herein is our love made perfect, that we may have boldness in the day of judgment: because as he is, so are we in this world. {our love: Gr. love with us}
There is no fear in love; but perfect love casteth out fear: because fear hath torment. He that feareth is not made perfect in love.
19 We love him, because he first loved us.
20 If a man say, I love God, and hateth his brother, he is a liar: for he that loveth not his brother whom he hath seen, how can he love God whom he hath not seen?
21 And this commandment have we from him, That he who loveth God love his brother also.

If you look up the type of love God is talking it is the agapao love or the love of God. The only way we can have or even know of this love is to know the author of it. The key to an anointing that engulfs our lives and affects everyone we meet is operating in this agapao love. We do not have the luxury of separating the person form the sin. We have to wholly love. We cannot participate and handle sin but we can show the sinner the love of God.
You may ask how I flow in this next step anointing. The answer is simple. When you rise up in the morning, ask God to allow you to walk in the anointing of great love. As your mind is focused that day on God and how he will manifest himself, faith is constantly active. Look for people near you to react to your presence especially when you have said or did

nothing. We have to understand it is not about your wondrous spiritual words, or even your righteous lifestyle, it is the Spirit of you Father in you that do the work. You will notice that people will sense something when they come around you. Some may say it is a peace; some may say they feel weird or freaked out around you. That is good. See this anointing is about your confidence in Christ Jesus. Just like the shadow of Peter passing by those people. They received their healing because of the close proximity of Peter. Just being around Jesus causes faith to be built and thus if Jesus is dominant in our lives, his spirit will cause those crying out to feel that virtue leave you without your ability to do or say.

Acts 5:
11 And great fear came upon all the church, and upon as many as heard these things.
12 And by the hands of the apostles were many signs and wonders wrought among the people; (and they were all with one accord in Solomon's porch.
13 And of the rest durst no man join himself to them: but the people magnified them.
14 And believers were the more added to the Lord, multitudes both of men and women.)
15 Insomuch that they brought forth the sick into the streets, and laid them on beds and couches, that at the least the shadow of Peter passing by might overshadow some of them
16 There came also a multitude out of the cities round about unto Jerusalem, bringing sick folks, and them which were vexed with unclean spirits: and they were healed every one.
There are only so many people we can speak to, lay hands on, prophesy to and personally minister to, but the anointing can. We just have to be vessels of that anointing. Does that make us radioactive? Maybe we are just anointing- active?

Mark 5:
28 For she said, If I may touch but his clothes, I shall be whole.
29 And straightway the fountain of her blood was dried up; and she felt in her body that she was healed of that plague.

30 And Jesus, immediately knowing in himself that virtue had gone out of him, turned him about in the press, and said, Who touched my clothes?

31 And his disciples said unto him, Thou seest the multitude thronging thee, and sayest thou, Who touched me?

32 And he looked round about to see her that had done this thing.

33 But the woman fearing and trembling, knowing what was done in her, came and fell down before him, and told him all the truth.

Can you handle this? This is the type of anointing I am talking about. It's on you and ministering for you even when you are not trying to minister. The key is their faith. If you read about the life of Rev. Smith Wigglesworth's, you'll understand this anointing. He could sit on the back of a train or bus and people start repenting of their sins without him saying a word! There is a cost for this anointing, are you willing to make the sacrifice to have it? Now that you know, it is in your hands!

Chapter IV

CUTTINGS, PAINTINGS AND PIERCING?

This study answers a question many Christians have asked. Is it wrong to have a pretty tattoo? Will it send me to Hell? Well, let's see.

Written By Dr. Ronald Sanders PhD
© By the Library of Congress 2006

What does the bible say about such things as tattoos, cutting your flesh, and having body piercing? Let's see.

Leviticus 19:
26 Ye shall not eat *any thing* with the blood: neither shall ye use enchantment, nor observe times.
27 Ye shall not round the corners of your heads, neither shalt thou mar the corners of thy beard.
28 Ye shall not make any cuttings in your flesh for the dead, nor print any marks upon you: I *am* the LORD.
29 Do not prostitute thy daughter, to cause her to be a whore; lest the land fall to whoredom, and the land become full of wickedness. {prostitute: Heb. profane}

Verse 27 sounded a little strange, so I looked it up to understand it. It seems to have been the custom to surgically alter the shape of their heads by removing skin from the high places to make it circular. They also cut the flesh to surgically graft masks to their face or head.
Verse 28 includes a number of things. First, we are not to cut our flesh, whether out of anger, remorse, or pleasure. Many as a sign of pity will cut themselves for attention. This is forbidden. This is to include cutting or etching designs in our flesh. The only two instances in the word that give headway to alter the flesh. *One is for circumcision*, which is done for sanitary reasons. The second is for a *bond servant. By the piercing of the ear*. We will discuss later. In this verse, we see we are not to print anything on our bodies. What is tattoos? Isn't it printing objects and/or words on the body?These cuttings into the flesh would include body piercing. They disfigure the body. This is and was a cult practice in the world. To glorify their Gods, and try to get favor of their Gods. It began in Genesis with the druid priests and satanic worship. It carries all through the bible. This spirit that comes upon a person to mar their bodies is the same perverse spirit that is the root ofa homosexual spirit.

Genesis 9:

22 And Ham, the father of Canaan, saw the nakedness of his father, and told his two brethren without.

23 And Shem and Japheth took a garment, and laid *it* upon both their shoulders, and went backward, and covered the nakedness of their father; and their faces *were* backward, and they saw not their father's nakedness.

24 And Noah awoke from his wine, and **knew what his younger son had done unto him**.

25 And he said, Cursed *be* Canaan; a servant of servants shall he be unto his brethren.

Done unto him is an action word in the Hebrew. It means that something was "to fashion, accomplished, to make". Ham did something to Noah that caused Noah to curse Ham or Canaan as he was known. He was the first homo mentioned. There was three cities in Abraham's day that God hated with a passion. These cities were Sodom, Gomorrah, and Zoar. Each of these cities were known for homosexual activities.

Genesis 19:

4 But before they lay down, the **men of the city**, *even* the men of Sodom, compassed the house round, both old and young, all the people from every quarter:

5 And they called unto Lot, and said unto him, Where *are* the men which came in to thee this night? bring them out unto us, **that we may know them**.

6 And Lot went out at the door unto them, and shut the door after him,

7 And said, I pray you, brethren, do not so wickedly.

8 Behold now, I have two daughters which have not known man; let me, I pray you, bring them out unto you, and do ye to them as is good in your eyes: only unto these men do nothing; for therefore came they under the shadow of my roof.

9 And they said, Stand back. And they said again, This one fellow came in to sojourn, and he will needs be a judge: now will we deal worse with thee, than with them. And they pressed

sore upon the man, even Lot, and came near to break the door.

The men of the city wanted to know the two strangers which were men. Fresh meat. Lot offered them his two virgin daughters of which they refused. We know that any hot-blooded ready-to-go men would not refuse a virgin! They did! Now I know what you're thinking. What does this have to do with body piercing, tattoos, and cuttings. Go with me and see the spirit that is on an individual.

Romans 1:
21 Because that, when **they knew God, they glorified** *him not as God*, neither were thankful; but became **vain in their imagination**s, and their **foolish heart** was darkened.
22 Professing themselves to be wise, they became fools,
23 And **changed the glory** of the uncorruptible God into an image made like to corruptible man, and to birds, and fourfooted beasts, and creeping things.
24 Wherefore God also **gave them up to uncleanness** through the **lusts of their own hearts, to dishonour their own bodies between themselves**:
25 Who changed the truth of God into a lie, and worshipped and **served the creature more than the Creator**, who is blessed for ever. Amen. {more: or, rather}
26 For this cause God gave them up unto **vile affections**: for even **their women did change the natural use into that which is against nature:**
27 And likewise also **the men, leaving the natural use of the woman, burned in their lust one toward another; men with men working that which is unseemly,** and receiving in themselves that recompence of their error which was meet.
28 And even as they did **not like to retain God in** *their* **knowledge**, God gave them over to a reprobate mind, to do those things which are not convenient; {to retain: or, to acknowledge} {a reprobate...: or, a mind void of judgment or, an unapproving mind}

29 Being filled with all unrighteousness, fornication, wickedness, covetousness, maliciousness; full of envy, murder, debate, deceit, malignity; whisperers,

30 Backbiters, haters of God, **despiteful, proud,** boasters, inventors of evil things, **disobedient to parents,**

31 Without understanding, **covenantbreakers, without natural affection, implacable,** unmerciful: {without natural...: or unsociable}

32 Who knowing the judgment of God, that they which commit such things are worthy of death, not only do the same, but have pleasure in them that do them. {have...: or, consent with}

Notice the chain of rebellion.

Maliciousness is one having a vicious disposition.

Malignity is having bad character, evil or pessimistic behavior.

Proud is not willing to listen.

Disobedient to parents is truly a sign of rebellion against authority.

Covenant breakers is a liar. One who can't be trusted at his word.

Without natural affection is one who is unsociable, who's sexual desires supersede the normal.

implacable is anyone who will not come into a covenant relationship. Whether marriage vows, Christian walk, a legal contract, or just keeping your word. Not trustworthy.

Now that we have looked at all that, let us consider those who have tattoos or have etched engravings into their skin. They will fall into one or more of the previous mentioned categories. We have not even gotten to piercing yet. Tattoos are representative of two things.

One, rebellion against God. My body isn't good enough. I need to make it better. Cursing God's creation.

Two, rebellion against authority. Rising up against "the system." I want to do my own thing, and I don't want anyone to try and tell me what to do.

Notice this is all lumped into the same category as homosexuality? Which is direct rebellion against the creation of God. The first thing they will tell you is, "That God made me this way". God created he them male and female. They will be called man and woman. The two equal one in God. He called them Adam. To be one, must comprise of a male and a female. Not butch and butchette. See Genesis 1: 27- 28; 2: 18- 25; 3: 12, 17; 5: 2

I Kings 18:

24 And **call ye on the name of your Gods**, and I will call on the name of the LORD: and the God that answereth by fire, let him be God. And all the people answered and said, It is well spoken. {It is...: Heb. The word is good}

25 And Elijah said unto the prophets of Baal, Choose you one bullock for yourselves, and dress it first; for ye *are* many; and call on the name of your Gods, but put no fire *under.*

26 And they took the bullock which was given them, and they dressed it, and called on the name of Baal from morning even until noon, saying, O Baal, hear us. But *there* was no voice, nor any that answered. And **they leaped upon the altar** which was made. {hear: or, answer} {answered: or, heard} {leaped...: or, leaped up and down at the altar}

27 And it came to pass at noon, that Elijah mocked them, and said, Cry aloud: for he is a God; either he is talking, or he is pursuing, or he is in a journey, or peradventure he sleepeth, and must be awaked. {aloud: Heb. with a great voice} {he is talking: or, he meditateth} {is pursuing: Heb. hath a pursuit}

28 And they **cried aloud**, and **cut themselves** after their manner **with knives and lancets, till the blood gushed out upon them**. {the blood...: Heb. poured out blood upon them}

29 And it came to pass, when midday was past, and they prophesied until the *time* of the offering of the *evening* sacrifice, that *there was* neither voice, nor any to answer, nor any that regarded. {offering: Heb. ascending} {that regarded: Heb. attention}

30 And Elijah said unto all the people, Come near unto me. And all the people came near unto him. And he repaired the altar of the LORD *that was* broken down.

Cult practices have used cuttings and carvings in the flesh for thousands of years. A desire to please and appease your flesh. You won't find a place in the word that cutting the flesh to appease God is ever required. I know what you're thinking. What about circumcision. Circumcision made the children different from any other nation. They were the first to institute established sanitation laws. Circumcision greatly reduces the chance of infections and a variety of other venereal diseases related to uncleanliness. A little research will reveal that over seventy-five percent of God's laws to the Jews are related to sanitation. They were the cleanest and most healthiest people on the face of the earth.

The idea of inflicting pain to appease a God has been practiced from the beginning of our time. The dummies can't understand it's just a statue they're worshipping and not a living God.

Jeremiah 16:
5 For thus saith the LORD, Enter not into the house of mourning, neither go to lam ent nor bemoan them: for I have taken away my peace from this people, saith the LORD, *even* lovingkindness and mercies. {mourning: or, mourning feast}
6 Both the great and the small shall die in this land: they shall not be buried, neither shall *men* lament for them, nor cut themselves, nor make themselves bald for them:
7 Neither shall *men* **tear *themselves* for them in mourning**, to comfort them for the dead; neither shall men give them the **cup of consolation to drink** for their father or for their mother. {tear...: or, break bread for them}
8 Thou shalt not also go **into the house of feasting**, to sit with them to eat and to drink.

One thing that can be observed as symptom of heaviness or rebellion is the desire to abuse the human body. Whether Hitler and his obsession with power to be the greatest, or here where God foreboded them from mutilating their bodies for those who were dead, one underlying truth still remains, all the demonic torture you inflict, won't solve any problem. In our society, we use many colors to hide the same torture we put our bodies through. We are just trying to prove something to ourselves. When we get depressed or despondent, we want to abuse something. Whether in over eating, cutting ourselves with needles, knives, drugs, alcohol, piercing or tattoos, it all boils down to the same problem. We have insecurities in our lives, and we want to hide them. We have discussed some about the rebellion of man against God as supreme and our hidden desire to do what we want and not have anyone tell us what to do. Here, they were wanting to cut themselves, eat till they were sick, or drink till they were pickled to hide their pain and show the world their level of commitment to their cause.

Proverbs 4:
13 Take **fast hold of instruction**; let *her* not go: keep her; for she *is* thy life.
14 Enter not into the path of the wicked, and go not in the way of evil *men*.
15 Avoid it, pass not by it, turn from it, and pass away.
16 For **they sleep not, except they have done mischief**; and **their sleep is taken away, unless they cause *some* to fall**.
17 For they eat the bread of wickedness, and drink the **wine of violence**.
18 But the path of the just *is* as the shining light, that shineth more and more unto the perfect day.
19 The way of the wicked *is* as darkness: they know not at what they stumble.
20 My son, attend to my words; incline thine ear unto my sayings.
21 Let them not depart from thine eyes; keep them in the midst of thine heart.
22 For they *are* life unto those that find them, and ***health to all their flesh***. {health: Heb. medicine}
23 Keep thy heart with all diligence; for out of it *are* the issues of life. {with...: Heb. above all keeping}
24 Put away from thee **a froward mouth, and perverse lips** put far from thee. {a froward...: Heb. frowardness of mouth and perverseness of lips}

Violence begets violence. Misery loves company. If I'm miserable, I'm not going to be alone. Does some of these saying rings true? That uncontrollable impulse to do something is generally brought on from restlessness in your spirit. Your problems lie deeper than the marking of the flesh. A spirit man is crying out for rest. Are you having trouble falling asleep or staying asleep? Check out your spirit man, there may be a problem.

Matthew 26:
52 Then said Jesus unto him, Put up again thy sword into his place: for all **they that take the sword shall perish with the sword**.

Violence begets violence. When you look for violence, you find and can't seem to free yourself from it. It's a trap that has no escape. Just like bad marriages. When you find out your perfect mate is a gate to hell, and you are falling fast and you think that divorce is the final savior. All too soon, you find another perfect mate to find out they were the exact same as the last except in difference packaging! We are creatures of habit. Unless someone whom we call a mediator steps in and drags us out of that endless cycle of death, we will do the same damnable thing repeatedly. Jesus is our only way out! Alone, we are doomed to repeat the same cycle of suffering only to hope for a quiet and quick death! To die is what you need, but not the way you think!

II Corinthians 5:
17 Therefore if any man *be* in Christ, *he is* **a new creature**: old things are passed away; behold, all things are become **new**. {he is: or, let him be}
18 And all things *are* of God, who hath reconciled us to himself by Jesus Christ, and hath given to us the ministry of reconciliation;

Passed away means died. If any be in Christ he is made new! Your emotions, self-confidence, hope for a peaceful life, a chance to see good days, and reeeeest!

I Corinthians 3:

16 Know ye not that ye are the temple of God, and *that* the Spirit of God dwelleth in you?

17 If any man **defile** the **temple** of God, him **shall God destroy**; for the **temple** of God is holy, which *temple* ye are. {defile: or, destroy}

Our bodies are a temple. Whether we abuse it with excessive food, sports, drugs, alcohol, or we disfigure our bodies, we are destroying the temple God gave to you. If you feel the need to disfigure yourself, there's always arthritis, cerebella palsy, and other disfiguring diseases we can pray for. God made you special and unique. Find satisfaction in who you are.

I Peter 3:

2 While they behold your chaste conversation *coupled* with fear.

3 Whose **adorning** let it not be that **outward** *adorning* of plaiting the hair, and of wearing of gold, or of putting on of apparel;

4 But *let it be* the hidden man of the heart, in that which is not corruptible, *even the ornament* of a meek and quiet spirit, which is in the sight of God of great price.

5 For after this manner in the old time the holy women also, who trusted in God, adorned themselves, being in subjection unto their own husbands:

As with any cults, they are always around. In the New Testament, the Romans and Greeks were into gold beads, and precious stones sewed into their hair and clothing. It was about the money. The harlots of that day were distinguishable among the Jews by the wearing of gold and colored beads in their hair. Paul wanted to make sure that they as Christians were not mistaken for that type of individual. Some were so devoted to the occult, that they would permanently tattoo their faces as an eye liner. Paul said;

Romans 14:
16 **Let not** then **your good be evil spoken of:**
17 For the kingdom of God is not meat and drink; but righteousness, and peace, and joy in the Holy Ghost.
18 For he that in these things serveth Christ is acceptable to God, and approved of men.

The crowd you hang around and look like will be the crowd you will be labeled as being. If we see a person with purple hair standing up in a rooster comb, chains on his side, ragged blue jeans, and tattoos all over, we will assume he is a punk rocker or want to be thug. Trying to disguise his fears with this rigid frigid exterior. If you talked to him as an individual and not out of fear, you will find he is probably an o.k. guy and glad to help. The type of tattoos in popularity today give the connotation of being easily laid. When I see a woman with these cute little tattoos on her leg, back, breast, stomach and so forth, I think of what she has hidden that I can't see, and will she let me see? If you will, a billboard for sex. If you lack the confidence to allure a man or woman with your looks and personality, then advertise! That way, you let their "fingers do the walking through the yellow pages." All the reasons for disfiguring your body thus discussed bring us to one simple conclusion. There is a spiritual problem when someone desires to disfigure him or herself!

Mark 5:
2 And when he was come out of the ship, immediately there met him out of the tombs a man with an unclean spirit,
3 Who had *his* dwelling among the tombs; and no man could bind him, no, not with chains:
4 Because that he had been often bound with fetters and chains, and the chains had been plucked asunder by him, and the fetters broken in pieces: neither could any *man* tame him.
5 And always, night and day, he was in the mountains, and in the **tombs**, crying, and **cutting himself with stones**.
6 But when he saw Jesus afar off, he ran and worshipped him,

7 And cried with a loud voice, and said, What have I to do with thee, Jesus, *thou* Son of the most high God? I adjure thee by God, that thou torment me not.

8 For he said unto him, Come out of the man, *thou* unclean spirit.

9 And he asked him, What *is* thy name? And he answered, saying, My name is Legion: for we are many.

Matthew 17:

15 Lord, have mercy on my son: for he is **lunatick,** and **sore vexed**: for ofttimes he **falleth into the fire, and oft into the water**.

16 And I brought him to thy disciples, and they could not cure him.

17 Then Jesus answered and said, O faithless and perverse generation, how long shall I be with you? how long shall I suffer you? bring him hither to me.

18 And Jesus rebuked the devil; and he departed out of him: and the child was cured from that very hour.

Here are two more examples of tattooing and tormenting the body to get satisfaction. We today are too civilized to take a needle or razor to cut ourselves. We hire someone to do it for us. To make it look pretty. I guess this is where I wanted to make my point. God made you beautiful. Therefore, what if the whole world does not see it. Some will. Be proud of who you are and do not yield yourselves as instruments unto Satan. It is like that first drink. It was o.k., but then you had to continue for friend's sake or appetite's sake. The next thing you know, it is an imbedded part of your life. To calm your nerves, to have a good time, to be excepted by your friends, to forget the stress of the day, or just to relax after a hard day's work. One thing always leads to another, without exemption. Most of the people you meet with tattoos, carving, excessive eating, driven lifestyles, abundance of make-up and jewelry, work-a-hollics, violent, s-m sexual appetites, homosexual appetites, always despondent or depressed, always negative and pessimistic, and the list goes on, have a spiritual problem. Stemming from oppression to possessed.

Exodus 21:
5 And if the servant shall plainly say, I love my master, my wife, and my children; I will not go out free: {shall...: Heb. saying shall say}
6 Then his master shall bring him unto the judges; he shall also bring him to the door, or unto the door post; and **his master shall bore his ear through with an aul; and he shall serve him for ever.**

This is an example of piercing. In Old Testament times, it was a sign of being a slave. We see earrings today and think nothing of it. Yet an increasing number of piercing is becoming common. If the word is true, then there is more than meets the eye concerning body and facial piercing. At what point is it o.k., and at which point does it constitute a spiritual problem? There are sixteen examples in the bible of people wearing ear or nose rings. In each case, they were a part of the jewelry ensemble. One-half of the cases it became a thing of pride. The earrings became a calf idol in one situation. In others, they were taken as a sign of victory over their enemies. When the people were lifted up in pride, the very sound of earrings, bracelets, anklets, and jewelry became a stench in God's nostrils. Here are all the scriptures listed in order; (Genesis 24: 22, 24: 30, 24: 47, 35: 4, Exodus 32: 2- 3, 35: 22, Numbers 31: 50, Judges 8: 24- 26, Job 42: 11, Proverbs 25: 12, Isaiah 3: 20, Ezekiel 16: 12, Hosea. 2: 13). The bible uses situations of earrings in people's ears and nose, but nowhere else? Maybe there is a fine line between simply beautiful and a desire to abuse our bodies. We have discussed already that abuse is sin. Keep in mind that the bible does in fact show a bearing that the presence of an earring can be a sign of being a bond slave for life. There are a couple of listings for this. Here is one of them.

Exodus 21:

5 And if the servant shall plainly say, I love my master, my wife, and my children; I will not go out free: {shall...: Heb. saying shall say}

6 Then his master shall bring him unto the judges; he shall also bring him to the door, or unto the door post; and his master shall **bore** his ear through with an aul; and he shall serve him for ever.

Who's servant are you? When does a simple earring become the bond to serve Satan for life? You have to answer that one. At the end of this study you will see the line Satan is drawing for you. If you are comfortable with tattoos, body piercing, cuttings and carvings on your flesh, then you definitely will not have a problem with this occurrence that will come in the near future. However, for now, here is a simple scripture that tells us where we should line up at.

Philippians 4:

4 Rejoice in the Lord always: *and* again I say, Rejoice.

5 Let your **moderation** be known unto all men. The Lord *is* at hand.

6 Be careful for nothing; but in every thing by prayer and supplication with thanksgiving let your requests be made known unto God.

7 And the **peace** of God, which passeth all understanding, shall **keep your hearts and minds** through Christ Jesus.

8 Finally, brethren, whatsoever things *are* true, whatsoever things *are* honest, whatsoever things *are* just, whatsoever things *are* pure, whatsoever things *are* lovely, whatsoever things *are* of good report; if *there be* any virtue, and if *there be* any praise, think on these things. {honest: or, venerable}

9 Those things, which ye have both learned, and received, and heard, and seen in me, do: and the God of peace shall be with you.

Herein is the middle of the road. If your life doesn't have this simple ingredient of moderation, then it is difficult to rejoice always. You have to accomplish something to rejoice. It only lasts as long as the accomplishment does, then back to the excessive. True peace comes from within, not from without. It's a knowing, a confidence, a calm. Moderation in simple English is modesty.

If you fall into any of the categories mentioned, try Jesus, he'll give you a sense of purpose and order.

Matthew 11:
25 At that time Jesus answered and said, I thank thee, O Father, Lord of heaven and earth, because thou hast hid these things from the wise and prudent, and hast revealed them unto babes.
26 Even so, Father: for so it seemed good in thy sight.
27 All things are delivered unto me of my Father: and no man knoweth the Son, but the Father; neither knoweth any man the Father, save the Son, and *he* to whomsoever the Son will reveal *him.*
28 **Come unto me**, all *ye* **that labour** and are **heavy laden**, and I will **give you rest**.
29 Take my yoke upon you, and learn of me; for I am meek and lowly in heart: and ye shall **find** rest unto your souls.
30 For my yoke *is* easy, and my burden is light.

The first thing you have to do is ask. Jesus wants to give purpose and peace. As a Christian, we have found the author of rest. We must then allow that rest to overflow us and fill us. His yoke or lifestyle is easy. It is light, not hard to live. It just takes a made up mind.

John 6:

37 All that the Father giveth me shall come to me; and **him that cometh to me I** will in **no wise cast out**.

Come today, ask Jesus to forgive you of your sins and give you peace. He will!

Revelation 13:

15 And he had power to give life unto the image of the beast, that the image of the beast should both speak, and cause that as many as would not worship the image of the beast should be killed. {life: Gr. breath}

16 And he causeth all, both small and great, rich and poor, free and bond, **to receive a mark in their right hand, or in their foreheads**: {to receive: Gr. to give them}

17 And that no man might buy or sell, save he that had the mark, or the name of the beast, or the number of his name.

Revelation 14:

9 And the third angel followed them, saying with a loud voice, If any man worship the beast and *his* image, and receive his **mark in his forehead, or in his hand**,

10 The same shall drink of the wine of the wrath of God, which is poured out without mixture into the cup of his indignation; and he shall be tormented with fire and brimstone in the presence of the holy angels, and in the presence of the Lamb:

11 And the smoke of their torment ascendeth up for ever and ever: and they have no rest day nor night, who worship the beast and his image, and whosoever receiveth the mark of his name.

12 Here is the patience of the saints: here are they that keep the commandments of God, and the faith of Jesus.

If we already have the ability to not only tag animals, but also to implant microchips under their skin that gives detailed information about the animal's history, how much harder will it be to tag you? If you as an individual become comfortable with tattoos, which use needles, piercings which pierce the skin, and cuttings, which cause raised scars on the skin, how much more easily will it be to receive the mark of the beast? You will because your family depends on you to feed them. My question is, is it worth you going to hell for an eternity without hope to rebel against God for a few morsels of food? I have watched people get saved for years. The first thing they do as new born converts is put on adequate clothing, remove body piercing, try to cover up tattoos, even change hair styles. If God forgives and abolishes the dependencies of alcohol, drugs, sex outside of marriage, anger, fear, abuse, wrongful conduct, and the such like, then we need to simply address what is obvious. It keeps you out of relationship with God, and that will carry you to hell! Wear your earrings, jewelry, make-up and pretty clothing in modesty, and let God bless you. Because you have to remember, you are the only Jesus this world will ever see, and if the Jesus they see in you is no different from where they already are, why will they want to change masters? We are first and foremost witnesses.

Chapter V

A LITTLE WAGER NEVER HURT ANYBODY?

This study answers a question many Christians have asked. Is it wrong to gamble or play the lottery? Well, let's see.

Written By Dr. Ronald Sanders PhD
© By the Library of Congress 2006

A LITTLE WAGER NEVER HURT ANYBODY?

Many have asked the question, is there anything wrong with occasionally playing the lottery or gambling. What are games of chance, and does the bible say anything about this? Since the word gamble, wager, slots, or even poker is not found in the bible, we have to rely on more than one scripture to get an understanding. We do find that the words casting lots is found 24 times, but really doesn't refer to actual gambling. We may have to begin with the spiritual aspect of gambling to get an understanding of the physical phenomenon of gambling.

Romans 8:
13 For if ye live after the flesh, ye shall die: but if ye through the Spirit do mortify the deeds of the body, ye shall live.
14 For as many as are led by the Spirit of God, they are the sons of God.
15 For ye have not received the **spirit** of **bondage** again to fear; but ye have received the **Spirit** of adoption, whereby we cry, Abba, Father.
16 The Spirit itself beareth witness with our spirit, that we are the children of God:

One of the most common attributes we see in gambling is fear. How do we see fear? When we have played for example a slot machine, and it does not produce a winning combination, we wonder if we try again will it come up a winner. When we walk away, we feel an overwhelming fear that the next person may win our money. Many will sit for hours at the same machine and wait to win. Over ninety percent of the time, you will sit and play as long as you have money, yours or the winnings you've gotten. There is an inbred desire in mankind to get rich quick without working for it. The expression "Strike it Big" comes to mind. When you enter a gambling establishment, notice what you feel in the spirit realm as soon as you walk in. You will feel a strange sensation come over you. This desire dates back approximately sixty-five hundred years ago. Let us see where it all began.

Genesis 3:

1 Now the serpent was more subtil than any beast of the field which the LORD God had made. And he said unto the woman, Yea, hath God said, Ye shall not eat of every tree of the garden?

2 And the woman said unto the serpent, We may eat of the fruit of the trees of the garden:

3 But of the fruit of the tree which *is* in the midst of the garden, God hath said, Ye shall not eat of it, neither shall ye touch it, lest ye die.

4 And the serpent said unto the woman, Ye shall not surely die:

5 For God doth know that in the day ye eat thereof, then your eyes shall be opened, and ye shall be as Gods, knowing good and evil.

6 And when the woman saw that the tree *was* good for food, and that it *was* pleasant to the eyes, and a tree to be desired to make *one* wise, she took of the fruit thereof, and did eat, and gave also unto her husband with her; and he did eat.

7 And the eyes of them both *were* opened, and they knew that they were naked; and they sewed fig leaves together, and made themselves aprons.

8 And they heard the voice of the LORD God walking in the garden in the cool of the day: and Adam and his wife hid themselves from the presence of the LORD God amongst the trees of the garden.

9 And the LORD God called unto Adam, and said unto him, Where *art* thou?

10 And he said, I heard thy voice in the garden, and I was afraid, because I was naked; and I hid myself.

11 And he said, Who told thee that thou *wast* naked? Hast thou eaten of the tree, whereof I commanded thee that thou shouldest not eat?

12 And the man said, The woman whom thou gavest *to be* with me, she gave me of the tree, and I did eat.

Notice that I separated this scripture into two separate parts. First, the conversation with Satan. Notice God's description of Satan. He was subtle, which is shrewd, crafty, or sly. He eased up to Eve and made her feel comfortable. That is why you feel that spirit of fear and bondage ease up to you when you enter the doors of those establishments. Satan used what she knew against her. He started out with quoting truth in a question to get her defenses up. Then he eased her conscience while he talked about the word of God. As she relaxed, and her trust in Satan grew, he began to implement subtle lies so she would begin to question the real motives of Gods law. The words "And when the woman saw" it his way. Satan had educated her to question the truth of God's word and make her wonder what God wasn't telling her. She wanted to know why God would keep secrets from her. We translate that into; this next pull may be the million-dollar payoff. The tree was a tree and didn't look much different from the last one she ate from, but this one will make me wise or rich. This one will set me for life, and I won't have to depend on anyone.

I Samuel 15:
22 And Samuel said, Hath the LORD *as great* delight in burnt offerings *and* sacrifices, as in obeying the voice of the LORD? Behold, to obey is better than sacrifice, and to hearken than the fat of rams.
23 For **rebellion** *is as* the sin of witchcraft, and stubbornness *is as* iniquity and idolatry. Because thou hast rejected the word of the LORD, he hath also rejected thee from *being* king.

Eve rebelled against God. She didn't want to obey anyone; she wanted to be her own boss. Wise enough to rule and know good and evil. To be a God. Man from the beginning has desired to be independent. Gambling is a dream of being rich and independent. Something for nothing. Next, we will see what happens when our dreams of glamour fail. Embarrassment and shame as was the case of Adam and Eve. The very thing they were trying to get free of, God imposed upon them to keep them submissive. In the sweat of your brow you will eat your bread all your days. The woman was cursed with having to submit to a husband, father or a pastor all her days.

I Timothy 6:
7 For we brought nothing into *this* world, *and it is* certain we can carry nothing out.
8 And having food and raiment let us be therewith content.
9 But they that will be rich fall into temptation and a snare, and *into* many foolish and hurtful lusts, which drown men in destruction and perdition.
10 For the love of **money** is the **root** of all evil: which while some coveted after, they have erred from the faith, and pierced themselves through with many sorrows.

The lack of contentment is a fierce driving force. It's not that God doesn't desire to bless us, but our attitude should not be one of greed and lust. There is no evil in money, until it is lusted after. Many will work two full time jobs, and do whatever it takes to make as much money as humanly possible. Then they'll stay out of church on Sunday so they can spend it. There excuse is, I work all week and don't have time to spend with my family, so Sunday is a day of rest, and that's what we do. We make Sunday a family day, and we don't want to spend it together in church.

Proverbs 15:
26 The thoughts of the wicked *are* an abomination to the LORD: but *the words* of the pure *are* pleasant words.
27 **He that is greedy of gain troubleth his own house; but he that hateth gifts shall live.**
28 The heart of the righteous studieth to answer: but the mouth of the wicked poureth out evil things.
29 The LORD *is* far from the wicked: but he heareth the prayer of the righteous.
30 The light of the eyes rejoiceth the heart: *and* a good report maketh the bones fat.
 31 The ear that heareth the reproof of life abideth among the wise.

32 He that refuseth instruction despiseth his own soul: but he that heareth reproof getteth understanding.

33 The fear of the LORD *is* the instruction of wisdom; and before honour *is* humility.

The first thing that gambling does is to puff one up and cause pride; the enemy of humility. The thoughts of the wicked are to get gain and with it many gifts. A lustful spirit takes hold. Lust is a drive that makes every muscle in the body to tighten. You know something I've begun to notice about this study? Many are tied up into multi-level marketing programs that promise easy money by reaping the benefits of other people's labor. This study seems to address this subject also, doesn't it?

Isaiah 56:

11 Yea, *they are* greedy dogs *which* can never have enough, and they *are* shepherds *that* cannot understand: they all look to their own way, every one for his gain, from his quarter.

12 Come ye, *say they*, I will fetch wine, and we will fill ourselves with strong drink; and tomorrow shall be as this day, *and* much more abundant.

This one last quarter. Maybe I'll win with this lucky quarter. Some people will never have enough. The spiritual defense they use is; well if I win, then it will bring more tithes to the church. One question comes to mind. If you don't pay tithes on one hundred dollars, then what makes you think you'll pay tithes on one million dollars? It doesn't take a rocket scientist to figure out that line of bologna. Greed is all consuming.

Psalm 107:

35 He turneth the wilderness into a standing water, and dry ground into watersprings.

36 And there he maketh the hungry to dwell, that they may prepare a city for habitation;

37 And sow the fields, and plant vineyards, which may yield fruits of increase.

38 He blesseth them also, so that they are multiplied greatly; and suffereth not their cattle to decrease.

39 Again, they are minished and brought low through oppression, affliction, and sorrow.

40 He poureth contempt upon princes, and causeth them to wander in the wilderness, where there is no way.

41 Yet setteth he the poor on high from affliction, and maketh *him* families like a flock.

42 The righteous shall see *it*, and rejoice: and all iniquity shall stop her mouth.

43 Whoso *is* wise, and will observe these *things*, even they shall understand the lovingkindness of the LORD

Chapter VI

PROMISSORY NOTES, INTEREST AND LENDING?

The Lord wants us out of debt however we live in a society that everything is based on debt. To what degree and how should we be indebted? Should we lend or stand loans for other Christians? What measures am I allowed to pursue to collect debts from other Christians? We hope to answer your questions in this study.

Written By Dr. Ronald Sanders PhD

I. SURETY MEANS:

6148 `arab {aw-rab'}
Meaning: 1) to pledge, exchange, mortgage, engage, occupy, undertake for, give pledges, be or become surety, take on pledge, give in pledge 1a) (Qal) 1a1) to take on pledge, go surety for 1a2) to give in pledge 1a3) to exchange 1a4) to pledge 1b) (Hithpael) 1b1) to exchange pledges 1b2) to have fellowship with, share

Surety is one who stands a security or loan for another. Co-signer.

Proverbs 6:
1 My son, if thou be **surety** for thy friend, *if* thou hast stricken thy hand with a stranger,
2 Thou art snared with the words of thy mouth, thou art taken with the words of thy mouth.
3 Do this now, my son, and deliver thyself, when thou art come into the hand of thy friend; go, humble thyself, and make sure thy friend. {and make...: or, so shalt thou prevail with thy friend}
4 Give not sleep to thine eyes, nor slumber to thine eyelids.
5 Deliver thyself as a roe from the hand *of the hunter*, and as a bird from the hand of the fowler.

Here, being a co-signer for a friend or relative may cost your friendship. You are snared or trapped by the words of your mouth. In another scripture, you'll see that to spare your friendship, you must be willing to pay this loan yourself. Here, you are likened to a female dear chased by a hunter. You're a target.

Proverbs 11:
13 A talebearer revealeth secrets: but he that is of a faithful spirit concealeth the matter.
14 Where no counsel *is*, the people fall: but in the multitude of counsellors *there* is safety.
15 He that is surety for a stranger shall **smart** *for it*: and he that hateth suretiship is sure.

7321 ruwa` {roo-ah'}
Meaning: 1) to shout, and raise a sound, cry out, give a blast 1a) (Hiphil) 1a1) to shout a war-cry or alarm of battle 1a2) to sound a signal for war or march 1a3) to shout in triumph (over enemies) 1a4) to shout in applause 1a5) to shout (with religious impulse) 1a6) to cry out in distress 1b) (Polal) to utter a shout 1c) (Hithpolel) 1c1) to shout in triumph 1c2) to shout for joy 2) (Niphal) destroyed

08735 Stem - Niphal (See 08833) Mood - Imperfect (See 08811) Count - 1602

7451 ra` {rah}
Meaning: adj 1) bad, evil 1a) bad, disagreeable, malignant 1b) **bad, unpleasant, evil (giving pain, unhappiness, misery)** 1c) evil, displeasing 1d) bad (of its kind - land, water, etc) 1e) bad (of value) 1f) worse than, worst (comparison) 1g) sad, unhappy 1h) evil (hurtful) 1i) bad, unkind (vicious in disposition) 1j) bad, evil, wicked (ethically) 1j1) in general, of persons, of thoughts 1j2) deeds, actions n m 2) evil, distress, misery, injury, calamity 2a) evil, distress, adversity 2b) evil, injury, wrong 2c) evil (ethical) n f 3) evil, misery, distress, injury 3a) evil, misery, distress 3b) evil, injury, wrong 3c) evil (ethical) "Shall smart," is defined as giving a shout of misery or pain. First thing we need to do is; count the cost. Can we afford to pay this debt off? Can we keep the integrity of our friendship if we have to pay that debt for them? And, is it worth the chance?

Proverbs 17:
17 A friend loveth at all times, and a brother is born for adversity. 18 A man void of understanding striketh hands, *and* becometh **surety** in the presence of his friend.

The key is, a friend loveth at all times, even though brothers are born to fight. Brothers who are friends will love at all times, and bind up each others wounds. Here though the scriptures place co-signing with someone who is not too bright.

Proverbs 20:
16 Take his garment that is **surety** *for* a stranger: and take a pledge of him for a strange woman.
17 Bread of deceit *is* sweet to a man; but afterwards his mouth shall be filled with gravel. {deceit: Heb. lying, or, falsehood}
18 *Every* purpose is established by counsel: and with good advice make war.
Proverbs 27:

13 Take his garment that is **surety** for a stranger, and take a pledge of him for a strange woman.

When you stand a loan, you're apt to loose your shirt. That's what this means in the Hebrew. When a woman is involved, you will! Here, you are strongly warned not to deal with a person stricken by love (lust). His brain is not functioning. When you're in a desperate situation, you'll promise the sun and moon to get out of it. Knowing there is no way to fulfill your obligations. If you sign for a person, don't do it if they're under duress. Their mind is not clear, and wisdom is far from them.

Hebrews 7:
22 By so much was Jesus made a **surety** of a better testament.

Jesus being surety for us cost him his shirt, which is what the executioners gambled for. His problem was, it cost him his life. He had to count the cost of our friendship, and he was willing to pay the price for our friendship.

John 15: 12- 17,

12 This is my commandment, That ye love one another, as I have loved you.

13 Greater love hath no man than this, that a man lay down his life for his friends.

14 **Ye are my friends**, if ye do whatsoever I command you.

15 Henceforth I call you not servants; for the servant knoweth not what his lord doeth: but I have called you friends; for all things that I have heard of my Father I have made known unto you.

16 Ye have not chosen me, but I have chosen you, and ordained you, that ye should go and bring forth fruit, and *that* your fruit should remain: that whatsoever ye shall ask of the Father in my name, he may give it you.

17 These things I command you, that ye love one another.

"A friend loveth at all times." Jesus fulfilled this scripture from proverbs. He co-signed heaven for us. We didn't have enough collateral to get there on our own, so he stood the loan! This was not even enough to ensure our heavenly home. He had to leave this surety in his will, so that Satan could not have repossessed our possession of it. To keep Satan from being executor of the estate, he had to ensure we would receive his will; He Came Back From The Dead To Be The Executor Of The Estate.

Hebrews 9:

14 How much more shall the blood of Christ, who through the eternal Spirit offered himself without spot to God, purge your conscience from dead works to serve the living God? {spot: or, fault}

15 And for this cause he is the mediator of the new testament, that by means of death, for the redemption of the transgressions *that were* under the first testament, they which are called might receive the promise of eternal inheritance.

16 For where a testament *is*, there must also of necessity be the death of the **testator**. {be: or, be brought in}

17 For a testament *is* of force after men are dead: otherwise it is of no strength at all while the testator liveth.

18 Whereupon neither the first *testament* was dedicated without blood. {dedicated: or, purified}

27 And as it is appointed unto men once to die, but after this the judgment:

28 So Christ was once offered to bear the sins of many; and unto them that look for him shall he appear the second time without sin unto salvation.

John 14:

1 Let not your heart be troubled: ye believe in God, believe also in me.

2 In my Father's house are many mansions: if *it were* not *so*, I would have told you. I go to prepare a place for you.

3 And if I go and prepare a place for you, I will come again, and receive you unto myself; that where I am, *there* ye may be also.

4 And whither I go ye know, and the way ye know.

5 Thomas saith unto him, Lord, we know not whither thou goest; and how can we know the way?

6 Jesus saith unto him, I am the way, the truth, and the life: no man cometh unto the Father, but by me.

Here is the explanation of the will before he died, and the promise that he would be back to enforce his will. Satan has no chance of breaking the will. No higher court than God. Jesus has introduced us to God himself, and we know him (verses 7- 11). The will was signed in blood. In Indian heritage, no greater vow is known than a vow of blood. Whether we are blood brothers with the mingling of each others blood, or blood dropped as a sign of a life vow. You are promising your life as collateral for the fulfilling of the vow.

Proverbs 22:

26 Be not thou *one* of them that strike hands, *or* of them that are sureties for debts.

27 If thou hast nothing to pay, why should he take away thy bed from under thee?

28 Remove not the ancient landmark, which thy fathers have set.
29 Seest thou a man diligent in his business? he shall stand before kings; he shall not stand before mean *men*.

It was not your debt, why loose your bed over another person's debt? If you stand before a king, he will be fair, but ruthless businessmen are merciless, (credit cards, finance co.). In addition, will take all you have.

Ecclesiastes 5:
3 For a dream cometh through the multitude of business; and a fool's voice *is known* by multitude of words.
4 When thou vowest a vow unto God, defer not to pay it; for *he hath* no pleasure in fools: pay that which thou hast vowed.
5 Better *is it* that thou shouldest not vow, than that thou shouldest vow and not pay.
6 Suffer not thy mouth to cause thy flesh to sin; neither say thou before the angel, that it *was* an error: wherefore should God be angry at thy voice, and destroy the work of thine hands?

This usury is to God; a vow that you are promising to God. I think at one time all of us vow unto God. The question is, did we honor it? God once winked at ignorance, and I think he winks at sinners who promise the world and deliver nothing. God calls those who promise wonderful things to him fools, because he knows they do not intend to pay the vow. Many times God will fulfill their needs, knowing he would never receive his portion. He is merciful, isn't he? The sad fact is that the works of their hands will be cursed. Have you ever heard it said, "heartaches comes in bunches like bananas and clusters like grapes"? If the truth was known, they made a vow to God that they would not pay. He hears and honors their cries, yet the laws of God are already set into place.

Mark 8:
36 For what shall it profit a man, if he shall gain the whole world, and lose his own soul?
37 Or what shall a man give in **exchange for his soul?**

38 Whosoever therefore shall be ashamed of me and of my words in this adulterous and sinful generation; of him also shall the Son of man be ashamed, when he cometh in the glory of his Father with the holy angels.

In this, many will promise their soul for a loved one, and when the crisis is over, they forget the promise. What did they exchange their soul for?

II. USURY MEANS:

5392 neshek {neh'-shek}
Meaning: 1) interest, usury

Lend means:
3867 lavah {law-vaw'}
Meaning: 1) to join, be joined 1a) (Qal) to join, be joined, attend 1b) (Niphal) to join oneself to, be joined unto 2) to borrow, lend 2a) (Qal) to borrow 2b) (Hiphil) to cause to borrow, lend to

Brother means:
0251 'ach {awkh}
Meaning: 1) brother 1a) brother of same parents 1b) half-brother (same father) 1c) relative, kinship, same tribe 1d) each to the other (reciprocal relationship) 1e) (fig.) of resemblance

We have the same father God, thus is those who are Christians.

Leviticus 25:
35 And if thy brother be waxen poor, and fallen in decay with thee; then thou shalt relieve him: *yea, though he be* a stranger, or a sojourner; that he may live with thee.
36 Take thou no usury of him, or increase: but fear thy God; that thy brother may live with thee.
37 Thou shalt not give him thy money upon **usury**, nor **lend** him thy victuals for increase.
38 I *am* the LORD your God, which brought you forth out of the land of Egypt, to give you the land of Canaan, *and* to be your God.

When we sell to other Christians, we are instructed to charge no interest. If we lend out something, we are not to expect more in return than what was lent. This applies to the household of faith, not to sinners.

Exodus 22:

25 If thou lend money to *any of my people that is* poor by thee, thou shalt not be to him as an usurer, neither shalt thou lay upon him usury.

Loan sharks and pawnshops have gotten rich off Christians down through the years. Their wealth is limited because of non-functioning products, and plagued with stolen goods. If they had done what God said for them to do, their prosperity would have been immeasurable.

Deuteronomy 23:

19 Thou shalt not **lend** upon **usury** to thy brother; usury of money, usury of victuals, usury of any thing that is lent upon usury:
20 Unto a stranger thou mayest lend upon usury; but unto thy brother thou shalt not lend upon usury: that the LORD thy God may bless thee in all that thou settest thine hand to in the land whither thou goest to possess it.

Here, permission is given to lend to the world and charge a fair interest. They are not of the household of faith. You know the funny thing? When the world finds out that you will lend interest free to Christians, they will try to pass themselves off as Christians. The wonderful thing about it is, Christianity just doesn't fit them right. They are dabbling into a realm that they are so clueless of. We know our own and are known of our own.

Ezekiel 18:

12 Hath oppressed the poor and needy, hath spoiled by violence, hath not restored the pledge, and hath lifted up his eyes to the idols, hath committed abomination,

13 Hath given forth upon usury, and hath taken increase: shall he then live? he shall not live: he hath done all these abominations; he shall surely die; his blood shall be upon him. 14 Now, lo, *if* he beget a son, that seeth all his father's sins which he hath done, and considereth, and doeth not such like, 18:16 Neither hath oppressed any, hath not withholden the pledge, neither hath spoiled by violence, *but* hath given his bread to the hungry, and hath covered the naked with a garment,

17 *That* hath taken off his hand from the poor, *that* hath not received usury nor increase, hath executed my judgments, hath walked in my statutes; he shall not die for the iniquity of his father, he shall surely live.

18 *As for* his father, because he cruelly oppressed, spoiled his brother by violence, and did *that* which *is* not good among his people, lo, even he shall die in his iniquity.

This is interesting scripture. Here, it sounds as if it is a sin to charge other Christians interest? If iniquity is sin, and he dies in it, then where will his iniquity carry him? However, this sin is not a sin that is automatically visited unto the third and forth generation.

Exodus 34:
7 Keeping mercy for thousands, forgiving iniquity and transgression and sin, and that will by no means clear **the guilty**; visiting **the** iniquity of **the** fathers upon **the** children, and upon **the** children's children, **unto the third** and to **the fourth** *generation.*

This sin is an individual sin. Each generation can repent of this sin and do justice.

Matthew 25:
27 Thou oughtest therefore to have put my money to the exchangers, and *then* at my coming I should have received mine own with usury.

Now, we are not to charge the Christians interest, yet our Lord expects us to get interest from what he blesses us with. If we give of our substance to Christians, God has to give us the usury or interest, because we cannot. However, those in the world we must charge interest to, according to this scripture.

Luke 6:
38 **Give**, and **it shall be given** unto you; **good measure, pressed** down, and **shaken** together, and **running** over, **shall** men give into your bosom. For with the same measure that ye mete withal it shall be measured to you again.
If this rule of giving is true, then when we bless the church, then God blesses us four to one from the world. They will bring in the interest to us. Cool!

III. TAXES

Matthew 17:

24 And when they were come to Capernaum, they that received tribute *money* came to Peter, and said, Doth not your master pay **tribute**?

25 He saith, Yes. And when he was come into the house, Jesus prevented him, saying, What thinkest thou, Simon? of whom do the kings of the earth take custom or tribute? of their own children, or of strangers?

26 Peter saith unto him, Of strangers. Jesus saith unto him, Then are the children free. 27 Notwithstanding, lest we should offend them, go thou to the sea, and cast an hook, and take up the fish that first cometh up; and when thou hast opened his mouth, thou shalt find a piece of money: that take, and give unto them for me and thee.

The scribes, Pharisees, wanted to entrap Jesus in this tax evasion question. Al Capone went to prison for tax evasion, not for all the crimes he committed. He still spent life in prison. Jesus knew the thoughts and intents of their hearts. Jesus made a statement to us here. If we owe taxes, pay them. If we can get deductions and deferrals, do it. We are to be honest in our dealings with our government.

Romans 14:

16 **Let not** then your good be **evil spoken** of:

17 For the kingdom of God is not meat and drink; but righteousness, and peace, and joy in the Holy Ghost.

 18 For he that in these things serveth Christ *is* acceptable to God, and approved of men.

How much influence would Christ have had if he had not paid his taxes? It would have killed his influence. Yet, when paying taxes with fish, caused the people to marvel at how easily we can obey the laws of the land and still give God the glory.

Luke 7:
41 There was a certain creditor which had two debtors: the one owed five hundred pence, and the other fifty. 42 And when they had nothing to pay, he frankly forgave them both. Tell me therefore, which of them will love him most?
43 Simon answered and said, I suppose that *he*, to whom he forgave most. And he said unto him, Thou hast rightly judged.

We can be on both ends of this scripture. We can be the one who forgives the debt; seeing there's no way that they can pay the debt. We can be the one who is in debt that we cannot pay. Which one would you rather be? If we are accountable to God for our debts and finances, we can be the one who forgives the debts and not the one in over his head.

Romans 13:
4 For he is the minister of God to thee for good. But if thou do that which is evil, be afraid; for he beareth not the sword in vain: for he is the minister of God, a revenger to *execute* wrath upon him that doeth evil.

5 Wherefore *ye* must needs be subject, not only for wrath, but also for conscience sake.

6 For for this cause pay ye tribute also: for they are God's ministers, attending continually upon this very thing.

7 Render therefore to all their dues: tribute to whom tribute *is due*; custom to whom custom; fear to whom fear; honour to whom honour.

8 Owe no man any thing, but to love one another: for he that loveth another hath fulfilled the law.

It is so much easier to love when you are not over your head in debt. Here, we are to pay our taxes and bills. Lest be inflicted by the continual harassments of collectors and IRS. We are to be at peace with ourselves and God. We need to learn to control our outflow of finances by not buying or charging. God ordained law and order. He ordained police and government officials. He ordained debt collectors, even though they don't ask to be ordained! Reduce your debt and spending, and find a peaceful walk with God.

IV. LENDING

Psalm 37:
21 The wicked borroweth, and payeth not again: but the righteous sheweth mercy, and giveth.

Let us learn a rule of thumb here. If someone wants to borrow from us, we are to lend it, knowing we may never get it back. Not be willing to lend anything that we expect it to come back. Yet the church world here is obligated to bring it back, yet we are not obligated to ask for it back. They should bring it back of their own accord.

Exodus 22:
14 And if a man borrow *ought* of his neighbour, and it be hurt, or die, the owner thereof *being* not with it, he shall surely make *it* good.
15 *But* if the owner thereof *be* with it, he shall not make *it* good: if it *be* an hired *thing*, it came for his hire.

If you borrow something from someone, and you break it, fix it. Do not carry it back to the lender broke! This is God's command. If you lend something and you go over and help them use it, and it breaks, then it is your liability. If you give tools for an employee to use and they break it working for you, you suffer the loss of it. They were hired by you to use that equipment. Unless malice or vandalism is involved, then they will be responsible for the loss and pay for it. This is outside of the scope of using equipment as a hire. Remember, if you borrow something; be willing to carry it back in better shape than when you borrowed it!

Deuteronomy 15:
6 For the LORD thy God blesseth thee, as he promised thee: and thou shalt lend unto many nations, **but thou shalt not borrow**; and thou shalt reign over many nations, **but they shall not reign over thee**.
7 If there be among you a poor man of one of thy brethren within any of thy gates in thy land which the LORD thy God

giveth thee, thou **shalt not harden thine heart, nor shut thine hand from thy poor brother:**
8 But thou shalt open thine hand wide unto him, and shalt **surely lend** him sufficient for his need, *in that* which he wanteth.

But thou shalt not borrow. In our society, these words are taboo. We live by the credit card. If we open our hearts to those who are in need, God said he would prosper us. In other places, he even said that our crops would not waste in the field. God will even give us good weather to prosper us. He says to lend, but doesn't say how to get it back?

Deuteronomy 28:
12 The LORD shall open unto thee his good treasure, the heaven to give the rain unto thy land in his season, and to bless all the work of thine hand: and thou shalt lend unto many nations, and thou shalt not borrow.
13 And the LORD shall make thee the head, and not the tail; and thou shalt be above only, and thou shalt not be beneath; if that thou hearken unto the commandments of the LORD thy God, which I command thee this day, to observe and to do *them*:

In the previous scripture God said that we would reign over many nations and they will not reign over us. Who reigns over us? Our lenders do. They own a portion of our lives. We are not reined over by other nations, but by our lenders. Here, God said he would open to us his good treasure. He will bless the work of our hand. If nothing is in our hand to bless, then how can we be blessed? We have to be busy for God to bless us. He wants to make you the head, always leading and showing the way to others. Not bound but free.

Luke 6:
30 Give to every man that asketh of thee; and of him that taketh away thy goods ask *them* not again.

Again, here is the scripture that says when we lend, be willing to give it to them. If we are not willing to give it away, do not lend it. More friends are lost over borrowing and not repaying or bringing it back, than is lost in our wars.

Luke 6:
34 And if ye lend *to them* of whom ye hope to receive, what thank have ye? for sinners also lend to sinners, to receive as much again.
35 But love ye your enemies, and do good, and lend, hoping for nothing again; and your reward shall be great, and ye shall be the children of the Highest: for he is kind unto the unthankful and *to* the evil.

This is very hard. I don't mind lending to Christians and they don't give it back, but to sinners! Please tell me he did not mean what he said? Then again, how much more will they see the love of God in you if you are not like the world and act as a taskmaster? This is separate from the previous chapter on usury and interest. This is the loaning of non-business things. We are to be wise in business. The key here is; "As much again". Receiving back what was lent out. This is not referring to interest bearing lending to receive usury. This is to your neighbor, who needs the hedge trimmers or food.

Proverbs 19:
17 He that hath pity upon the poor lendeth unto the LORD; and that which he hath given will he pay him again.

There is two parties involved here, talking about a third person as a subject; us as the first "He"; God as the precipitant of our lending. When we come into covenant with the Lord, then we receiver his covenant back (Hebrew). Lendeth is two-fold. We are lending to the Lord and coming into covenant with God in this lending. The poor are the precipitants of our giving, but God views it as he is receiving it. There are to he's here. Notice that the first he is us, and the second he is God. In the last of this verse, "And that which he hath given will he pay him again", the second He is God. We give and he repays. If the poor pays us again, then that is a profit. We will not lose. So lend, not unto those who need, but as unto the Lord. Then we will receive again from God even better than was lent!

Chapter VII

TRAGEDY TO TRIUMPH THE BOOK OF RUTH

Revised From October 20, 2003 Writings
By Dr. Ronald Sanders PhD
Finished On June 20th, 2005
Updated January 6th, 2011

It is our sincere prayer that this study will inspire you and encourage you as we move into this second book. Notice one thing as you read. Ruth was just trying to get through the next day after such a horrific tragedy. She was not trying to make any kind of statement or agenda. She was just trying to survive and take care of her friend. Thank you for taking the time to read this study.

Tragedy to Triumph – book of Ruth

CHAPTER ONE

In this study, we will endeavor to unfold some of the marvels of this book. This is one of the most unique books in the Bible. We will go verse by verse. As you read a verse in the Bible, I will have commentary as to what God has revealed to me about it.

Ruth 1:
1 Now it came to pass in the days when the judges ruled, that there was a famine in the land. And a certain man of Bethlehemjudah went to sojourn in the country of Moab, he, and his wife, and his two sons.

Elimelech – Hebrew. Means "My God is king".
Elimelech carries his family to the land of Moab because of famine.
Two other examples of moving because of famine.
Jacob and his sons went to Egypt. Genesis 47:4

2 And the name of the man was Elimelech, and the name of his wife Naomi, and the name of his two sons Mahlon and Chilion, Ephrathites of Bethlehemjudah. And they came into the country of Moab, and continued there.

Abram also went to Egypt.

Genesis 12:4
In both cases here, it was the perfect will of God for them to move, just as it was for Elimelech.

3 And Elimelech Naomi's husband died; and she was left, and her two sons.
4 And they took them wives of the women of Moab; the name of the one was Orpah, and the name of the other Ruth: and they dwelled there about ten years.

It was after the death of Elimelech that his sons Mahlon and Chilion married two Moabite women, Orpah and Ruth. One reason they may have waited was because it was against Jewish customs to marry women outside of their tribes, and especially women of Moab.

Deuteronomy 23:3
3 An Ammonite or Moabite shall not enter into the congregation of the LORD; even to their tenth generation shall they not enter into the congregation of the LORD forever:

Even though Elimelech was well known in the land of Bethlehem-Judah, he was a stranger in the land of Moab. Since the term sojourned was used, it leads to the conclusion that Elimelech was a migrant worker. The word country means fields in Hebrew.

It is also noted that sometimes God has to move us so that we can be in his perfect will. If Elimelech had not moved to the land of Moab, then Ruth would not have become the mother of Obed, grandfather of King David, and the root of Jesus.

4 And they took them wives of the women of Moab; the name of the one was Orpah, and the name of the other Ruth: and they dwelled there about ten years.
5 And Mahlon and Chilion died also both of them; and the woman was left of her two sons and her husband.

Mahlon means weak or sickly.
Chilion means failing or pining.
After they were married ten years, they both died. It is a wonder they lived the period of time they did, since they both were sickly. You have to remember that a Hebrew name is more than just a name, but a lifestyle. That is why many times God changes people's names to mean something else. Their name molds their lives. We find that neither Orpah nor Ruth had any children by Mahlon or Chilion.

6 Then she arose with her daughters in law, that she might return from the country of Moab: for she had heard in the country of Moab how that the LORD had visited his people in giving them bread.

Naomi hears that the famine is over in Bethlehem-Judah. God has to get Ruth back to the city of Bethlehem because her son would be the forerunner of Jesus, just as Mary and Joseph had to go to Bethlehem from Nazareth for the Son of God to be born.

Luke 2:
1 And it came to pass in those days, that there went out a decree from Caesar Augustus, that all the world should be taxed.
2 (And this taxing was first made when Cyrenius was governor of Syria.)
3 And all went to be taxed, every one into his own city.
4 And Joseph also went up from Galilee, out of the city of Nazareth, into Judaea, unto the city of David, which is called Bethlehem; (because he was of the house and lineage of David:)
5 To be taxed with Mary his espoused wife, being great with child.
6 And so it was, that, while they were there, the days were accomplished that she should be delivered.

Here we see the Lord as each are set at an appointed place. Both had a necessity to reach Bethlehem-Judah. Jesus would be the fulfillment of a covenant he made with Ruth and her seed, so the seed had to travel to a land where there was no promise of tomorrow, yet God had ordained that each would inherit the promise by simple blind obedience.

7 Wherefore she went forth out of the place where she was, and her two daughters in law with her; and they went on the way to return unto the land of Judah.

Both daughter-in-laws leave Moab without hesitation to follow Naomi to Bethlehem. When Orpah and Ruth were asked by Naomi to turn back to their own land, there were several reasons for her request. First they too would be lonely in Bethlehem-Judah. Seeing the Jews was not allowed to marry the Moabites. Two, they would be leaving their land of nativity and their families behind.

8 And Naomi said unto her two daughters in law, Go, return each to her mother's house: the LORD deal kindly with you, as ye have dealt with the dead, and with me.
9 The LORD grant you that ye may find rest, each of you in the house of her husband. Then she kissed them; and they lifted up their voice, and wept.

Orpah means fawn. Ruth means friend. Naomi's request was simple. They were young enough to remarry and start families of their own. Naomi was concerned for their security and welfare, seeing she did not know what would be in store for her when she returned empty handed and broke. When you lose a loved one, let alone three, you come to realize how important family is. You will find that the relationship between Naomi and her daughter-in-laws super-cedes a normal relationship. Three things to keep in mind; one, they rose up to move without hesitation; two, Naomi loved them as daughters. They kissed each other and lifted up their voices in wailing to weep at the probability of severing their relationship; three, Ruth and Orpah loved Naomi enough to forever forsake their own families and friends.

10 And they said unto her, Surely we will return with thee unto thy people.
11 And Naomi said, Turn again, my daughters: why will ye go with me? are there yet any more sons in my womb, that they may be your husbands?

12 Turn again, my daughters, go your way; for I am too old to have an husband. If I should say, I have hope, if I should have an husband also to night, and should also bear sons;
13 Would ye tarry for them till they were grown? would ye stay for them from having husbands? nay, my daughters; for it grieveth me much for your sakes that the hand of the LORD is gone out against me.

Naomi was successful at convincing Orpah to go home by telling her that it would grieve her more if she went with her to a land where she had no husbands to offer her.

14 And they lifted up their voice, and wept again: and Orpah kissed her mother in law; but Ruth clave unto her.

Ruth had already made up her mind that if going meant she would be a widow for the rest of her life, she was willing to make the sacrifice just to be there to care for Naomi.

15 And she said, Behold, thy sister in law is gone back unto her people, and unto her Gods: return thou after thy sister in law.
16 And Ruth said, Intreat me not to leave thee, or to return from following after thee: for whither thou goest, I will go; and where thou lodgest, I will lodge: thy people shall be my people, and thy God my God:
17 Where thou diest, will I die, and there will I be buried: the LORD do so to me, and more also, if ought but death part thee and me.

"Entreat me not to leave thee or return from following after thee. For whether thou goest, I will go." V.16

II Kings 2: 1- 14

1 And it came to pass, when the LORD would take up Elijah into heaven by a whirlwind, that Elijah went with Elisha from Gilgal.

2 And Elijah said unto Elisha, Tarry here, I pray thee; for the LORD hath sent me to Bethel. And Elisha said *unto him*, **As the LORD liveth**, **and *as* thy soul liveth, I will not leave thee**. So they went down to Bethel.

3 And the sons of the prophets that were at Bethel came forth to Elisha, and said unto him, Knowest thou that the LORD will take away thy master from thy head to day? And he said, Yea, I know *it*; hold ye your peace.

4 And Elijah said unto him, Elisha, tarry here, I pray thee; for the LORD hath sent me to Jericho. And he said, **As the LORD liveth, and as thy soul liveth, I will not leave thee**. So they came to Jericho.

5 And the sons of the prophets that were at Jericho came to Elisha, and said unto him, Knowest thou that the LORD will take away thy master from thy head to day? And he answered, Yea, I know it; hold ye your peace.

6 And Elijah said unto him, Tarry, I pray thee, here; for the LORD hath sent me to Jordan. And he said, **As the LORD liveth, and as thy soul liveth, I will not leave thee**. And they two went on.

7 And fifty men of the sons of the prophets went, and stood to view afar off: and they two stood by Jordan. {to view: Heb. in sight, or, over against}

8 And Elijah took his mantle, and wrapped *it* together, and smote the waters, and they were divided hither and thither, so that they two went over on dry ground.

9 And it came to pass, when they were gone over, that Elijah said unto Elisha, Ask what I shall do for thee, before I be taken away from thee. And Elisha said, I pray thee, let a double portion of thy spirit be upon me.

10 And he said, Thou hast asked a hard thing: *nevertheless*, if thou see me *when I am taken* from thee, it shall be so unto thee; but if not, it shall not be so. {Thou hast...: Heb. Thou hast done hard in asking}

11 And it came to pass, as they still went on, and talked, that, behold, *there appeared* a chariot of fire, and horses of fire, and parted them both asunder; and Elijah went up by a whirlwind into heaven.

12 And Elisha saw *it*, and he cried, My father, my father, the chariot of Israel, and the horsemen thereof. And he saw him no more: and he took hold of his own clothes, and rent them in two pieces.

13 He took up also the mantle of Elijah that fell from him, and went back, and stood by the bank of Jordan; {bank: Heb. lip}

14 And he took the mantle of Elijah that fell from him, and smote the waters, and said, Where *is* the LORD God of Elijah? and when he also had smitten the waters, they parted hither and thither: and Elisha went over.

(Three times Elijah asked Elisha to stay behind for his own safety and each time Elisha said, "As the Lord liveth and as thy soul liveth, I will not leave thee." In v.10 Elisha is given the promise of a double portion if he sees Elijah go up into heaven.)

Ruth says I will not leave thee, and because of her firm stand Ruth, as a stranger becomes the forerunner and bloodline of Jesus. "Where thou lodgest, I will lodge." Ruth didn't know what was ahead for her, but if it meant sleeping in the streets as a homeless person, she was willing to stand by Naomi. If we look 1235 years into the future, we see her seed has the same made up mind and makes a similar statement to do what it takes to accomplish what God has ordained for him.

Matthew 8: 18- 22
18 Now when Jesus saw great multitudes about him, he gave commandment to depart unto the other side.

19 And a certain scribe came, and said unto him, Master, I will follow thee whithersoever thou goest.

187

20 And Jesus saith unto him, The foxes have holes, and the birds of the air *have* nests; but the Son of man hath not where to lay *his* head.

21 And another of his disciples said unto him, Lord, suffer me first to go and bury my father.

22 But Jesus said unto him, Follow me; and let the dead bury their dead.

"**Thy people shall be my people**." There is more here than just to go home with Naomi. Ruth is willing to change cultures. She is willing to deny all her teachings, beliefs, and culture just to adapt to Naomi's people's customs. She could never be more than just a servant in Bethlehem-Judah.

Deuteronomy 23: 3- 6

3 An **Ammonite or Moabite shall not enter into the congregation of the LORD; even to their tenth generation** shall they not enter into the congregation of the LORD for ever:

4 **Because they met you not with bread and with water in the way, when ye came forth out of Egypt; and because they hired against thee Balaam the son of Beor of Pethor of Mesopotamia, to curse thee.**

5 Nevertheless the LORD thy God would not hearken unto Balaam; but the LORD thy God turned the curse into a blessing unto thee, because the LORD thy God loved thee.

6 **Thou shalt not seek their peace nor their prosperity all thy days for ever**. {prosperity: Heb. good}

God said that the Jews were not allowed to marry the Moabites. They were not allowed to worship with them. She would not be allowed to be anything else but a servant. She would always be considered an outcast. There was an even greater miracle about her commitment to Naomi. Only about eighty years previously we find;

Judges 3: 12- 30

12 And the children of Israel did evil again in the sight of the LORD: and the **LORD strengthened Eglon the king of Moab against Israel,** because they had done evil in the sight of the LORD.

13 And he gathered unto him the children of Ammon and Amalek, and went and smote Israel, and possessed the city of palm trees.

14 So **the children of Israel served Eglon the king of Moab eighteen years.**

15 But when the children of Israel cried unto the LORD, the LORD raised them up a deliverer, Ehud the son of Gera, a Benjamite, a man lefthanded: and by him the children of Israel sent a present unto Eglon the king of Moab. {a Benjamite: or, the son of Jemini} {lefthanded: Heb. shut of his right hand}

16 **But Ehud made him a dagger which had two edges, of a cubit length; and he did gird it under his raiment upon his right thigh**.

17 And he brought the present unto Eglon king of Moab: and **Eglon** *was* **a very fat man.**

18 And when he had made an end to offer the present, he sent away the people that bare the present.

19 But he himself turned again from the quarries that *were* by Gilgal, and said, I have a secret errand unto thee, O king: who said, Keep silence. And all that stood by him went out from him. {quarries: or, graven images}

20 And Ehud came unto him; and he was sitting in a summer parlour, which he had for himself alone. And Ehud said, I have a message from God unto thee. And he arose out of his seat. {a summer...: Heb. a parlour of cooling}

21 And Ehud put forth his left hand, and took the dagger from his right thigh, and thrust it into his belly:

22 And **the haft also went in after the blade; and the fat closed upon the blade, so that he could not draw the dagger out of his belly; and the dirt came out**. {the dirt...: or, it came out at the buttocks}

23 Then Ehud went forth through the porch, and shut the doors of the parlour upon him, and locked them.

24 When he was gone out, **his servants came**; and when they saw that, behold, the doors of the parlour were locked, they said, **Surely he covereth his feet in his summer chamber. {covereth...: or, doeth his easement}**

25 And they tarried till they were ashamed: and, behold, he opened not the doors of the parlour; therefore they took a key, and opened *them*: and, behold, their lord *was* fallen down dead on the earth.

26 And Ehud escaped while they tarried, and passed beyond the quarries, and escaped unto Seirath.

27 **And it came to pass, when he was come, that he blew a trumpet in the mountain of Ephraim, and the children of Israel went down with him from the mount, and he before them.**

28 **And he said unto them, Follow after me: for the LORD hath delivered your enemies the Moabites into your hand. And they went down after him, and took the fords of Jordan toward Moab, and suffered not a man to pass over.**

29 And **they slew of Moab at that time about ten thousand men, all lusty**, and all men of valour; and there escaped not a man. {lusty: Heb. fat}

30 So Moab was subdued that day under the hand of Israel. And **the land had rest fourscore years.**

The same Jews that she was willing to serve, **had only eighty years before, went through her land and killed all the men. Ruth was willing to lay aside prejudice and embrace her archenemies.** See also **Numbers 22: through Numbers 31: 1- 12**

"And thy God shall be my God." The Moabites worshipped Baal-Peor. In her native religion, they were allowed to have orgies, prostitution, and sacrificial sex. Their religion dealt a great deal with self-mutilation and human suffering. Some areas they even had human sacrifices to Baal. Her sacrifice here was a total sacrifice of will. She loved Naomi to such a depth that her life no longer had significance to her. If she had gone to Bethlehem and they required her life to be taken, she was willing to be sacrificed.

"**Where thou diest, will I die**." This is simple proof that Ruth took her commitment seriously. She had no intention of ever returning back home. She would live out her life with a strange people just because her mother-in-law her loved the Bethlemites. Another interesting development that had to taken place. Naomi had spoken so much of her God that Ruth had to have enough confidence in God that she knew God was a just God. That her life was safe in his hands, seeing he was actually a living God and not just an idol. The other point of interest is that Naomi knew from Ruth's declaration, that she had no intentions of turning back with Orpah. It reminds me of another person who made a similar statement.

Mark 8: 31- 38,
31 And he began to teach them, that the **Son of man must suffer many things, and be rejected of the elders**, and *of the chief priests, and scribes, and be killed*, and after three days rise again.
32 And he spake that saying openly. And Peter took him, and began to rebuke him.
33 But when he had turned about and looked on his disciples, he rebuked Peter, saying, Get thee behind me, Satan: for thou savourest not the things that be of God, but the things that be of men.
34 And when he had called the people *unto him* with his disciples also, he said unto them, Whosoever will come after me, let him deny himself, and take up his cross, and follow me.
35 For whosoever will save his life shall lose it; but whosoever shall lose his life for my sake and the gospel's, the same shall save it.
36 For what shall it profit a man, if he shall gain the whole world, and lose his own soul?

37 Or what shall a man give in exchange for his soul?

38 Whosoever therefore shall be ashamed of me and of my words in this adulterous and sinful generation; of him also shall the Son of man be ashamed, when he cometh in the glory of his Father with the holy angels.

Ruth had the same made up mind as Jesus. It didn't matter that she was going into the unknown. She would walk in with Naomi with her head held high, and not afraid.

I Peter 4: 19,
19 Wherefore let them that suffer according to the will of God **commit the keeping of their souls *to him* in well doing, as unto a faithful Creator.**

Ruth had set her face like a flint, not to be moved by fear or doubt. She on that road that day committed her soul unto the faithful creator, just as Jesus her grandson 30 generations later would do. God saw so much faith and determination in Ruth that God just had to have her as a part of the bloodline of Jesus. Jesus had to have the same ability to look into the unknown and say I refuse to run! Its amazing how overwhelmed God was with Ruth on that day. He no doubt already began to work on the heart of Boaz and his servants of whom she would find great favor with. Boaz's servants were the ones that testified of her faithful work habits and Godly spirit. Of which, Boaz would shortly fall in love with.

"The Lord do so to me, and more also, if ought but death part thee from me…" We see so many covenants in the Bible, yet few involve a covenant of death as sworn before God. Her covenant was sealed by her life.

She asked only two things of Naomi.

1)   And Ruth said, Entreat me not to leave thee,
2)   *Or* to return from following after thee:

Ruth promises a covenant of five things that change the history of God's heart. This covenant shaped a nation.

1)   For whither thou goest, I will go;
2)   And where thou lodgest, I will lodge:
3)   Thy people *shall be* my people, and thy God my God:
4)   Where thou diest, will I die, and there will I be buried:
5)   The LORD do so to me, and more also, *if ought* but death part thee and me.

By her determination, God knew he could do no less than to give his son for her, seeing she gave her life for him. Ruth just doing what she thought was right for that moment for a friend in whom she loved; however, her choices would change the direction of salvation forever to a people who were stubborn, hard-headed, and rebellious. God would spare them because of one heathen woman who loved!

Just a mere 9 generations before a young man by the name of Isaac had made such a faith stands.

Genesis 22: 7- 18,

7 And Isaac spake unto Abraham his father, and said, My father: and he said, Here am I, my son. And he said, **Behold the fire and the wood: but where *is* the lamb for a burnt offering?** {lamb: or, kid}

8 And Abraham said, My son, **God will provide himself a lamb** for a burnt offering: so they went both of them together.

9 **And they came** to the place which God had told him of; and Abraham built an altar there, and laid the wood in order, and bound Isaac his son, and laid him on the altar upon the wood.

10 And Abraham stretched forth his hand, and took the knife to slay his son.

11 And the angel of the LORD called unto him out of heaven, and said, **Abraham, Abraham: and he said, Here *am* I.**

12 And he said, **Lay not thine hand upon the lad, neither do thou any thing unto him: for now I know that thou fearest God, seeing thou hast not withheld thy son, thine only *son* from me**.

13 And **Abraham lifted up his eyes, and looked**, and **behold behind** *him* **a ram caught in a thicket by his horns:** and Abraham went and took the ram, and offered him up for a burnt offering in the stead of his son.

14 And Abraham called the name of that place **Jehovahjireh:** as it is said *to* this day, In the mount of the LORD it shall be seen. {Jehovahjireh: that is, The Lord will see, or, provide}

15 And <u>the angel of the LORD</u> **called unto Abraham out of heaven the second time**,

16 And said, **By myself have I sworn, saith the LORD, for because thou hast done this thing, and hast not withheld thy son, thine only** *son*:

17 **That in blessing I will bless thee, and in multiplying I will multiply thy seed as the stars of the heaven, and as the sand which is upon the sea shore; and thy seed shall possess the gate of his enemies**; {shore: Heb. lip}

18 **And in thy seed shall all the nations of the earth be blessed; because thou hast obeyed my voice**.

Isaac here had already heard what his father had said, and he knew there was no sacrifice. He trusted his father, just as Ruth trusted Naomi. She was the sacrifice to be carried on a journey just as Isaac was carried on a journey to be sacrificed. God swore by himself, who could not die, Ruth swore on her life that could die. God's vow was greater. God saw this sacrificial faith over many generations, and each time God's heart broke. No doubt God wept over this commitment to him. No fight, just compliance to commit to him who is just.

18 When she saw that she was stedfastly minded to go with her, then she left speaking unto her.

Even though Naomi did not reply to Ruth's vow, I am sure that Naomi felt relief from that sick feeling in the pit of her stomach. **She knew she would not have to make that humiliating and lonely journey alone. Someone was willing to help her bear her overwhelming grief and burden of devastating sorrow.** Ruth was thinking that I just want to serve my mother as her servant, to love her in her years of loneliness and see that the pain of her heart be eased. She came to Moab full with a husband and two sons. She prospered and saw her sons marry two wonderful daughters. Just to lose all she called dear! Now, to return home as a beggar, condemned to live on the streets in shame.

Deuteronomy 15: 11- 18,
11 For the poor shall never cease out of the land: therefore I command thee, saying, Thou shalt open thine hand wide unto thy brother, to thy poor, and to thy needy, in thy land.
12 *And* if thy brother, an Hebrew man, or an Hebrew woman, be sold unto thee, and serve thee six years; then in the seventh year thou shalt let him go free from thee.
13 And when thou sendest him out free from thee, thou shalt not let him go away empty:
14 Thou shalt furnish him liberally out of thy flock, and out of thy floor, and out of thy winepress: *of that* wherewith the LORD thy God hath blessed thee thou shalt give unto him.
15 And thou shalt remember that thou wast a bondman in the land of Egypt, and the LORD thy God redeemed thee: therefore I command thee this thing to day.
16 **And it shall be, if he say unto thee, I will not go away from thee; because he loveth thee and thine house, because he is well with thee;**
17 **Then thou shalt take an aul, and thrust *it* through his ear unto the door, and he shall be thy servant for ever. And also unto thy maidservant thou shalt do likewise**.
18 It shall not seem hard unto thee, when thou sendest him away free from thee; for he hath been worth a double hired servant *to thee*, in serving thee six years: and the LORD thy God shall bless thee in all that thou doest.

Naomi was going home to see what would become of her. **Ruth on the other hand didn't need a ring in her ear. She has been thrust through the heart**. An earring would have made no difference to Ruth.

19 So they two went until they came to Bethlehem. And it came to pass, when they were come to Bethlehem, that all the city was moved about them, and they said, Is this Naomi?

20 And she said unto them, Call me not Naomi, call me Mara: for the Almighty hath dealt very bitterly with me.

21 I went out full, and the LORD hath brought me home again empty: why then call ye me Naomi, seeing the LORD hath testified against me, and the Almighty hath afflicted me?

22 So Naomi returned, and Ruth the Moabitess, her daughter in law, with her, which returned out of the country of Moab: and they came to Bethlehem in the beginning of barley harvest.

Notice two things, **Naomi in Hebrew means, pleasant or my delight. Ruth in Hebrew means friend or friendship.** When the people of Bethlehem saw Ruth and Naomi, they saw **"Pleasant friend"**. We see that all the town was moved and noised round about at her entering in. She was loved and missed by all. They would yell, "My delight is back!". Naomi was a virtuous woman. Naomi's first response to the welcome of friendship was, I am no longer pleasant, but **Mara, which is bitter**. The Lord has visited me and my end was bitter. Those of Bethlehem saw not bitterness, but still delight. With the presence of Ruth and Naomi the people saw pleasant friends. God saw them as the "Gate called Beautiful".

Acts 3:1- 2
Now Peter and John went up together into the temple at the hour of prayer, *being* the ninth *hour*.

2 And a certain man lame from his mother's womb was carried, whom they laid daily at the **gate** of the temple **which is called Beautiful**, to ask alms of them that entered into the temple;

7 And he took him by the right hand, and lifted *him* up: and immediately his feet and ankle bones received strength.

8 And he leaping up stood, and walked, and entered with them into the temple, walking, and leaping, and praising God.
9 And all the people saw him walking and praising God:

Beautiful in the Greek **means, "Right time or season". Naomi and Ruth were at the right time and season**. God had set them up for a blessing that would last an eternity. **They only had to do as the lame man and enter in**. They did. Inside the gate is beautiful. **The same place those 30 generations later, a man called Jesus would enter the gate of Bethlehem and be born to a woman named Mary.** Just as Naomi and Ruth entered in ashamed, and were made glad, Jesus would enter in glad and be made a shame for them. He took their shame and bore it himself!

Isaiah 53: 2- 3,

2 For he shall grow up before him as a tender plant, and as a root out of a dry ground: he hath no form nor comeliness; and when we shall see him, *there is* no beauty that we should desire him.
3 **He is despised and rejected of men; a man of sorrows, and acquainted with grief**: and **we hid as it were our faces from him; he was despised, and we esteemed him not.** {we hid...: or, he hid as it were his face from us: Heb. as an hiding of faces from him, or, from us}

CHAPTER TWO

1 And Naomi had a kinsman of her husband's, a mighty man of wealth, of the family of Elimelech; and his name was Boaz.

Boaz means swiftness.
Boaz was a man of great wealth and influence.

2 And Ruth the Moabitess said unto Naomi, Let me now go to the field, and glean ears of corn after him in whose sight I shall find grace. And she said unto her, Go, my daughter.

Ruth volunteers to go into the field to pick up food after the harvesters. Ruth was hoping to find a field in which they would allow her to glean. **The law of the Lord is that the Jewish farmers were to plant their crops in squares, but would only harvest circles. Leaving the four corner triangles for the poor, widows, strangers, and orphans**. God said he would bless the crops that they produced more in that center than any average crop would if they harvested the whole field.

Leviticus 19: 9- 10,
9 And when ye reap the harvest of your land, **thou shalt not wholly reap the corners of thy field, neither shalt thou gather the gleanings of thy harvest**.
10 And thou shalt not glean thy vineyard, neither shalt thou gather *every* grape of thy vineyard; thou shalt leave them for the poor and stranger: I *am* the LORD your God.

Leviticus 24: 19- 22,
19 **When thou cuttest down thine harvest in thy field, and hast forgot a sheaf in the field, thou shalt not go again to fetch it:** it shall be for the stranger, for the fatherless, and for the widow: that the LORD thy God may bless thee in all the work of thine hands.
20 **When thou beatest thine olive tree, thou shalt not go over the boughs again**: it shall be for the stranger, for the fatherless, and for the widow. {go...: Heb. bough it after thee}

21 **When thou gatherest the grapes of thy vineyard, thou shalt not glean *it* afterward**: it shall be for the stranger, for the fatherless, and for the widow. {afterward: Heb. after thee}
22 And thou shalt remember that thou wast a bondman in the land of Egypt: therefore I command thee to do this thing.

When they went into the field, and missed picking up some of the harvest that fell to the ground, they were not allowed to go back and pick up the scraps. That also belonged to the poor, strangers, and widows.
Let us look a little deeper into the heritage of Ruth the Moabitess. We know she came from the land of Moab. Where did the Moabites people originate, and why did God despise them so much?

Genesis 19:
32 **Come, let us make our father drink wine, and we will lie with him, that we may preserve seed of our father**.
33 **And they made their father drink wine that night: and the firstborn went in, and lay with her father; and he perceived not when she lay down, nor when she arose.**
34 **And it came to pass on the morrow, that the firstborn said unto the younger**, Behold, I lay yesternight with my father: let us make him drink wine this night also; and go thou in, *and* lie with him, that we may preserve seed of our father.
35 And they made their father drink wine that night also: and **the younger arose, and lay with him; and he perceived not when she lay down, nor when she arose.**
36 **Thus were both the daughters of Lot with child by their father**.
37 And **the firstborn bare a son, and called his name Moab**: the same is the father of the Moabites unto this day.
38 And **the younger, she also bare a son, and called his name Benammi**: the same *is* the **father of the children of Ammon unto this day**.

The two daughters of Lot got pregnant by Lot while he was drunk as a skunk. The two nations that would be a thorn in the side of the Israelites for an eternity were originated here because two daughters were hot to trot, and had nowhere else to run. It may have been said that it was an act of preservation, but they were not the last three Israelites left on the face of the earth.

If that wasn't bad enough, the story doesn't end there. When the scriptures say;

Numbers 32:
23 But if ye will not do so, behold, ye have sinned against the LORD: and **be sure your sin will find you out.**

The sin may have started in private, in the comforts of their home, but sin is like a cancer, it will spread.

Numbers 22:
1 And the children of Israel set forward, and pitched in the plains of **Moab** on this side Jordan by Jericho.
2 And **Balak the son of Zippor** saw all that Israel had done to the Amorites.
3 And **Moab** was sore afraid of the people, because they were many: and Moab was distressed because of the children of Israel.
4 And **Moab** said unto the elders of Midian, Now shall this company lick up all *that* are round about us, as the ox licketh up the grass of the field. **And Balak the son of Zippor** *was* **king of the Moabites** at that time.

5 **He sent messengers therefore unto Balaam the son of Beor to Pethor**, which *is* by the river of the land of the children of his people, to call him, saying, Behold, there is a people come out from Egypt: behold, they cover the face of the earth, and they abide over against me: {face: Heb. eye}
6 **Come now therefore, I pray thee, curse me this people; for they** *are* **too mighty for me**: peradventure I shall prevail, that we may smite them, and that I may drive them out of the land: for I wot that he whom thou blessest is blessed, and he whom thou cursest is cursed.

7 And the elders of **Moab** and the elders of Midian departed with the rewards of divination in their hand; and they came unto Balaam, and spake unto him the words of Balak.

8 And he said unto them, Lodge here this night, and I will bring you word again, as the LORD shall speak unto me: and the princes of **Moab** abode with Balaam.

9 And God came unto Balaam, and said, What men *are* these with thee?

10 And Balaam said unto God, Balak the son of Zippor, king of **Moab** , hath sent unto me, *saying,*

11 Behold, *there is* a people come out of Egypt, which covereth the face of the earth: come now, curse me them; peradventure I shall be able to overcome them, and drive them out. {I shall...: Heb. I shall prevail in fighting against him}

12 And God said unto Balaam, **Thou shalt not go with them; thou shalt not curse the people: for they** *are* **blessed.**

13 And Balaam rose up in the morning, and said unto the princes of Balak, Get you into your land: for the LORD refuseth to give me leave to go with you.

Well, we all know the story. Balaam ended up going with them and blessing the people of God. The problem still endures; let's see what happened. Strike one.

Numbers 25:

1 And Israel abode in Shittim, and the people began to commit whoredom with the **daughters of Moab**.

2 **And they called the people unto the sacrifices of their Gods: and the people did eat, and bowed down to their Gods.**

3 And **Israel joined himself unto Baalpeor**: and the anger of the LORD was kindled against Israel.

4 And the **LORD said unto Moses, Take all the heads of the people, and hang them up before the LORD against the sun,** that the fierce anger of the LORD may be turned away from Israel.

5 And Moses said unto the judges of Israel, **Slay ye every one his men that were joined unto Baalpeor.**

The children of Israel were prone to idol worship. Here a little sex hath made them crazy. Instead of being led of the Lord, they were led by something else? It will always lead you astray! God had less than favorable feelings toward the Moabites already, but now, they are taking away his sheep. Strike two.

Deuteronomy 23:
1 He that is wounded in the stones, or hath his privy member cut off, shall not enter into the congregation of the LORD.
2 **A bastard shall not enter into the congregation of the LORD; even to his tenth generation shall he not enter into the congregation of the LORD**.
3 An Ammonite or **Moabite shall not enter into the congregation of the LORD; even to their tenth generation shall they not enter into the congregation of the LORD for ever:**
4 Because they met you not with bread and with water in the way, when ye came forth out of Egypt; and because they hired against thee Balaam the son of Beor of Pethor of Mesopotamia, to curse thee.
5 Nevertheless the LORD thy God would not hearken unto Balaam; but the LORD thy God turned the curse into a blessing unto thee, because the LORD thy God loved thee.
6 **Thou shalt not seek their peace nor their prosperity all thy days for ever**. {prosperity: Heb. good}

Strike three you're out. God gives commands unto the children of Israel concerning the Moabites. You don't worship with them; they are not allowed to come into the sanctuary with you, unless their family has been with you for at least ten generations. This means the great great great great great great great great grand sons may be in church with you. God's way of thinking is, it's going to take ten generations to wash away the customs and traditions of idolatry and adultery from the bloodline. Remember that Ruth had just left the land of Moab. She was first generation Moabitess. She was considered a stranger and not even a welcome one when she came to

Bethlehem-Judah. God has seen a lot of bad blood with the Moabite people. There has been nothing but bloodshed since Moses passed through their land. They were a violent people and superstitious people.

3 And she went, and came, and gleaned in the field after the reapers: and her hap was to light on a part of the field belonging unto Boaz, who was of the kindred of Elimelech.

As Ruth is gleaning, she ends up in a field owned by Boaz. Notice the word hap.

Hap-
4745 hr,q.mi miqreh {mik-reh'}
Meaning: 1) unforeseen meeting or event, accident, happening, chance, fortune 1a) accident, chance 1b) fortune, fate

She was so engrossed in supplying food for Naomi and keeping up with the reapers so was unaware of crossing into another man's field. The fact is she probably would not even known if there was another field seeing she was not familiar with the customs or even how boundaries worked. Sometimes God can use our ignorance more than he can our intelligence. This reminds me of a wonderful scripture.

Psalm 37:
22 For *such as be* blessed of him shall inherit the earth; and *they that be* cursed of him shall be cut off.
23 The **steps** of a *good* **man** are **ordered by the LORD: and he delighteth in his way.**
24 **Though he fall, he shall not be utterly cast down: for the LORD upholdeth** *him with* **his hand.**
25 I have been young, and *now* am old; yet have I not seen the righteous forsaken, nor his seed begging bread.
26 *He is* ever merciful, and lendeth; and his seed *is* blessed.
27 Depart from evil, and do good; and dwell for evermore.

Watch this scripture. Ruth's steps were ordered or directed by the Lord. Even if God has to keep your mind off what you're doing to direct your paths, he will

Guess what she runs into?

She ends up in Boaz's field. We see from this verse that Boaz is a close kin to Elimelech who was Ruth's father-in-law. The word Boaz in Hebrew means;

Boaz

1162 z[;Bo Bo`az {bo'az}

Meaning: Boaz = "fleetness" 1) ancestor of David, kinsman-redeemer to Ruth, daughter-in-law of Naomi 2) name of the left of two brazen pillars, 18 cubits high, erected in the porch of Solomon's temple

Fleetness or quick and agile. It also means the two brazen pillars in Solomon's temple which has not even been built yet! Prophecy is about to be written. If brazen pillars were anything to do with his appearance, then all the Israelite women were hot on his trail. Notice that Ruth showed no such intentions at the onset of their meeting.

4 And, behold, Boaz came from Bethlehem, and said unto the reapers, The LORD be with you. And they answered him, The LORD bless thee.

5 Then said Boaz unto his servant that was set over the reapers, Whose damsel is this?

6 And the servant that was set over the reapers answered and said, It is the Moabitish damsel that came back with Naomi out of the country of Moab:

This is the introduction of Boaz into this story. We learn a lot about this man in just the few words he spoke to his reapers who were his servants. **His greeting was that of "The Existing One be with you".** He had an excellent working relationship with his workers and servants. In verse 5 we see his attention is changed from the conversation with his servants to this beautiful young woman in his field. He begins to enquire of the servants as to whom this woman was and if she was married or another man's servant. The word Moabitish damsel means;

Moab
4125 ybia'Am Mow'abiy {mo-aw-bee'} fem. Mow'abiyah {mo-aw-bee-yaw'} or Mowabiyth {mo-aw-beeth'}
Meaning: Moabite = "**from father: what father**?" 1) an citizen of Moab 2) an inhabitant of the land of Moab

Who's your daddy? That's a bad way to be introduced, isn't it; however the next parts of her introduction from these servants make up for all the questionable cultural issues.

The Israelites considered the Moabites as bastard children. Not worthy of being a part of the heritage of God, nor of the sacred bloodline that Christ would descend from.

Notice the character of Ruth.
First, she asks permission to glean or follow behind the reapers to gather what is left behind or deemed unsuitable. She did not ask to go into the four corners of the field and gather the best even though she had that right.

Leviticus 23:
22 And when ye reap the harvest of your land, thou shalt not make clean riddance of the **corners of thy field when thou reapest, neither shalt thou gather any gleaning of thy harvest: thou shalt leave them unto the poor, and to the stranger**: I *am* the LORD your God.

She had the right according to Leviticus to go into the corners of the field and gather of the first fruit instead she was willing to leave that for those who were from that city. She was content with picking up what others didn't want. In Israel God commanded the farmers to plant in squares but reap in circles. This leaves the four corners of each field to be harvested by the poor and strangers in the land.
The fact that she did not assume she had the right to follow the reapers was a sign of humility in itself. She

**was accountable to the reapers and placed herself at
their mercy and grace.** This shows a tremendous amount of
faith on her part.

**Secondly, she had followed them all daylong gleaning and
picking thru what was left behind with no complaints and
only a minimal amount of time resting**. The reapers were
obviously amazed at her stamina and persistence to provide
for her mother-in-law.

*7 And she said, I pray you, let me glean and gather
after the reapers among the sheaves: so she came,
and hath continued even from the morning until
now, that she tarried a little in the house.
8 Then said Boaz unto Ruth, Hearest thou not, my
daughter? Go not to glean in another field, neither
go from hence, but abide here fast by my maidens:
9 Let thine eyes be on the field that they do reap, and
go thou after them: have I not charged the young
men that they shall not touch thee? and when thou
art athirst, go unto the vessels, and drink of that
which the young men have drawn.
10 Then she fell on her face, and bowed herself to the
ground, and said unto him, Why have I found grace
in thine eyes, that thou shouldest take knowledge of
me, seeing I am a stranger?
11 And Boaz answered and said unto her, It hath
fully been shewed me, all that thou hast done unto
thy mother in law since the death of thine husband:
and how thou hast left thy father and thy mother,
and the land of thy nativity, and art come unto a
people which thou knewest not heretofore.
12 The LORD recompense thy work, and a full
reward be given thee of the LORD God of Israel,
under whose wings thou art come to trust.
13 Then she said, Let me find favour in thy sight, my
lord; for that thou hast comforted me, and for that
thou hast spoken friendly unto thine handmaid,
though I be not like unto one of thine handmaidens.*

14 And Boaz said unto her, At mealtime come thou hither, and eat of the bread, and dip thy morsel in the vinegar. And she sat beside the reapers: and he reached her parched corn, and she did eat, and was sufficed, and left.

She had won the respect of all the men there. They evidently saw many young women come to the field to gather food but were lazy and wanted someone else to do their work. No doubt, some of these young women who were at the age to marry flirted with the workers in the field. Yet we see no indication that Ruth used her feminine personality to get what she wanted. The word **maiden** gives us a clue of the type of women in the field gleaning.

Maiden
5291 hr'[]n: na`arah {nah-ar-aw'}
Meaning: 1) girl, damsel, female servant 1a) girl, damsel, little girl 1a1) of young woman, marriageable young woman, concubine, prostitute 1b) maid, female attendant, female servant

With this definition in mind we see a wide variety of typical Israelite women. Ruth had charisma and integrity, a rare trait among women from any time era.
I like what Boaz did for Ruth. He leveled an unfair playing field that gave Ruth explicit permission to be treated and respected just as any other woman from Israel should be with one exception. The men working under Boaz's employ were not to harass, intimidate or to approach with unGodly motives! She was safe from sexual advances.
 This favor of Boaz no doubt made the Israelite women less than happy with Ruth, yet there was noting they could do about it. As humans are characteristically predictable, these same women probably called Ruth names and talked to her as if she were less than human. See, when we find favor of

the Lord no one can break our spirit. God will always send an intercessor to defend and deliver us through whatever temptation comes our way and his name is Jesus.

Boaz asked Ruth to not worry about having to go to another field to find enough food. He assures her that his field will yield enough to sustain her and Naomi.

15 And when she was risen up to glean, Boaz commanded his young men, saying, Let her glean even among the sheaves, and reproach her not:
16 And let fall also some of the handfuls of purpose for her, and leave them, that she may glean them, and rebuke her not.
17 So she gleaned in the field until even, and beat out that she had gleaned: and it was about an ephah of barley.

When God gives us instructions, it may not seem like the right thing. When God is in charge, he has already made provision to fulfill his word with abundant provision. Ruth was not aware of Boaz's intentions. He instructed the harvesters to leave behind some of the best harvest so Ruth could glean it. God wanted the best because Ruth was willing to be content whatever God blessed her with, large or small. God's heart melted at the faith and commitment of Ruth.

Verse 9 shows us a spiritual principle when our spirits are righteous.

John 4:
33 Therefore said the disciples one to another, Hath any man brought him *ought* to eat?
34 Jesus saith unto them, **My meat is to do the will of him that sent me, and to finish his work.**
35 Say not ye, There are yet four months, and *then* cometh harvest? behold, I say unto you, Lift up your eyes, and look on the fields; for they are white already to harvest.
36 And he that reapeth receiveth wages, and gathereth fruit unto life eternal: that both he that soweth and he that reapeth may rejoice together.

37 And herein is that saying true, One soweth, and another reapeth.

38 **I sent you to reap that whereon ye bestowed no labour: other men laboured, and ye are entered into their labours.**

When we walk righteously before God there is a spiritual principle that we inherit. God's blessing come on us and overtakes us. We begin to see fruits of other people's labors. We are not just reaping our harvest but seeing other gifts being added to us.

Matthew 25:

20 And so he that had received **five talents** came and brought other **five talents**, saying, Lord, thou deliveredst unto me **five talents**: behold, I have gained beside them **five talents** more.
21 His lord said unto him, Well done, thou good and faithful servant: thou hast been faithful over a few things, I will make thee ruler over many things: enter thou into the joy of thy lord.
27 Thou oughtest therefore to have put my money to the exchangers, and *then* at my coming I should have received mine own with usury.
28 Take therefore the talent from him, and give *it* unto him which hath ten talents.
29 For unto every one that hath shall be given, and he shall have abundance: but from him that hath not shall be taken away even that which he hath.

There is always some in the kingdom who are just trying to maintain their relationship with God but not increase. They are the ones that you reap harvests from. They won't receive the increase of God because of the level of commitment God requires to walk in the place of blessing. They are satisfied being a luke-warm Christian still able to do things of the world to satisfy their flesh. In the book of Ruth, Ruth made a commitment to Naomi and to God. That commitment would transcend all her desires and dreams to become what God desires for her. Little did she know at that time, his desires would far surpass any imagination she could want? We need to watch the life of Ruth and see that daily she found favor with God and man. She walked in a continual place of blessing. When trials and tribulations came her way, she just did a sidestep and kept trusting God.

Verse **15** uses a special word. That word is "**Reproach her not**" in the Hebrew reproach means:

Meaning: 1) **to insult, shame, humiliate, blush, be ashamed, be put to shame**, be reproached, be put to confusion, be humiliated 1a) (Niphal) 1a1) to be humiliated, be ashamed 1a2) to be put to shame, be dishonoured, be confounded 1b) (Hiphil) 1b1) to put to shame, insult, humiliate, cause shame to 1b2) to exhibit shame 1c) (Hophal) 1c1) to be insulted, be humiliated 1c2) to be put to shame, be dishonoured, be confounded

As we have already discussed, Ruth was an outsider. She was from an accursed people. Yet Boaz re-emphasizes to his men not to insult her, hurt her feelings, or humiliate her in any way. Now the beautiful thing about this is that Ruth did not know that these men were so instructed. If she did, then she could have had a haughty spirit. She worked humbly and quietly doing her everyday duties trying to be a "Friend" (Ruth) to all she meets. The entire time God had worked on the other end of the circumstances causing her to walk with the favor and love of God. There was an invisible shield of favor around her because her ways pleased the Lord.

Proverbs. 16:
6 By mercy and truth iniquity is purged: and by the fear of the LORD *men* depart from evil.
7 When a **man's ways please** the LORD, **he maketh even his enemies to be at peace with him.**
8 Better *is* a little with righteousness than great revenues without right.
9 A man's heart deviseth his way: but **the LORD directeth his steps**.

We have seen that by chance that Ruth crossed over into Boaz' field. Yea right, by chance "My foot"! The Lord directs your path. Nothing is by chance when God is in the lead. Can you imagine that even those busybody women gleaning beside Ruth knew that their privilege of gleaning could be revoked if they tried to verbally or physically assault Ruth? You know that the men of Boaz would have called them to the side and spoken rashly with anyone who stood against Ruth the Moabites. Instead, she would have had more friends than she knew what to do with because of God's favor on her life they were getting blessed also. See, your blessings run over on all those around you. Those who want to be blessed will stay near the source of their blessings.

Verse **14- 17** continues. When you're faithful to God, he will supply all your need. Ruth got the honor of eating the best that was offered. Boaz made sure she had parched corn by handing it to her personally. Do you ever feel like your work and labour is in vain? I imagine Ruth had been there a few times. In verse 16 Boaz goes even one step further. He instructs these same workers to drop some of the best harvest on purpose so she could pick it up and not to look back or go back to get it. What would have happened if Ruth were too lazy to pick it up? That's right; she would soon loose the privilege of harvesting the best. She would be back to gleaning leftovers. Be encouraged because:

Hebrews 6:
9 But, beloved, **we are persuaded better things of you**, and things that accompany salvation, though we thus speak.
10 **For God *is* not unrighteous to forget your work and labour of love, which ye have shewed toward his name, in that ye have ministered to the saints, and do minister.**
11 And we desire that every one of you do shew the same diligence to the full assurance of hope unto the end:
12 That ye be not slothful, but followers of them who through faith and patience inherit the promises.

God desires better things for you. Your work and labour is not in vain. God doesn't forget. He will reward you for your efforts and love. God encourages us to be diligent with confidence that God does reward if we remain faithful and patient. Blessings don't always come when we expect them, but that does not mean they are not coming. The blessings of God are like the vision God has given you for ministry. We have to remind ourselves of God's promises.

Habakkuk 2:

1 I will stand upon my watch, and set me upon the tower, and will watch to see what he will say unto me, and what I shall answer when I am reproved.

2 And the LORD answered me, and said, **Write** the **vision**, and **make** *it* **plain upon tables**, that he may run that readeth it.

3 For the vision *is* yet **for an appointed time**, but at the end it shall speak, and **not lie**: **though it tarry, wait for it**; because it **will surely come, it will not tarry**.

4 Behold, his soul *which* is lifted up is not upright in him: but **the just shall live by his faith.**

Who is "his faith"? At first we would think its God's faith. But this is not entirely complete. His faith here is your own faith. According as you will believe God so shall you receive. There is a harvest time for all seed that is sown, so is there an appointed time for your harvest. It shall surely come!

18 And she took it up, and went into the city: and her mother in law saw what she had gleaned: and she brought forth, and gave to her that she had reserved after she was sufficed.

19 And her mother in law said unto her, Where hast thou gleaned to day? and where wroughtest thou? blessed be he that did take knowledge of thee. And she shewed her mother in law with whom she had wrought, and said, The man's name with whom I wrought to day is Boaz.

20 And Naomi said unto her daughter in law, Blessed be he of the LORD, who hath not left off his kindness to the living and to the dead. And Naomi said unto her, The man is near of kin unto us, one of our next kinsmen.
21 And Ruth the Moabitess said, He said unto me also, Thou shalt keep fast by my young men, until they have ended all my harvest.
22 And Naomi said unto Ruth her daughter in law, It is good, my daughter, that thou go out with his maidens, that they meet thee not in any other field.
23 So she kept fast by the maidens of Boaz to glean unto the end of barley harvest and of wheat harvest; and dwelt with her mother in law.

When Ruth brought home such a large amount of barley, she was amazed. Seeing this was an unusual occurrence just gleaning the fields for scraps. You know**, God wants his blessings on our life to be evident to all those around us**. If she had brought home an average amount of barley, Naomi would have missed what God was trying to do for them.

Ephesians 3:
11 According to the **eternal purpose which he purposed in Christ Jesus** our Lord:
12 In whom **we have boldness and access with confidence by the faith** of him.
13 Wherefore I desire**16 That he would grant you, according to the riches of his glory,** for you, which is your glory.
14 For this cause I bow my knees unto the Father of our Lord Jesus Christ,
15 Of whom the whole family in heaven and earth is named,
16 That he would grant you, according to the riches of his glory, to be strengthened with might by his Spirit in the inner man;
17 That Christ may dwell in your hearts by faith; that ye, being rooted and grounded in love,

18 **May be able to comprehend** with all saints what *is* **the breadth, and length, and depth, and height;**
19 **And to know the love of Christ, which passeth knowledge, that ye might be filled with all the fulness of God.**
20 **Now unto him that is able to do exceeding abundantly above all that we ask or think, according to the power that worketh in us,**
21 Unto him *be* glory in the church by Christ Jesus throughout all ages, world without end. Amen.

This scripture is so powerful and so eloquently fits what God is doing in the lives of Ruth and Naomi. This abundance of barley only wet the appetite of these two women. He has so much more in store for us than we can even allow ourselves to comprehend. God was setting these two up for a miracle. They came back home with nothing, yet at home was where the abundance of God was waiting them. In our lives, things go wrong, and the only way God can get us to the place of blessing is to allow all we are attempting to do to backfire. When we stop trying to figure out God's will and just walk in it, then his blessings will truly come on us and overtake us. He desires his fullness to hit us like a tidal wave and be swept away by his unimaginable love for us.

CHAPTER THREE

1 Then Naomi her mother in law said unto her, My daughter, shall I not seek rest for thee, that it may be well with thee?

2 And now is not Boaz of our kindred, with whose maidens thou wast? Behold, he winnoweth barley to night in the threshingfloor.

3 Wash thyself therefore, and anoint thee, and put thy raiment upon thee, and get thee down to the floor: but make not thyself known unto the man, until he shall have done eating and drinking.

4 And it shall be, when he lieth down, that thou shalt mark the place where he shall lie, and thou shalt go in, and uncover his feet, and lay thee down; and he will tell thee what thou shalt do.

5 And she said unto her, All that thou sayest unto me I will do.

6 And she went down unto the floor, and did according to all that her mother in law bade her.

7 And when Boaz had eaten and drunk, and his heart was merry, he went to lie down at the end of the heap of corn: and she came softly, and uncovered his feet, and laid her down.

When you're introduced into other cultures, there is so many little things that seem insignificant yet are major traditions. Here Naomi informs Ruth that she is trying to make sure that she is taken care of. That she will not have to be a stranger and foreigner forever. Seeing **Boaz was of near kin, he had the right to take Ruth to be his wife and rise up a child unto her late husband.**

Genesis 38:
6 And Judah took a wife for **Er** his firstborn, whose name *was* Tamar.

7 And Er, Judah's firstborn, was wicked in the sight of the LORD; and the LORD slew him.

8 And **Judah said unto Onan, Go in unto thy brother's wife, and marry her, and raise up seed to thy brother.**

9 And **Onan knew that the seed should not be his; and it came to pass, when he went in unto his brother's wife, that he spilled it on the ground, lest that he should give seed to his brother.**

10 And the thing which he did displeased the LORD: wherefore he slew him also.

11 Then said Judah to Tamar his daughter in law, **Remain a widow at thy father's house, till Shelah my son be grown**: for he said, Lest peradventure he die also, as his brethren *did*. And Tamar went and dwelt in her father's house.

13 And it was told Tamar, saying, Behold thy father in law goeth up to Timnath to shear his sheep.

14 And she put her widow's garments off from her, and covered her with a vail, and wrapped herself, and sat in an open place, which *is* by the way to Timnath; for she saw that Shelah was grown, and she was not given unto him to wife.

15 When Judah saw her, he thought her to be an harlot; because she had covered her face.

16 And he turned unto her by the way, and said, Go to, I pray thee, let me come in unto thee; (for he knew not that she *was* his daughter in law.) And she said, What wilt thou give me, that thou mayest come in unto me?

17 And he said, I will send thee a kid from the flock. And she said, Wilt thou give me a pledge, till thou send *it?*

18 And he said, What pledge shall I give thee? And she said, Thy signet, and thy bracelets, and thy staff that *is* in thine hand. And he gave *it* her, and came in unto her, and she conceived by him.

19 And she arose, and went away, and laid by her vail from her, and put on the garments of her widowhood.

23 And Judah said, Let her take *it* to her, lest we be shamed: behold, I sent this kid, and thou hast not found her.

24 And it came to pass about three months after, that it was told Judah, saying, **Tamar thy daughter in law hath played the harlot; and also, behold, she is with child by whoredom. And Judah said, Bring her forth, and let her be burnt.**

25 **When she was brought forth**, she sent to her father in law, saying, By the man, whose these *are, am* I with child: and she said, **Discern, I pray thee, whose *are* these, the signet, and bracelets, and staff**.

26 And **Judah acknowledged *them*, and said, She hath been more righteous than I; because that I gave her not to Shelah my son**. And he knew her again no more.

This is the story of Tamer, who seven generations before Ruth had exercised and established her right to have a son after her dead husband. Er had died before giving her a male child, which would have been in the bloodline of Christ. So God commanded Onan his brother to marry her and get her pregnant so that Er would have a son to continue the bloodline of Christ him being the surrogate father. Evidently Onan wasn't too keen on the idea. When it came time to impregnate her, he decided not to let Tamar have his seed. As a result of his disobedience God struck him "Deader than a doorknob".

Incidentally the custom of the Jews is; Jews were not allowed to use any form of birth control to hinder the woman from getting pregnant. They were not even allowed to "Spill it on the ground". If she married a man, she had the right to have a male child. In those days a woman who did not have a male child was less than dirt. Women of that day were sold and traded like cattle or property. She had few redeeming qualities and child birth was the greatest. Thank God Jesus set new laws into action.

Matthew 5:
27 Ye have heard that it was said by them of old time, Thou shalt not commit adultery:

28 But I say unto you, That whosoever **looketh on a woman to lust after her hath committed adultery with her already in his heart.**

The custom was, if it looked like it might be good, you could marry her to find out. If you marry it's not a sin to have sex with her. If it's not what you expected it to be you send her back home with a writing of divorce and the man had not sinned! You can see why this commandment Jesus established did not settle well with the Jews. They were trying to justify themselves by marriage and Jesus said you are still an adulterer because you just wanted her for sex!

Then to seal the deal:

Ephesians 5:
31 For this cause shall a man leave his father and mother, and shall be joined **unto his wife**, and they two shall be **one flesh**.
32 This is a great mystery: but I speak concerning Christ and the church.
33 Nevertheless let **every one of you in particular so love his wife** even as himself; and the wife see that she reverence her husband.

The emphasis is on his own wife, not wives.

II Timothy 4:
5 For this cause left I thee in Crete, that thou shouldest set in order the things that are wanting, and ordain elders in every city, as I had appointed thee:
6 If any be blameless, the **husband** of **one wife**, having faithful children not accused of riot or unruly.
7 For a bishop must be blameless, as the steward of God; not selfwilled, not soon angry, not given to wine, no striker, not given to filthy lucre;

Notice the order, which Paul uses. **First he tells the men that they can only have one wife not a harem.** He then talks about a bishop after establishing an unmovable precedent as a Christian. He tells Timothy to set this in order. This is the ordinance of God not of himself.

With Genesis 3:8 in mind we see why Naomi is trying to get Ruth to find where Boaz is going to rest. Notice that in verse seven she is instructed to uncover his feet. That does not uncover his private parts but lets him know her intentions of wanting to be his wife. **It seems to me she was trying to bear herself by humbling herself to lie at his feet. We have paralleled Ruth with Jesus all through this study so let's do it again, ok?**

Luke 7:
37 And, **behold, a woman in the city, which was a sinner, when she knew that *Jesus* sat at meat in the Pharisee's house,** brought an alabaster box of ointment,
38 And **stood at his feet behind *him* weeping, and began to wash his feet with tears, and did wipe *them* with the hairs of her head, and kissed his feet, and anointed *them* with the ointment.**
39 Now when the Pharisee which had bidden him saw *it*, he spake within himself, saying, This man, **if he were a prophet, would have known who and what manner of woman *this is* that toucheth him: for she is a sinner.**
40 And Jesus answering said unto him, Simon, I have somewhat to say unto thee. And he saith, Master, say on.
41 There was a certain creditor which had two debtors: the one owed five hundred pence, and the other fifty.
42 And when they had nothing to pay, he frankly forgave them both. Tell me therefore, which of them will love him most?
43 Simon answered and said, I suppose that *he*, to whom he forgave most. And he said unto him, Thou hast rightly judged.
44 And he turned to the woman, and said unto Simon, Seest thou this woman? I entered into thine house, thou gavest me no water for my feet: **but she hath washed my feet with tears, and wiped *them* with the hairs of her head.**
45 Thou gavest me no kiss: but **this woman since the time I came in hath not ceased to kiss my feet.**
46 My head with oil thou didst not anoint: but **this woman hath anointed my feet with ointment.**

47 Wherefore I say unto thee, **Her sins, which are many, are forgiven; for she loved much: but to whom little is forgiven,** *the same* **loveth little.**
48 And he said unto her, Thy sins are forgiven.
49 And they that sat at meat with him began to say within themselves, Who is this that forgiveth sins also?
50 And he said to the woman, Thy faith hath saved thee; go in peace.

Jesus received the same honor as Ruth bestowed upon boas. She humbled herself at his mercy just as this woman in the New Testament. The result was the same. Their shame and disgrace was taken away. All of Ruth's fears and sorrows were about to be forgotten.

8 And it came to pass at midnight, that the man was afraid, and turned himself: and, behold, a woman lay at his feet.
9 And he said, Who art thou? And she answered, I am Ruth thine handmaid: spread therefore thy skirt over thine handmaid; for thou art a near kinsman.
10 And he said, Blessed be thou of the LORD, my daughter: for thou hast shewed more kindness in the latter end than at the beginning, inasmuch as thou followedst not young men, whether poor or rich.
11 And now, my daughter, fear not; I will do to thee all that thou requirest: for all the city of my people doth know that thou art a virtuous woman.

Ruth lies at Boaz' feet. He is startled when he realizes someone is there. He questions her and finds out vital information such as I am kin to you, **and I desire that you would take me as your wife. Spreading your skirt over me sounds like another scripture David her great-great grandson wrote.**

Psalm 91:

1 **He that dwelleth** in the secret place of the most High **shall abide under the shadow of the Almighty.**

2 **I will say** of the LORD, **He is my refuge and my fortress:** my God; **in him will I trust.**

3 Surely **he shall deliver thee** from the snare of the fowler, *and* from the noisome pestilence.

4 **He shall cover thee with his feathers,** and **under his wings shalt thou trust: his truth** *shall be thy* **shield** and buckler.

Notice the words he and his. This scripture is covenant relationship with Christ at its best. The first "he" is we speaking of God. "He" now becomes God's covenant with us written through David. David prophetically writes to us in songs. Boaz spread his garment over Ruth just as God spreads covering of anointing over us. We too become one with God through Christ. Ruth could trust Boaz' covering just as we can trust God's covering over us.

Deuteronomy 28:

1 And it shall come to pass, if thou shalt hearken diligently unto the voice of the LORD thy God, to observe *and* to do all his commandments which I command thee this day, that the LORD thy God will set thee on high above all nations of the earth:

2 And all these blessings shall come on thee, and overtake thee, if thou shalt hearken unto the voice of the LORD thy God.

3 **Blessed** *shalt* thou *be* in the city, and **blessed** *shalt* thou *be* in the field.

4 **Blessed** *shall* be the fruit of thy body, and the fruit of thy ground, and the fruit of thy cattle, the increase of thy kine, and the flocks of thy sheep.

5 **Blessed** *shall be* thy basket and thy store.

6 **Blessed** *shalt* thou *be* when thou comest in, and blessed *shalt* thou *be* when thou goest out.

7 The LORD shall cause thine enemies that rise up against thee to be smitten before thy face: they shall come out against thee one way, and flee before thee seven ways.

8 The LORD shall command the **blessing** upon thee in thy storehouses, and in all that thou settest thine hand unto; and he shall **bless** thee in the land which the LORD thy God giveth thee.

9 The LORD shall establish thee an holy people unto himself, as he hath sworn unto thee, if thou shalt keep the commandments of the LORD thy God, and walk in his ways.

10 And all people of the earth shall see that thou art called by the name of the LORD; and they shall be afraid of thee.

11 And the LORD shall make thee plenteous in goods, in the fruit of thy body, and in the fruit of thy cattle, and in the fruit of thy ground, in the land which the LORD sware unto thy fathers to give thee.

12 The LORD shall open unto thee his good treasure, the heaven to give the rain unto thy land in his season, and to bless all the work of thine hand: and thou shalt lend unto many nations, and thou shalt not borrow.

13 And the LORD shall make thee the head, and not the tail; and thou shalt be above only, and thou shalt not be beneath; if that thou hearken unto the commandments of the LORD thy God, which I command thee this day, to observe and to do *them:*

This is the covenant God made with Moses, the children of Israel and this is the same covenant God makes with us when we allow God's covering over us. To stay under his covering is simple. Do what the word tells you to do. How can it be any simpler? God wants to make you the anointing of blessing. Let me explain. If Deuteronomy 28: is true, and we know that it is, then everything we involve ourselves in, everything we touch, everything Godly we speak will prosper and come to pass. Does that excite you as much as it does me?

Notice in **verse 10** that Boaz is somewhat older than Ruth. He even comments that you have not chased after the young men for looks or money but have chosen me. He was so amazed at this obviously beautiful Ruth that he commits himself to her immediately. **Verse 11** shows the impact area that Ruth's life has effected. Boaz sees the whole city being touched by the genuine life of Ruth. He actually feels honored to be her betrothed, yet in **verse 12** realities sets back in. He realizes that his hopes and desires toward Ruth may not come to flourishing. There is another "Old geezer" standing between him and his lady love.

12 And now it is true that I am thy near kinsman: howbeit there is a kinsman nearer than I.
13 Tarry this night, and it shall be in the morning, that if he will perform unto thee the part of a kinsman, well; let him do the kinsman's part: but if he will not do the part of a kinsman to thee, then will I do the part of a kinsman to thee, as the LORD liveth: lie down until the morning.
14 And she lay at his feet until the morning: and she rose up before one could know another. And he said, Let it not be known that a woman came into the floor.

Shows wisdom. Ruth was instructed to stay the night with him and rest. Then they arise before daybreak, before any one could make out the shadows and recognize Ruth. In this manner, his near kinsman could not accuse him of any wrong doing. Ruth would not have a soiled reputation.

Romans 14:
16 **Let not** then your **good** be **evil spoken** of:

Sometimes it's not the wrong thing but the wrong way. There are many things as Christians that we can do and there would be no sin; however, that does not means we are free to do those things because it would appear to someone looking on as sin. Thus would destroy the testimony and work you are trying to accomplish for God. Paul says;

I Corinthians 6:

11 And such were some of you: but ye are washed, but ye are sanctified, but ye are justified in the name of the Lord Jesus, and by the Spirit of our God.

12 All things are lawful unto me, but all things are not expedient: all things are lawful for me, but I will not be brought under the power of any.

It's just not worth taking the chance of embarrassing Jesus so I just choose not to do it.

15 Also he said, Bring the vail that thou hast upon thee, and hold it. And when she held it, he measured six measures of barley, and laid it on her: and she went into the city.

16 And when she came to her mother in law, she said, Who art thou, my daughter? And she told her all that the man had done to her.

17 And she said, These six measures of barley gave he me; for he said to me, Go not empty unto thy mother in law.

18 Then said she, Sit still, my daughter, until thou know how the matter will fall: for the man will not be in rest, until he have finished the thing this day.

Verses 13 & 18 are giving the same instructions. Hold your peace and stay still. Don't talk to anyone about what has happened and don't get hasty.

II Corinthians 13:

1 This *is* the third *time* I am coming to you. In the mouth of **two** or **three witnesses shall every word be established**.

When God confirms a thing, we need to hear and obey. When you get instructions as simple as shut up and get still and yet so important. Ruth's life and the life of her mother-in-law were at stake.

Mathew. 27:

24 When Pilate saw that he could prevail nothing, but *that* rather a tumult was made, he took water, and washed *his* hands before the multitude, saying, I am innocent of the blood of this just person: **see ye** *to it.*

See
3700 ovpta,nomai optanomai {op-tan'-om-ahee} or **o;ptomai** optomai {op-tom-ahee}
Meaning: 1) to look at, behold 2) to allow one's self to be seen, to appear

Ye
5210 u`mei/j humeis {hoo-mice'}
Meaning: 1) you

This phrase used by Pilate means to stand still and consider your ways. Not to make a rash decision that you can't take back. This is the same instruction that Ruth took to heart.

Notice that Boaz would not send her away empty handed. She carried all the grain her outer garment could hold. I like it when God said that "These blessings shall come on thee and overtake thee", Deuteronomy 28: 2.

CHAPTER FOUR

1 Then went Boaz up to the gate, and sat him down there: and, behold, the kinsman of whom Boaz spake came by; unto whom he said, Ho, such a one! turn aside, sit down here. And he turned aside, and sat down.

2 And he took ten men of the elders of the city, and said, Sit ye down here. And they sat down.

3 And he said unto the kinsman, Naomi, that is come again out of the country of Moab, selleth a parcel of land, which was our brother Elimelech's:

4 And I thought to advertise thee, saying, Buy it before the inhabitants, and before the elders of my people. If thou wilt redeem it, redeem it: but if thou wilt not redeem it, then tell me, that I may know: for there is none to redeem it beside thee; and I am after thee. And he said, I will redeem it.

5 Then said Boaz, What day thou buyest the field of the hand of Naomi, thou must buy it also of Ruth the Moabitess, the wife of the dead, to raise up the name of the dead upon his inheritance.

6 And the kinsman said, I cannot redeem it for myself, lest I mar mine own inheritance: redeem thou my right to thyself; for I cannot redeem it.

7 Now this was the manner in former time in Israel concerning redeeming and concerning changing, for to confirm all things; a man plucked off his shoe, and gave it to his neighbour: and this was a testimony in Israel.

When Boaz sees his kinsman he says "ho, such a one! Turn aside, sit down here. In modern English he would have said, "Yo', you there, come here and cop a squat, I need to talk at you!" watch the wisdom of Boaz. He entices the kinsman with the chance of getting a piece of land before it goes onto the open market. We would call this insider trading. The kinsman was excited. He must have already owned a great amount of property at this time and Boaz was appealing to his business interest. Once the kinsman was thinking about all he owned then Boaz settled the account by telling him that the parcel of land was also the inheritance of Mahlon. He had to purchase it not only from the mother but according to Jewish law; he had to marry Ruth because she had no male child. The kinsman then realized that a child born to him would also become an heir of all he had not just this small parcel of land. His other children would be affected by this transaction. He would be a rightful heir and the land would no longer be in the kinsman's family but in Naomi's family because he had to name Ruth's firstborn after Elimelech's son Mahlon. Boaz was truly shrewd in business. As we know, the kinsman chose not to redeem the land in front of ten witnesses. In Israel he only had to be witnessed by two or three witnesses.

8 Therefore the kinsman said unto Boaz, Buy it for thee. So he drew off his shoe.
9 And Boaz said unto the elders, and unto all the people, Ye are witnesses this day, that I have bought all that was Elimelech's, and all that was Chilion's and Mahlon's, of the hand of Naomi.

This is an interesting way to seal a deal. I guess it's better than spitting in your hand and shaking on it. Yet the loser was obvious. He had to walk down the street wobbling with only one shoe on. Can you imagine how many shoes you would go through if you made a lot of deals? You would have to add the price of a new set of shoes when making a deal in Bethlehem just to break even. So off goes the kinsman bouncing with one shoe.

10 Moreover Ruth the Moabitess, the wife of Mahlon, have I purchased to be my wife, to raise up the name of the dead upon his inheritance, that the name of the dead be not cut off from among his brethren, and from the gate of his place: ye are witnesses this day.

11 And all the people that were in the gate, and the elders, said, We are witnesses. The LORD make the woman that is come into thine house like Rachel and like Leah, which two did build the house of Israel: and do thou worthily in Ephratah, and be famous in Bethlehem:
12 And let thy house be like the house of Pharez, whom Tamar bare unto Judah, of the seed which the LORD shall give thee of this young woman.
13 So Boaz took Ruth, and she was his wife: and when he went in unto her, the LORD gave her conception, and she bare a son.

Boaz not only gets the land, the beautiful bride, and he gets the spiritual blessing of Abraham pronounced upon him by the elders of Bethlehem. They prophesy to Boaz that Ruth will be as Rachel, Leah who established the nation of Israel, and Tamar whose descendants will birth Jesus Christ the son of God. According to:

Matthew 1: 2- 6;
2 **Abraham** begat Isaac; and **Isaac begat Jacob**; and Jacob begat Judas and his brethren; (Jacob's Name Was Changed By God To Israel.)
3 And Judas begat Phares and Zara of Thamar; and Phares begat Esrom; and Esrom begat Aram; (Pregnant From Her Father-In-Law)
4 And Aram begat Aminadab; and Aminadab begat Naasson; and Naasson begat Salmon;

5 And Salmon begat Booz of Rachab; and Booz begat Obed of Ruth; and Obed begat Jesse; (Rachab was the harlot from Jericho. Ruth from Moab.)
6 And Jesse begat David the king; and David the king begat Solomon of her *that had been* **the wife** of Urias; (David Had An Affair With Bathsheba And Then Had Solomon.)

There are only five women mentioned in the bloodline of Jesus from Abraham, to whom the promise of Jesus was given. Each one of these special women had one thing in common, faith. I guess when the bible says:

Proverbs 18:
22 *Whoso* **findeth a wife findeth a good** *thing*, and **obtaineth favour of the LORD.**

It must really be a good thing. Boaz found favour with Ruth, Naomi, elders of Bethlehem (The birthplace of Jesus), the kinsman and God. How awesome is that? You know what else is amazing? We have waited all this time to find out who Ruth was the widow of. His name ladies and gentlemen is Mahlon. Any mention of these two sons was grouped together and never separate. This is the first time you actually find out which one was Ruth's husband. He was the sick one and Chilion was the pining one. Both of these sons were pitiful looking husbands. One was sickly and the other was feeble.

After all this grandstanding that God has done, he made sure that this prophesies would come to pass, because Ruth got pregnant on her wedding night. Wow, an explosion of great passion that would be talked about for three thousand years. So, I wonder what they named him? Mmm, Obed was his name. Let's separate his name. O' bed! In English for those of you who haven't figured it out. **Oh' what a bed!** (This is from the book of Ronald chapter one.)

14 And the women said unto Naomi, Blessed be the LORD, which hath not left thee this day without a kinsman, that his name may be famous in Israel.
15 And he shall be unto thee a restorer of thy life, and a nourisher of thine old age: for thy daughter in law, which loveth thee, which is better to thee than seven sons, hath born him.
16 And Naomi took the child, and laid it in her bosom, and became nurse unto it.

17 And the women her neighbours gave it a name, saying, There is a son born to Naomi; and they called his name Obed: he is the father of Jesse, the father of David.

18 Now these are the generations of Pharez: Pharez begat Hezron,

19 And Hezron begat Ram, and Ram begat Amminadab,

20 And Amminadab begat Nahshon, and Nahshon begat Salmon,

21 And Salmon begat Boaz, and Boaz begat Obed,

22 And Obed begat Jesse, and Jesse begat David.

Is so important. The women of Bethlehem begin to prophesy to Ruth and Naomi. They give the child his name, Obed. They have already spoken a name for his descendants, namely Jessie and David who became king.

"Fleetness" and "Friend" gave birth to "Serving" to be the heritage of "My delight". These are the names of our hero's. Boaz and Ruth gave birth to Obed to be the heritage of Naomi. We know that in three generations a king will come; Ruth's great grand son.

This gives all new meaning to a scripture that David inspired Solomon to write.

Proverbs 5:

15 Drink waters out of thine own cistern, and running waters out of thine own well.

16 Let thy fountains be dispersed abroad, *and* rivers of waters in the streets.

17 Let them be only thine own, and not strangers' with thee.

18 Let thy fountain be blessed: and rejoice with the wife of thy youth.

19 *Let her be as* the loving hind and pleasant roe; let her breasts satisfy thee at all times; and be thou ravished always with her love.

Solomon saw the fruitfulness of Ruth and Boaz. He saw the same desire with David and Bathsheba. The fountains here are the fountains from your loins. Dispersed into the streets is what effect your children will have on your city. Let everyone be blessed by the wife of my youth. We know that Boaz' wife Ruth dispersed abroad and produced Jesus Christ the messiah. This poem of Solomon is dedicated to Ruth and Boaz. How can we not be awestruck by the life and faithfulness of Ruth. If we could live our lives after the faith of this wonderful woman, then what impact would you have on the world we know?

Chapter VIII

GRASSHOPPERS AND LOCUSTS, THE MINI-GIANTS OF GOD!

In this study, we will look at what odds are stacked against you and what your attitude should betoward these seemly insurmountable odds. Sometimes we find the weakest among us are indeed the strongest?

Wrritten By: Dr. Ronald Sanders PhD
© by the Library of Congress 2005

GRASSHOPPERS AND LOCUSTS, THE MINI-GIANTS OF GOD!

Psalm 42:

2 My soul thirsteth for God, for the living God: when shall I come and appear before God?

3 My tears have been my meat day and night, while they continually say unto me, Where is thy God?

4 When I remember these *things,* I pour out my soul in me: for I had gone with the multitude, I went with them to the house of God, with the voice of joy and praise, with a multitude that kept holyday.

5 Why art thou **cast down**, O my **soul?** and *why* art thou disquieted in me? hope thou in God: for I shall yet praise him *for* the help of his countenance.

6 O my God, my **soul** is **cast down** within me: therefore will I remember thee from the land of Jordan, and of the Hermonites, from the hill Mizar.

7 Deep calleth unto deep at the noise of thy waterspouts: all thy waves and thy billows are gone over me.

8 Yet the LORD will command his lovingkindness in the daytime, and in the night his song *shall be* with me, *and* my prayer unto the God of my life.

9 I will say unto God my rock, Why hast thou forgotten me? why go I mourning because of the oppression of the enemy?

10 *As* with a sword in my bones, mine enemies reproach me; while they say daily unto me, Where is thy God?

11 Why art thou **cast down**, O my **soul**? and why art thou disquieted within me? hope thou in God: for I shall yet praise him, *who is* the health of my countenance, and my God.

Ever felt like this? Where are you God? I am so broken up that my appetite has fled from me. All I can do is cry? It seems as if everyone has risen up against me. I feel lower than scum.

Numbers 13:

27 And they told him, and said, We came unto the land whither thou sentest us, and surely it floweth with milk and honey; and this *is* the fruit of it.

28 Nevertheless the people *be* strong that dwell in the land, and the cities *are* walled, and very great: *and* moreover we saw the children of Anak there.

29 The Amalekites dwell in the land of the south: and the Hittites, and the Jebusites, and the Amorites, dwell in the mountains: and the Canaanites dwell by the sea, and by the coast of Jordan.

30 And Caleb stilled the people before Moses, and said, Let us go up at once, and possess it; for we are well able to overcome it.

31 But the men that went up with him said, We be not able to go up against the people; for they *are* stronger than we.

32 And they brought up an evil report of the land which they had searched unto the children of Israel, saying, The land, through which we have gone to search it, *is* a land that eateth up the inhabitants thereof; and all the people that we saw in it *are* men of a great stature.

33 And there we saw the giants, the sons of Anak, *which come* of the giants: and we were in our own sight as **grasshoppers**, and so we were in their sight.

Yea, that's what I feel like, a grasshopper. You can't get much smaller or insignificant than a grasshopper. Everyone seems larger than life, and I don't feel like I can do anything right!

You know something I have noticed? If we were grasshoppers, then we could feed off of the land that flowed with milk and honey and not have to worry about the giants. They are not a threat to a grasshopper, just to the humans. Seeing it's a land flowing with milk and honey, I can enjoy all I want and the giants of the land will scare off those who would take my blessing away. in the midst of my giants, I can feast!

Judges 7:

9 And it came to pass the same night, that the LORD said unto him, Arise, get thee down unto the host; for I have delivered it into thine hand.

10 But if thou fear to go down, go thou with Phurah thy servant down to the host:

11 And thou shalt hear what they say; and afterward shall thine hands be strengthened to go down unto the host. Then went he down with Phurah his servant unto the outside of the armed men that *were* in the host.

12 And the Midianites and the Amalekites and all the children of the east lay along in the valley like **grasshoppers** for multitude; and their camels *were* without number, as the sand by the sea side for multitude.

13 And when Gideon was come, behold, *there* was a man that told a dream unto his fellow, and said, Behold, I dreamed a dream, and, lo, a cake of barley bread tumbled into the host of Midian, and came unto a tent, and smote it that it fell, and overturned it, that the tent lay along.

14 And his fellow answered and said, This *is* nothing else save the sword of Gideon the son of Joash, a man of Israel: *for* into his hand hath God delivered Midian, and all the host.

15 And it was *so*, when Gideon heard the telling of the dream, and the interpretation thereof, that he worshipped, and returned into the host of Israel, and said, Arise; for the LORD hath delivered into your hand the host of Midian.

16 And he divided the three hundred men *into* three companies, and he put a trumpet in every man's hand, with empty pitchers, and lamps within the pitchers.

In verse twelve, we get the scene of Gideon surveying the land. His two observations are like unto locust engulfing the land and the sand of the sea. Notice that the sand of the sea is in direct similarity with the promise God made Abraham in Genesis. If that is true, then also the fact that Gideon saw himself as the grasshopper as being weak and unable to overcome this enormous enemy until… he heard the testimony of the soldier that had the dream about the wheel of bread rolling into the camp and destroying it. Gideon saw the fear in the hearts of his enemy and saw God at work. Thus, it didn't matter what he saw himself as, grasshopper or hurricane. He knew God had given him the battle.

Isaiah 40:

21 Have ye not known? have ye not heard? hath it not been told you from the beginning? have ye not understood from the foundations of the earth?

22 *It is* he that sitteth upon the circle of the earth, and the inhabitants thereof *are* as **grasshoppers**; that stretcheth out the heavens as a curtain, and spreadeth them out as a tent to dwell in:

If God sees you as a grasshopper, then you must just be a grasshopper? Is that a good thing?

Amos 7:

1 Thus hath the Lord God shewed unto me; and, behold, he formed **grasshoppers** in the beginning of the shooting up of the latter growth; and, lo, *it* was the latter growth after the king's mowings.

2 And it came to pass, *that* when they had made an end of eating the grass of the land, then I said, O Lord God, forgive, I beseech thee: by whom shall Jacob arise? for he *is* small.

He formed the grasshopper, and he saw that it was good, so I guess if I'm a grasshopper it must be good! Especially if I get to eat the tender sweet grass that even the king hadn't had yet.

Exodus 10:

11 Not so: go now ye *that are* men, and serve the LORD; for that ye did desire. And they were driven out from Pharaoh's presence.

12 And the LORD said unto Moses, Stretch out thine hand over the land of Egypt for the locusts, that they may come up upon the land of Egypt, and eat every herb of the land, *even* all that the hail hath left.

13 And Moses stretched forth his rod over the land of Egypt, and the LORD brought an east wind upon the land all that day, and all *that* night; *and* when it was morning, the east wind brought the locusts.

14 And the locusts went up over all the land of Egypt, and rested in all the coasts of Egypt: very grievous *were they*;

before them there were no such **locusts** as they, neither after them shall be such.

15 For they covered the face of the whole earth, so that the land was darkened; and they did eat every herb of the land, and all the fruit of the trees which the hail had left: and there remained not any green thing in the trees, or in the herbs of the field, through all the land of Egypt.

16 Then Pharaoh called for Moses and Aaron in haste; and he said, I have sinned against the LORD your God, and against you.

17 Now therefore forgive, I pray thee, my sin only this once, and intreat the LORD your God, that he may take away from me this death only.

18 And he went out from Pharaoh, and intreated the LORD.

19 And the LORD turned a mighty strong west wind, which took away the locusts, and cast them into the Red sea; there remained not one locust in all the coasts of Egypt.

Here God used grasshoppers or locust as they are also called, to drive a whole nation to repentance before God. If God can drive a nation with a locust, how much more effective can you be in our nation? The locust got fat and satisfied by the Lord. It's alright if the Lord wants to use me to take away an unbeliever's blessing and give it to me. I'm get fatter and he's paying for it. That's a God kind of party if I ever heard of one. When your life as a grasshopper has come to a completion, it's wonderful to know that all God has instilled into you will be passed on to another generation. Here the locust were driven into the sea, and no doubt eaten by schools of fish. What the locust has done, will live in the next generation, who will be even greater than you!

II Chronicles 7:

13 If I shut up heaven that there be no rain, or if I command the **locusts** to devour the land, or if I send pestilence among my people;

14 If my people, which are called by my name, shall humble themselves, and pray, and seek my face, and turn from their

wicked ways; then will I hear from heaven, and will forgive their sin, and will heal their land.

15 Now mine eyes shall be open, and mine ears attent unto the prayer *that is made* in this place.

16 For now have I chosen and sanctified this house, that my name may be there for ever: and mine eyes and mine heart shall be there perpetually.

Your life in Christ will send conviction to all that come near you. When you are near, Satan's blessing are cut off from all you come in contact with. Causing the sinner to want the Spirit of life that permeates from your very being! Knowing that your enthusiasm is contagious, powerful and marvelous. When we gather in the house of God, and come as one voice unto God in praises, we are like those locust that are making one sound that can be heard for miles and miles. God's ears will pay attention to our prayer made in his house, and God will even change the course of nature to bring pleasure to our hearts.

Proverbs 30:

21 For three *things* the earth is disquieted, and for four *which* it cannot bear:

22 For a servant when he reigneth; and a fool when he is filled with meat;

23 For an odious (HATEFUL, SPITEFUL) *woman* when she is married; and an handmaid that is heir to her mistress.

24 There be four *things which* <u>are little upon the earth</u>, but they *are* exceeding wise:

25 The <u>ants</u> *are* a people not strong, yet they prepare their meat in the summer;

26 The <u>conies</u> (ROCK BADGER) *are but* a feeble folk, yet make they their houses in the rocks;

27 The **locusts** have no king, yet go they forth all of them by bands;

28 The <u>spider</u> taketh hold with her hands, and is in kings' palaces.

29 There be three *things* which go well, yea, four are comely in going:

30 A lion *which is* strongest among beasts, and turneth not away for any;

31 A greyhound; an he goat also; and a king, against whom *there is* no rising up.

32 If thou hast done foolishly in lifting up thyself, or if thou hast thought evil, *lay* thine hand upon thy mouth

33 Surely the churning of milk bringeth forth butter, and the wringing of the nose bringeth forth blood: so the forcing of wrath bringeth forth strife.

Locust have no leader, yet they are in unity and always in a swarm. As individuals, they are easily squashed, yet in a swarm, they are a terror of nature. A fear and dread of all mankind. The amazing thing is, locust are not even harmful to humans, but can be eaten as food! There is so much power in unity, unlike a hateful and spiteful individual who demands it their way.

Psalm 78:

45 He sent divers sorts of flies among them, which devoured them; and frogs, which destroyed them.

46 He gave also their increase unto the caterpiller, and their labour unto the locust.

Psalm 109:

22 For I *am* poor and needy, and my heart is wounded within me.

23 I am gone like the shadow when it declineth: I am tossed up and down as the locust.

24 My knees are weak through fasting; and my flesh faileth of fatness.

25 I became also a reproach unto them: *when* they looked upon me they shaked their heads.

26 Help me, O LORD my God: O save me according to thy mercy:

27 That they may know that this *is* thy hand; *that* thou, LORD, hast done it

The nature of the locust:

- Carried by the winds.
- They cover the sky like an eclipse.
- Eat everything before them, with little discrimination.
- They have the sound of chariots and horsemen, and sounding of hurricane.
- They are always seen in swarms, never alone.
- Alone, they have no power, very easily crushed.
- They can hang on to almost anything.
- Beautiful to look upon, yet greatly feared.
- They flow in unity without a leader or boss.
- They are obedient to the Lord, and hear quickly.
- Used of God to reveal sin and shame.

Chapter IX

I WILL NOT MURMUR
BECAUSE THE AX HEAD SWIMS!

Do you really believe that you walk in Devine appointment?
Do you really believe that all things work together for good?
Well, read this study and allow God to minister to you.

Written By Dr. Ronald Sanders PhD
© By the Library of Congress

"I WILL NOT MURMUR, BECAUSE
THE AX HEAD SWIMS! "

Revelation from 8/3/97. The Lord spoke and said these words. When everything is going wrong, don't murmur! God will cause whatever situation there is, to float. Feel like you're sinking and there is no hope, don't murmur. Feel like you're drowning, and no one has cared enough to throw you a lifeline, don't murmur!

Exodus 15: 24,
24 And the people **murmured against Moses**, saying, <u>What shall we drink?</u>

Exodus 16: 2- 3,
2 And the whole congregation of the children of Israel murmured against Moses and Aaron in the wilderness:
3 And the children of Israel said unto them, Would to God we had died by the hand of the LORD in the land of Egypt, when we sat by the flesh pots, *and* when we did eat bread to the full; for ye have **brought us forth into this wilderness, to kill this whole assembly with hunger.**

Exodus 16: 8,
8 And Moses said, *This shall be*, when the LORD shall give you in the evening flesh to eat, and in the morning bread to the full; for that the LORD heareth your murmurings which ye murmur against him: and what *are* we? **your murmurings** *are* **not against us, but against the LORD.**

Numbers 11: 20, 33,
20 *But* even a whole month, until it come out at your nostrils, and it be loathsome unto you: **because that ye have despised the LORD** which *is* among you, and have wept before him, saying, Why came we forth out of Egypt? {whole...: Heb. month of days}
33 And while the flesh was yet between their teeth, ere it was chewed, the wrath of the LORD was kindled against the

people, and the LORD smote the people with a very great plague.

Exodus 17: 7,
7 And he called the name of the place Massah, and Meribah, because of the chiding of the children of Israel, and **because they tempted the LORD**, saying, Is the LORD among us, or not? {Massah: that is, Temptation} {Meribah: that is, Chiding, or, Strife}

Exodus 32: 9- 12, Also Numbers 14: 12- 16,
9 And the LORD said unto Moses, I have seen this people, and, behold**, it *is* a stiffnecked people:**
10 Now therefore let me alone, that my wrath may wax hot against them, and that I may consume them: and I will make of thee a great nation.
11 And Moses besought the LORD his God, and said, LORD, why doth thy wrath wax hot against thy people, which thou hast brought forth out of the land of Egypt with great power, and with a mighty hand? {the LORD: Heb. the face of the LORD}
12 Wherefore should the Egyptians speak, and say, For mischief did he bring them out, to slay them in the mountains, and to consume them from the face of the earth? Turn from thy fierce wrath, and repent of this evil against thy people.

Numbers 14: 22- 23, 29- 34,
22 Because all those men which have seen my glory, and my miracles, which I did in Egypt and in the wilderness, and **have tempted me now these ten times**, and have **not hearkened to my voice;**
23 Surely they shall not see the land which I sware unto their fathers, neither shall any of them that provoked me see it: {Surely...: Heb. If they see the land}
29 **Your carcases shall fall in this wilderness**; and all that were numbered of you, according to your whole number, from twenty years old and upward, which have murmured against me.

30 Doubtless ye shall not come into the land, *concerning* which I sware to make you dwell therein, save Caleb the son of Jephunneh, and Joshua the son of Nun. {sware: Heb. lifted up my hand}

31 But your little ones, which ye said should be a prey, them will I bring in, and they shall know the land which ye have despised.

32 But *as for* you, **your carcases, they shall fall in this wilderness.**

33 And your children shall wander in the wilderness forty years, and bear your whoredoms, until your carcases be wasted in the wilderness. {wander: or, feed}

34 After the number of the days in which ye searched the land, even forty days, each day for a year, shall ye bear your iniquities, *even* forty years, and ye shall know my breach of promise. {breach...: or, changing of my purpose}

As a history with the children of Israel, they murmured and complained while they were in Egypt, and never stopped after they had been delivered. They had the "Lot's wife syndrome ". Didn't know when they were free. They complained when God gave them the best water, from a rock. They complained when they had the best food, manna of heaven, which means, "We know not what it is". They had never been anything upon the earth like manna before. It was a special creation just for the children of Israel. They murmured when God performed miracles, they murmured when he didn't. The only thing they had to accept was, that God promised to bring them unto the land of Canaan. He would do whatever was necessary for them to get there. God is not stupid, as sometimes we treat him. God promised that.

Matthew 6: 30,
30 Wherefore, if God so clothe the grass of the field, which to day is, and to morrow is cast into the oven, *shall he* not much more *clothe* you, O ye of little faith?

God promised, and if we will not murmur and complain about what has come our way, shall he not even so take care of us?

25 times in the Old Testament, they murmured.
What is the problem with murmuring?

I Corinthians 10: 9- 13,
9 Neither let us tempt Christ, as some of them also tempted, and were destroyed of serpents.
10 Neither murmur ye, as some of them also murmured, and were destroyed of the destroyer.
11 Now all these things happened unto them for ensamples: and they are written for our admonition, upon whom the ends of the world are come. {ensamples: or, types}
12 Wherefore let him that thinketh he standeth take heed lest he fall.
13 There hath no temptation taken you but such as *is* common to man: but God is faithful, who will not suffer you to be tempted above that ye are able; but will with the temptation also make a way to escape, that ye may be able to bear *it*. {common...: or, moderate}

One of the hardest things to understand is, that, God will not send us through anything that he isn't already there waiting for us, and will lead us through. We must learn to trust God in every circumstance, even though we do not think it is a spiritual battle, but every event in our lives is a result of a spiritual battle. God sees the path we are walking, and knows every pitfall along the way. If we walked around every trial, then we would fall into the pitfalls Satan has prepared for us. An example of this would be; if we were walking along a narrow path, headed toward a given destination, and the path has a large hole, one in which would cause serious harm to us. As we go into the edge of the woods to avoid this hole, we get entangled with thorns and briars. We may even step into a small hole, turning our ankle over, and yet not spraining it. When we get back on the path, we see that someone else has fallen into the hole meant for us, and has suffered great harm. As we help them to safety, we then will realize that the briars, thorns, and small holes, we encountered, was a very small price to pay to save our lives. God sends us on detours many times to keep us from harm. It is not always the way we desire to go, but if we do not murmur against God, the pilot of our lives, then we will reach homeport in safety, only with a greater testimony of how great God is. Make up your mind,

**************** **"I will not murmur!"** *****************

It is not murmuring against the circumstances, it is murmuring against God! Because if we trust God for our lives, then he sent us through whatever we have gone through, because it was a place of safety, and he knew we had strength enough to overcome whatever obstacle that came our way. We know according to James the first chapter, God does not tempt us to do evil. So many times the route we have gone is to avoid temptations. By not murmuring, we do not have to endure many of the temptations of Satan. We go through many of the temptations when we don't trust God, and go our own way. Then God has to come and rescue us from destruction. That is just like God, isn't it? He's always there to rescue us when we royally mess up.

All this is fine, but what does it have to do with an ax head?

II Kings 6: 1- 7,
1 And the sons of the prophets said unto Elisha, Behold now, the place where we dwell with thee is too strait for us.
2 Let us go, we pray thee, unto Jordan, and take thence every man a beam, and let us make us a place there, where we may dwell. And he answered, Go ye.
3 And one said, Be content, I pray thee, and go with thy servants. And he answered, I will go.
4 So he went with them. And when they came to Jordan, they cut down wood.
5 But as one was felling a beam, the axe head fell into the water: **and he cried, and said, Alas, master! for it was borrowed.** {axe head: Heb. iron}
6 And the man of God said, Where fell it? And he shewed him the place. And he cut down a stick, and **cast *it* in thither; and the iron did swim.**

7 Therefore said he, Take *it* up to thee. And he put out his hand, and took it.

Here, we see prophets who were willing to do work needed for the temple and the dwelling thereof. At least one priest had to borrow an ax to participate in the work. Isn't it wonderful when someone is so excited about the work of the Lord, they will borrow tools just to help! We also see divine appointment. Elisha had not intended going to Jordan with them, seeing they invited him to go with them. In
Elisha's life, many doubted that Elijah had left the anointing of prophet to Elisha. Next you will see an illustration of how that this doubt was even taught to their children.

II Kings 2: 23- 24,

23 And he went up from thence unto Bethel: and as he was going up by the way, there came forth little children out of the city, and mocked him, and said unto him, Go up, thou bald head; go up, thou bald head.
24 And he turned back, and looked on them, and cursed them in the name of the LORD. And there came forth two she bears out of the wood, and tare forty and two children of them.

Some say that these little children were teens, but it does not actually say. The Hebrew just says from infancy to adolescence. It is possible that the forty-two children that died made a point to those in Bethel. Those children came out of bethel, or the house of God. Those who were in Bethel doubted that God had actually called Elisha to succeed Elijah. Even though Elisha did miracles as Elijah and other prophets. If you noticed that the children came out of the house of God. How many times have we come out of the house of God, complaining about what the teacher or preacher ministered on? A word to the wise, watch what we saw about the man or woman of God. God hears and responds. We know that Elisha was bald, because the children observed it. They wanted Elisha to do some great feat of magic to prove he really was God's prophet. In our language they would have said something like: " if you're really called of God to follow in the footsteps of Elijah, then you ascend into the clouds like you said Elijah did, you bald headed old cookie. Get a life, no one believes your lie." I guess they murmured one time too many. They would not have murmured if they hadn't been taught it by their parents. So we see that Bethel, supposedly being the house of God, did not receive a visitation of the Lord. Elisha passed by, and did not enter there. He had just left Jericho where the bad water was made pure. Jesus, "Did not many miracles," in Jerusalem. We desire the great blessing of God, but we want to have the right to judge whether it is what we want, not what God wants for us.

The prophets that went to the river Jordan had the privilege of seeing another miracle, a steel ax head floating on the top of the water. This is an impossibility according to nature. What ever battles we are facing in life, when we place our trust in the hands of God, we will also see our trials and battles float to the top. When all seems to fall apart, God will perform miracles to cause the impossible to be possible. So when all your heartaches get you down, let God float it. Many times we are like the man chopping that tree, trying with all our might, and getting nowhere. We have no steel in our ax. We are beating wood with wood. We need some of that Holy Ghost steel that moves every obstacle. The man became frantic when he lost his ax head, but he knew where to turn. When we lose what we have, turn to Jesus.

Romans 8: 28,
28 And we know that all things work together for good to them that love God, to them who are the **called** according to *his* purpose.

" Called" Means Invited, Appointed.

Ephesians 1: 4- 7,
4 According as he hath chosen us in him before the foundation of the world, that we should be holy and without blame before him in love:

5 Having predestinated us unto the adoption of children by Jesus Christ to himself, according to the good pleasure of his will.

6 To the praise of the glory of his grace, wherein he hath made us accepted in the beloved.

7 In whom we have redemption through his blood, the forgiveness of sins, according to the riches of his grace;

For some time we have made out that Romans 8: 28, belonged only to a special group of Christians. However, when we see that we were invited and appointed a Christian, it gives cause for rejoicing. God has purpose for your life. Your life was and is not by accident. God told Jeremiah that he knew him while he was in his mother's womb, and called him. God called you and beaconed you unto himself even while you were being formed in your mother's belly. If you are not serving God, then you are running from your first friend you ever knew, the first one to call you by name. That is the reason so many are miserable and do not even realize it. They are running from their first love.

God wants us to understand that he does not want us to worry, but to give it to him. We have to return to our mother's womb to understand and accept what God desires for our life. We felt safe, and the things of this world did not affect us. We trusted our mother. We must have the same trust in God! Is it always easy? No! Letting go is the hardest thing you will ever do. We are so accustomed to working it out, and fixing it ourselves, and only as a last resort turning it over to God. We need to reprogram our minds.

Chapter X

SHOUT!

There comes times in our lives that all we want to do is scream. When the entire world seems to fall down around you, and there seems no hope in sight? Think on this. God is just waiting for you to give a shout to him. You may think this is silly, so did many in biblical days, but it worked. So, get ready…

Written By: Dr. Ronald Sanders PhD

SHOUT!

Joshua 6: 5,
5 And it shall come to pass, that when they make a long *blast* with the ram's horn, *and* when ye hear the sound of the trumpet, all the people shall shout with a great shout; and the wall of the city shall fall down flat, and the people shall ascend up every man straight before him. {flat: Heb. under it}

Surrounded, and no way out, God commanded a shout of victory!

Joshua 6: 16, 20,
16 And it came to pass at the seventh time, when the priests blew with the trumpets, Joshua said unto the people, Shout; for the LORD hath given you the clty.
20 So the people shouted when *the priests* blew with the trumpets: and it came to pass, when the people heard the sound of the trumpet, and the people shouted with a great shout, that the wall fell down flat, so that the people went up into the city, every man straight before him, and they took the city. {flat: Heb. under it}

Shouted
7321- to mar (espec. by breaking); fig. to split the ears (with sound), shout (for alarm or joy): blow an alarm, cry (alarm, aloud, out),destroy, make a joyful noise, smart, shout (for joy), sound an alarm, triumph.

In the Hebrew, shout means; to sound an alarm, to shout for victory, to make a loud cry, to make an ear piercing sound. We see that this was not just a random shout, the people shouted unto God in praise and victory. It has always been amazing that in front of the mightiest army of that day, there were always musicians, praises, worshippers, and singers. What a way to enter the battlefield. There is no way of hiding from the enemy with so much sound. Let us liken our situations to this same. When we are in the midst of gigantic problems, seemingly no way over or around them, what would happen if we just got beside ourselves and declared a shout of victory before we knew we had it. With a sound of praise that everyone who knows our situation can hear. I wonder what the outcome of such unacceptable behavior would be? Very probably the same as Joshua and the army of God, victory. Well, what if I don't come up on the situation; it overtakes me, and does this same principle still work?

II Chronicles 13: 12- 15,
12 And, behold, God himself *is* with us for *our* captain, and his priests with sounding trumpets to cry alarm against you. O children of Israel, fight ye not against the LORD God of your fathers; for ye shall not prosper.
13 But Jeroboam caused an ambushment to come about behind them: so they were before Judah, and the ambushment *was* behind them.
14 And when Judah looked back, behold, the battle was before and behind: and they cried unto the LORD, and the priests sounded with the trumpets.
15 Then the men of Judah gave a shout: and as the men of Judah shouted, it came to pass, that God smote Jeroboam and all Israel before Abijah and Judah.

Jeroboam figured that the words of Judah were just empty sounds, the sound of a desperate army trying to save their own lives. They had long since forgotten that God had won battle after battle for them when they came out of Egypt. He figured that he could surround them and they could not live, and there was nothing God could do against such an entrapment. The most important thing here to remember is that God smote Israel, not the army of Judah. If we can just catch the concept that God can win for us, and learn to do what is necessary for God to accomplish in us and for us, his desires, then we can fulfill the word when it says;

Mathew 17: 20,

20 And Jesus said unto them, Because of your unbelief: for verily I say unto you, If ye have faith as a grain of mustard seed, ye shall say unto this mountain, Remove hence to yonder place; and it shall remove; and nothing shall be impossible unto you.

Faith in this sense has to be public. Others will see and hear this great shout of faith. How many people could stand at the base of a mountain and command it to remove to another place and no one hear? This root of faith is bold, not backing down to fear. It is, as the cliché' goes, "Taking the bull by the horns", kind of faith. Did you notice the last seven words? "And nothing shall be impossible unto you! " How do we understand this mind set of such enormous moving faith? How do we come to a place of confidence to know that it shall remove to yonder place? How do we build such an awestruck awareness of God and his awesome ability, and can have no doubt to his answering our prayers? Have you ever felt something so strong that you could actually taste it? I have, and yet it hasn't always happened, why? Did I become scared, forgetful of that feeling of confidence in God? I wonder if I became like Peter walking on the water, being distracted just long enough to reason things out, and fail. What did he mean when he said?

I Corinthians 1: 27,

27 But God hath chosen the foolish things of the world to confound the wise; and God hath chosen the weak things of the world to confound the things which are mighty;

If we refuse to add our unneeded opinion in, then God can help us get it right the first time. God's answers are always simple. A child can understand God's wonderful revelations and mysteries for our lives, thus even us adults can enjoy the simplicity of God.

Proverbs 15: 1,
1 A soft answer turneth away wrath: but grievous words stir up anger.

The best way to start a fight or argument is to begin yelling at an individual. It is our desire to destroy what Satan has in store for us. If we begin to get our voices up in prayer against Satan and his deeds, what kind of effect will it have on him?

Acts 4: 24, 25, 31,
24 And when they heard that, they lifted up their voice to God with one accord, and said, Lord, thou art God, which hast made heaven, and earth, and the sea, and all that in them is:
25 Who by the mouth of thy servant David hast said, Why did the heathen rage, and the people imagine vain things?
31 And when they had prayed, the place was shaken where they were assembled together; and they were all filled with the Holy Ghost, and they spake the word of God with boldness.

"Lifted" in the Greek; to lift, to take up or away, to raise(the voice), keep in suspense(the mind), to sail away(to raise anchor), to expiate sin, away with, bear(up), carry, lift up, loose, make to doubt, put away, remove, take(away, up).

I like the expression to sail away, to raise anchor. This in reference to prayer is awesome. If we lift our voices to God, not worrying about those around who listen, and sail away in the Spirit with the Lord, think of what fellowship and intimacy we can have with our Lord. I also like the term, to make to doubt. If we have raised our voices, and are in boisterous worship of God, no doubt it would cause Satan to doubt his ability to conquer and defeat us. Many say it is not necessary to pray loud, this is true; however, the more boisterous and powerful the prayer, the anointing rises with the sound of the voices.

Matthew 11: 12,
12 And from the days of John the Baptist until now the kingdom of heaven suffereth violence, and the violent take it by force. {suffereth...: or, is gotten by force, and they that thrust men}
Greek for force- to seize, catch (away, up), pluck, pull, take (by force).
Greek for violent- a forcer, energetic, violent.

When we act in a manor of which the New Testament was designed in, we will be forceful against principalities and powers. We can be fevering in prayer and not be boisterous, but we cannot be violent in prayer with out making some noise in prayer.

Psalm 47: 1- 8,
1 <To the chief Musician, A Psalm for the sons of Korah.> O clap your hands, all ye people; shout unto God with the voice of triumph. {for: or, of}
2 For the LORD most high *is* terrible; *he* is a great King over all the earth.
3 He shall subdue the people under us, and the nations under our feet.
4 He shall choose our inheritance for us, the excellency of Jacob whom he loved. Selah.
5 God is gone up with a shout, the LORD with the sound of a trumpet.
6 Sing praises to God, sing praises: sing praises unto our King, sing praises.
7 For God *is* the King of all the earth: sing ye praises with understanding. {with: or, every one that hath}
8 God reigneth over the heathen: God sitteth upon the throne of his holiness.

Jacob, whom he loved. Jacob, who's name God changed to Israel. He trusted God for the preservation of his life. When Laban tried to steal and keep Jacob from being blessed, God makes the cursed thing, the undesirable thing a blessing. it's simply amazing isn't it. When God is in the midst of our finances, and life, he'll even take what others think is a curse against us, and make it a curse against them. What the world views as a curse, God makes it a blessing. Laban kept cutting back Jacob's wages, until it looked like Jacob would never acquire enough to leave Laban. Instead, more sheep and goats were being born with stripes, spots, and blemishes than ever in their history, just so that Jacob was blessed. "He'll turn your curses into blessings."

Jesus came out of praise!

Genesis 49: 8- 10,
8 Judah, thou *art he* whom thy brethren shall praise: thy hand *shall be* in the neck of thine enemies; thy father's children shall bow down before thee.
9 Judah *is* a lion's whelp: from the prey, my son, thou art gone up: he stooped down, he couched as a lion, and as an old lion; who shall rouse him up?
10 The sceptre shall not depart from Judah, nor a lawgiver from between his feet, until Shiloh come; and unto him *shall* the gathering of the people *be*.

The law is subject and learning from praise. Jesus is Shiloh (tranquil). Promise came out of praise.
Mary was of the tribe of Levi, the law givers and priests, and Joseph was of the tribe of Judah, the praisers. Luke 1: 1,36. Luke 1: 27, ch. 3: 23, 30. If you want Jesus to come, get loud in praising him, and he'll be there in the midst. He is born of praise.

Chapter XI

A TIME TO STAND!

A pastor friend used to quote these cloacae, "Sometimes a good run is better than a bad stand". I wknow this can be true when dealing with situations and people. The title of this study indicates that there are tiems we need to stand. This is not popular in this day of "No Confrontations". I hear sime say as pastors that they di not want to deal with any confrontations. In our day we need to understand that everything isn't always easy. There is a time to stand.

Written By: Dr. Ronald Sanders PhD
© By the Library of Congress 2006

257

A TIME TO STAND!

How much are you willing to put up with?
When are you going to take a stand, and say no more?
Are you tired of the devil beating you over the head?
What are you going to do about it?

Judges 6: 11- 13,
11 And there came an angel of the LORD, and sat under an oak which *was* in Ophrah, that *pertained* unto Joash the Abiezrite: and his son Gideon threshed wheat by the winepress, to hide *it* from the Midianites. {Gideon: Gr. Gedeon} {to hide...: Heb. to cause it to flee}
12 And the angel of the LORD appeared unto him, and said unto him, The LORD *is* with thee, thou mighty man of valour.
13 And Gideon said unto him, Oh my Lord, if the LORD be with us, why then is all this befallen us? and where *be* all his miracles which our fathers told us of, saying, Did not the LORD bring us up from Egypt? but now the LORD hath forsaken us, and delivered us into the hands of the Midianites.

Gideon, agreed, enough was enough? He went from 32,000 to 300. What a army, but enough is enough. When enough is enough, then you will do what is necessary to get free. No one in their right mind would fight an army with only 300 men. When enough is enough, then you will believe God for miracles.

Here, the reduction from 32,000 to 300 is less than 1% of the original army.

Bears witness to the scripture;

Deuteronomy 32: 30- 31,
30 How should one chase a thousand, and two put ten thousand to flight, except their Rock had sold them, and the LORD had shut them up?
31 For their rock *is* not as our Rock, even our enemies themselves *being* judges.

Gideon inherited the promise given to Joshua. You can too.

Joshua 23: 10,
10 One man of you shall chase a thousand: for the LORD your God, he it is that fighteth for you, as he hath promised you.

Great, you may say, but my battles are not in the physical warfare. How does all this help me?

Ephesians 6: 10- 13,
10 Finally, my brethren, be strong in the Lord, and in the power of his might.
11 Put on the whole armour of God, that ye may be able to stand against the wiles of the devil.
12 For we wrestle not against flesh and blood, but against principalities, against powers, against the rulers of the darkness of this world, against spiritual wickedness in high *places*. {flesh...: Gr. blood and flesh} {spiritual...: or, wicked spirits} {high: or, heavenly}
13 Wherefore take unto you the whole armour of God, that ye may be able to withstand in the evil day, and having done all, to stand. {having...: or, having overcome all}
OUR WEAPONS ARE;

Stand,
> Don't run!

> **Job 8:7,**
> 7 Though thy beginning was small, yet thy latter end should greatly increase.

> **Zechariah 4: 6,**
> 6 Then he answered and spake unto me, saying, This is the word of the LORD unto Zerubbabel, saying, Not by might, nor by power, but by my spirit, saith the LORD of hosts. {might: or, army}

Truth

Psalm 84: 9- 11,

9 Behold, O God our shield, and look upon the face of thine anointed.

10 For a day in thy courts is better than a thousand. I had rather be a doorkeeper in the house of my God, than to dwell in the tents of wickedness. {I had...: Heb. I would choose rather to sit at the threshold}

11 For the LORD God is a sun and shield: the LORD will give grace and glory: no good thing will he withhold from them that walk uprightly.

That walk uprightly.

Righteousness.

Attitude of Godliness, not backing up.

II Corinthians 5: 21,

21 For he hath made him *to be* sin for us, who knew no sin; that we might be made the righteousness of God in him.

I John 3: 7,

7 Little children, let no man deceive you: he that doeth righteousness is righteous, even as he is righteous.

Setting Conditions For The Enemies' Surrender.

(Preparation of the gospel of peace.) The only peace we will except!

I John 5: 4,

4 For whatsoever is born of God overcometh the world: and this is the victory that overcometh the world, even our faith.

Philippians 4: 7,
7 And the peace of God, which passeth all understanding, shall keep your hearts and minds through Christ Jesus.

Faith.
Confidence

I John 5: 14- 15,
14 And this is the confidence that we have in him, that, if we ask any thing according to his will, he heareth us: {in: or, concerning}
15 And if we know that he hear us, whatsoever we ask, we know that we have the petitions that we desired of him.

Salvation.
Knowing you will not be taken captive. not going to fall to the enemy.

I John 4: 17- 18,
17 Herein is our love made perfect, that we may have boldness in the day of judgment: because as he is, so are we in this world. {our love: Gr. love with us}
18 There is no fear in love; but perfect love casteth out fear: because fear hath torment. He that feareth is not made perfect in love.

Spirit.
Will follow the anointing of the Holy Ghost, not the circumstances around me.

I Peter 1: 7- 9,
7 That the trial of your faith, being much more precious than of gold that perisheth, though it be tried with fire, might be found unto praise and honour and glory at the appearing of Jesus Christ:
8 Whom having not seen, ye love; in whom, though now ye see him not, yet believing, ye rejoice with joy unspeakable and full of glory:

9 Receiving the end of your faith, even the salvation of your souls.

Praying.

When no one else wants to listen, he will. Getting re-enforcements in the Spirit.

1 Corinthians 14: 15,

15 What is it then? I will pray with the spirit, and I will pray with the understanding also: I will sing with the spirit, and I will sing with the understanding also.

Psalm 34: 15, 17- 20,

15 The eyes of the LORD are upon the righteous, and his ears are open unto their cry.

17 The righteous cry, and the LORD heareth, and delivereth them out of all their troubles.

18 The LORD is nigh unto them that are of a broken heart; and saveth such as be of a contrite spirit. {unto...: Heb. to the broken of heart} {of a contrite...: Heb. contrite of spirit}

19 Many are the afflictions of the righteous: but the LORD delivereth him out of them all.

20 He keepeth all his bones: not one of them is broken.

Supplications.

Crying out to God, not to the enemy. Never let the enemy see you sweat!

James 1: 3- 4, 6,

3 Knowing this, that the trying of your faith worketh patience.

4 But let patience have her perfect work, that ye may be perfect and entire, wanting nothing.

6 But let him ask in faith, nothing wavering. For he that wavereth is like a wave of the sea driven with the wind and tossed.

Perseverance.

Strengthening one another to draw strength yourself.

Luke 9: 51,

51 And it came to pass, when the time was come that he should be received up, he stedfastly set his face to go to Jerusalem,

Boldness.

Isaiah 59: 19

So shall they fear the name of the LORD from the west, and his glory from the rising of the sun. When the enemy shall come in like a flood, the Spirit of the LORD shall lift up a standard against him.

Hebrews 4: 15- 16,

15 For we have not an high priest which cannot be touched with the feeling of our infirmities; but was in all points tempted like as we are, yet without sin.

16 Let us therefore come boldly unto the throne of grace, that we may obtain mercy, and find grace to help in time of need.

It is time for a new beginning. It is time to make a stand against the things that have held us in bondage, and launch out into greater depths with God.

In Peter's life, he had to find the place in ministry where he belonged. We find him in Acts 2: standing up with the eleven. He had the backing of the apostles. Before, he was the one who was looked at strangely. Now he is the leader of the new church.

Ruth 1: 13, 16, 18,

13 Would ye tarry for them till they were grown? would ye stay for them from having husbands? nay, my daughters; for it grieveth me much for your sakes that the hand of the LORD is gone out against me. {tarry: Heb. hope} {it grieveth...: Heb. I have much bitterness}

16 And Ruth said, Intreat me not to leave thee, *or* to return from following after thee: for whither thou goest, I will go; and where thou lodgest, I will lodge: thy people *shall be* my people, and thy God my God: {Intreat...: or, Be not against me}
18 When she saw that she was stedfastly minded to go with her, then she left speaking unto her. {was...: Heb. strengthened herself}

We find an example of Naomi, when she had every reason to give up, she still found hope in the smallest of things. She was looking for a reason to go on. As we know, it did not take much. The old cliché, "Misery loves company", wasn't what Naomi was looking, but a kindred spirit, who would be willing to walk through the dry places with her, and find comfort together.

Psalm 35: 1- 4,
1 <*A Psalm* of David.> Plead *my cause*, O LORD, with them that strive with me: fight against them that fight against me.
2 Take hold of shield and buckler, and stand up for mine help.
3 Draw out also the spear, and stop *the way* against them that persecute me: say unto my soul, I am thy salvation.
4 Let them be confounded and put to shame that seek after my soul: let them be turned back and brought to confusion that devise my hurt.

Isaiah 35:
4 S**ay to them *that* are of a fearful heart**, Be strong, fear not: behold, your God will come with vengeance, even God with a recompence; he will come and save you. {fearful: Heb. hasty}
We know that he is speaking of a time yet to come; however, if this is our heritage, then we can begin to partake now, that when the fullness of time is come, we will know how to fulfill the sweetness of his presence. Seeing we are under schoolmasters, we have to learn of things to come for our lives.

Galatians 4: 1- 2, 6- 7,
1 Now I say, *That* the heir, as long as he is a child, differeth nothing from a servant, though he be lord of all;

2 But is under tutors and governors until the time appointed of the father.
6 And because ye are sons, God hath sent forth the Spirit of his Son into your hearts, crying, Abba, Father.
7 Wherefore thou art no more a servant, but a son; and if a son, then an heir of God through Christ.

It is time for us to understand sonship; a state of being, not a state of hoping for. It is up to us to find a place in Christ, and stand.
Let us see the significance of Carmel and Sharon in the above scripture. Carmel is a fruitful, plentiful country, with an elevation of 1500 foot, can be considered a mountain range with twelve miles of plenty, beautiful to the eye, wondrous in location, and splendor in any definition. On this mountain we have seen re-united the people of God, back to God, fire fall from heaven to destroy two sets of fifty men and their captains, mercy granted to a captain of fifty, dead sons raised to life for a widow woman, a place where wives are found, and yet a land that was taken by war when Joshua came through to overthrow the kingdoms there. Too often, we see all the battles around us, and do not take the time to see the wondrous splendor that so greatly surrounds us. Even when men of war adjourn from the day of fighting, finding themselves enjoying the splendor of the harvests, the tasty fruits, enjoying the beautiful heavens, and all that is worth fighting for. We as Christians are in a constant spiritual warfare, and forget that entire God has created for us to enjoy.

Chapter XII

HOW TO HANDLE DOMESTIC DISTURBANCES

There is a right way and a wring way.
Which way will you do it?
How long will you tolerate junk?

Written by Dr. Ronald Sanders PhD
As directed and revealed by the Holy Spirit
02/12/03
© By Library of Congress 2006

At times, in God's house, we find little schisms in the body of Christ. How should we handle such schisms or contentions?

Matthew 5: 23- 24,
23 Therefore if thou bring thy gift to the altar, and there rememberest **that thy brother hath ought against thee;**
24 Leave there thy gift before the altar, and go thy way; first be reconciled to thy brother, and then come and offer thy gift.

Somehow, we always end up getting this scripture backwards. We always hear the words "If I ought with my brother", even though that is not what is said. If you are praying and either you know or God reveals to you that someone has something against you. You are to go to them, not wait for them to come to you. We are to go in love and say unto them. What have I done to offend you, and how can I make it right between us? In most cases, you should be the innocent party, or at least the party without any harsh feelings. Therefore, it is easier for you to go to them and talk without accusations, innuendoes, slurred comments, or anger. You are not the one, or at least should not be the one with the bad feelings. You can talk rational and calmly as God sees as pleasing to him. Discuss the problem, settle the problem, and then pray over the problem to restore your fellowship with him. This attitude of Christ makes us mindful of others, and their feelings. Some of the reason we are not receiving from God, may have to do with our dealings with others. We are causing harsh feelings to swell in others, to being sensitive to them, thus hindering our answers from God!

Proverbs 18: 19,
19 A brother offended *is harder to be won* than a strong city: and *their* contentions *are* like the bars of a castle.

When we look at this Old Testament scripture, we see a prevalent problem in our society. When we offend someone, we do not like their response, and thus we do not bother to try to tear sown the walls of partition between us. We just say, "If that's the way he's going to be, forget him!" The mentality that arose in the church some twenty years ago, "Well, I'm going to tell them like it is, no matter who it hurts", has caused great divisions in the body of Christ. How many denominations were formed out of this mentality? Too many; the bible says:

Ephesians 4: 13- 16,
13 Till we all come in the unity of the faith, and of the knowledge of the Son of God, unto a perfect man, unto the measure of the stature of the fulness of Christ: {in: or, into} {stature: or, age}
14 That we *henceforth* be no more children, tossed to and fro, and carried about with every wind of doctrine, by the sleight of men, and cunning craftiness, whereby they lie in wait to deceive;
15 **But speaking the truth in love**, may grow up into him in all things, which is the head, even Christ: {speaking...: or, being sincere}
16 From whom the whole body fitly joined together and compacted by that which every joint supplieth, according to the effectual working in the measure of every part, **maketh increase of the body unto the edifying of itself in love.**

In the twentieth and the twenty - first century, the reason we have not won the world to Jesus, I believe is this one thing called love. The world does not see the love of Christ in the church, and for the brethren, thus why they should change. They have more love for each other in the dance halls, and beer joints of the world than the church of Jesus Christ, who is the author of love. Telling the truth is mandatory. How many ways can we tell the truth? Countless; the truth does not change, it is unchangeable, but how we tell it changes with our moods. We can speak the truth cautiously, or callously. In verse fourteen, we see some vital motives for speaking the way we do, (by the sleight of men, and cunning craftiness, whereby they lie in wait to deceive). Sneaky, ulterior motives, or just to cut them to the quick; we exact vengeance many times by telling the truth. The truth can kill, and as Christians, we have made it an act of war. Our first scripture we used, makes it humiliating and humbling to go to someone we know is wounded by us, and apologize.

Thus far, we have seen two sides of our first scripture in Matthew 5: 23- 24. We are the innocent trying to restore a brother, or we are the instigators of trouble that left us feeling just right, while the wounds are exacted upon our brethren. In which case would make us ashamed to go back and make amends with them. In either case, we are humbling ourselves to minister to our brother in Christ, and taking the fault upon ourselves without finding any excuses for our actions.

Amos 3: 3
3 Can two walk together, except they be agreed?

The greatest hindrance in our services and our churches is not having unity. The quickest thing to destroy the anointing in a service is for someone to do something out of order. Someone who wants to testify and stands up to preach condemnation upon every person they are looking down their nose at. For every great move of God, you will find one thing common. They were all in one accord or all with one heart. Whether in the word or in the history books, unity is a mighty tool and weapon. Without it, we just exist.

Galatians 6: 1- 5,
1 Brethren, if a man be overtaken in a fault, ye which are spiritual, restore such an one in the spirit of meekness; considering thyself, lest thou also be tempted. {If: or, although}
2 Bear ye one another's burdens, and so fulfil the law of Christ.
3 For if a man think himself to be something, when he is nothing, he deceiveth himself.
4 But let every man prove his own work, and then shall he have rejoicing in himself alone, and not in another.
5 For every man shall bear his own burden.
We are to restore in a spirit of gentleness (Greek). Now apply this to what we are talking about, and it gives new light. Not just the person who is falling prey to sin that we are restoring, but what if we see two brethren who are offended. We, who are prayed up and fasting, approach these brethren, bind up

their wounds as restore means in the Greek. You will gain your brethren, and they can hear from God again. So they can stand to pray, forgiving their brother who wronged them. Sometimes love needs a little helping hand. Be careful, lest you become an enemy of them both! That is where the considering thyself, lest you also be tempted comes into play.

Genesis 43: 29- 30
29 And he lifted up his eyes, and saw his brother Benjamin, his mother's son, and said, *Is* this your younger brother, of whom ye spake unto me? And he said, God be gracious unto thee, my son.
30 And Joseph made haste; for his bowels did **yearn** upon his brother: and he sought *where* to weep; and he entered into *his* chamber, and wept there.

We need to yearn. We need to grow hot (Greek), when we think about repairing the body of Christ. Joseph, one of the most passionate love stories in the bible, has nothing to do with marriage or love- making. It has to do with restoration of hurting and emotionally shipwrecked brethren. Brethren who have had to live with a lie for twenty- two years. Every time they saw their father's face, it crushed their spirits, knowing what they did to their father and brother. A lie they could never come clean with. Would never make amends for. Joseph, who could have told the truth and destroyed forever his family, never opened his mouth. He just cried for them, repeatedly, just cried for them. He opened his eyes to the truth, and saw the agony his brethren were in, and wanted to repair the broken hopes and dreams of their lives. Joseph was the one in slavery, but his brothers would always be slaves, never ever again to hold their heads high, to be confident and proud of themselves. Living with a secret so dark, they die with sorrow so great, they knew they were worthy of death, but begged for mercy. Joseph never showed them mercy! He just loved them! A love they felt so unworthy of never again being able to accept unconditional love. Joseph just nourished them and their little ones. He never brings up the past to them, never remembering the past, by choice. Just loving them! Would to God, we could just grasp the heart of Joseph! Just loving them! Let me nourish and care for you. Let me show you Jesus, he so loves and cares so greatly for you! He's right here, in my heart. See him through me!

Matthew 18: 12- 17,
12 How think ye? if a man have an hundred sheep, and one of them be gone astray, doth he not leave the ninety and nine, and goeth into the mountains, and seeketh that which is gone astray?
13 And if so be that he find it, verily I say unto you, he rejoiceth more of that *sheep*, than of the ninety and nine which went not astray.
14 Even so it is not the will of your Father which is in heaven, that one of these little ones should perish.
15 Moreover if thy brother shall trespass against thee, go and tell him his fault between thee and him alone: if he shall hear thee, thou hast gained thy brother.
16 But if he will not hear *thee, then* take with thee one or two more, that in the mouth of two or three witnesses every word may be established.
17 And if he shall neglect to hear them, tell *it* unto the church: but if he neglect to hear the church, let him be unto thee as an heathen man and a publican.

The first scripture we used was in reference to words that hurt, whether purposely or accidentally. Here, we see someone that has done something to you. Whether he cheated you, lied about you, fought you, or stole from you. This incident went past the word stage. Jesus said to try to bring that sheep back that has tried to hurt you. That means you first have to pray through to where you are not holding resentment toward that brother. This is not a sinner who has wronged you, but a brother. Spiritually he is under conviction about the deed he did against you. In the Greek, it means to expose this fault to the one who caused it, if you go to them to make things right, and he will not hear you. Then you need a judge or witness to go with you. That witness cannot be someone who was involved in the mess too. This must be someone they respect. Then, if he will not hear you and your witnesses, then bring this matter to the church or the board. God does not condone a mess. He wants no schisms in the body of Christ. If the board or church cannot work out a resolve, then the guilty party is removed from the church. The publicans were dreaded and not liked at all. They were always trying to steal money out of your pocket, charging unjust taxes. We are to treat a disruptive person like that dreaded person. Have no fellowship with them.

I Corinthians 12: 25- 27,
25 That there should be no schism in the body; but *that* the members should have the same care one for another. {schism: or, division}
26 And whether one member suffer, all the members suffer with it; or one member be honoured, all the members rejoice with it.
27 Now ye are the body of Christ, and members in particular. God says that when one part of the body had disruptions, it affects all the parts of the body.

II Thessalonians 3: 6,
6 Now we command you, brethren, in the name of our Lord Jesus Christ, that ye withdraw yourselves from every brother that walketh disorderly, and not after the tradition which he received of us.
Here is confirmation that those who are troublemakers, stay away from.

I Timothy 5: 22
22 Lay hands suddenly on no man, neither be partaker of other men's sins: keep thyself pure.

When you are near those who are committing sin, then you are guilty by association.
We are not to condone their sin, nor be seen with those who are sinning.

Romans 14: 16

16 Let not then your good be evil spoken of:

Need I say more?

Philippians 4: 8

8 Finally, brethren, whatsoever things *are* true, whatsoever things *are* honest, whatsoever things *are* just, whatsoever things *are* pure, whatsoever things *are* lovely, whatsoever things *are* of good report; if *there be* any virtue, and if *there be* any praise, think on these things. {honest: or, venerable}

What things are of a good report? We have to be cautious about those who are hindering the anointing of God. We want to think on things that are good. If you're around those who are always trying to find fault, then how often do you hear things of a good report? Paul even stated that when sin is in the church and it has not been dealt with, then there is one thing to do.

I Corinthians 5: 1- 8,

1 It is reported commonly *that there* is fornication among you, and such fornication as is not so much as named among the Gentiles, that one should have his father's wife.
 And ye are puffed up, and have not rather mourned, that he that hath done this deed might be taken away from among you.
3 For I verily, as absent in body, but present in spirit, have judged already, as though I were present, *concerning* him that hath so done this deed, {judged: or, determined}
4 In the name of our Lord Jesus Christ, when ye are gathered together, and my spirit, with the power of our Lord Jesus Christ,
5 To deliver such an one unto Satan for the destruction of the flesh, that the spirit may be saved in the day of the Lord Jesus.
6 Your glorying *is* not good. Know ye not that a little leaven leaveneth the whole lump?

7 Purge out therefore the old leaven that ye may be a new lump, as ye are unleavened. For even Christ our Passover is sacrificed for us: {is sacrificed; or, is slain}
8 Therefore let us keep the feast, not with old leaven, neither with the leaven of malice and wickedness; but with the unleavened *bread* of sincerity and truth. {the feast: or, holyday}

When a so-called brother, especially a leader is in open sin, then we are to go to them and try to win the brother back to Christ as Gal. 6: 1- 5 says, when they will not adhere to them, then Matthew 18: 12- 17 is invoked. a sinner does by nature what is sin. A Christian by nature does righteousness, not sin. When a Christian is walking in sin, then he is no longer righteous, and should not be treated as such. We love the sinner, but not the sin. When a backslidden person will not come back to Christ, and he has a reputation in the church as a leader, then you have no choice but to turn him over to Satan that he may reap havoc on him to turn his heart back to God. There are too many people in the church in leadership positions that are not living for Christ. It is time to sift out the old leaven, and replace it with new leaven. God will judge a church by it's leadership. If sin is in leadership, then God will judge the whole church. We are to love sinners, try to lead them to Christ. Those in leadership in the church must be pulled out of leadership until they make their walk with God sure. Those who hate or despise Christ, Paul had a note for them.

I Corinthians 16: 22
22 If any man love not the Lord Jesus Christ, let him be Anathema Maranatha.

Cursed unto the coming of our Lord Jesus Christ. That "Isn't" pretty. God sifts out the church. He brings to the surface the tares. When God brings them to the surface, we must first try to win them back to Christ.

I Timothy 5: 19- 20,
19 Against an elder receive not an accusation, but before two or three witnesses. {before: or, under}
0 Them that sin rebuke before all, that others also may fear.

The reason the word says not to accuse a leader, except it be by two or more witnesses is simple. Leaders cannot please all the people all the time, thus they will have those who are at ought with them. This is different from sin. As we add verses, seventeen and eighteen to this scripture, we see:

17 Let the elders that rule well be counted worthy of double honour, especially they who labour in the word and doctrine.
18 For the scripture saith, Thou shalt not muzzle the ox that treadeth out the corn. And, The labourer is worthy of his reward.

A leader is worthy of any honor bestowed upon them, because of the high profile position and the likely hood that he/ she is not liked by all. I had a pastor that once said, " I'm going to please all the people at one time or another; some when I come, some while I'm here, and the rest when I leave." That is probably the best-case scenario a leader can hope for. When a leader is in sin, the bible in the previous verses says to rebuke them openly. I would like to think that they will have the opportunity to repent privately first, before it is brought before the church. When they have repented, then they will have to openly apologize to those under them, that there be no rumors or vices to later come up to destroy that individual. As leaders, we have to be transparent. For everyone to see us as we are. Thus, we have to live it closer, straighter, and stronger than the average person does. It is very much like trying to get respect as a youth serving God.

I Timothy 4: 9- 16,
9 This is a faithful saying and worthy of all acceptation.
10 For therefore we both labour and suffer reproach, because we trust in the living God, who is the Saviour of all men, specially of those that believe.

11 These things command and teach.

12 Let no man despise thy youth; but be thou an example of the believers, in word, in conversation, in charity, in spirit, in faith, in purity.

13 Till I come, give attendance to reading, to exhortation, to doctrine.

14 Neglect not the gift that is in thee, which was given thee by prophecy, with the laying on of the hands of the presbytery.

15 Meditate upon these things; give thyself wholly to them; that thy profiting may appear to all. {to all: or, in all things}

16 Take heed unto thyself, and unto the doctrine; continue in them: for in doing this thou shalt both save thyself, and them that hear thee.

An individual who wants to be a leader is asking for pain. It is hard enough just walking in God's presence and staying away from the world. When you are in leadership, you are watched under a magnifying glass. The results though, are you get to go to heaven and take others with you. That makes all the labour worth the pain. The pain is being reticuled, belittled, others think you are stupid, and many times walking alone. However, the benefits are truly out of this world. The joy of knowing you had a hand in getting someone to heaven, and improving the life of those around you.

Chapter XIII

BUILD MY CHURCH!

The principles of what a church should be built upon, not of doctrines and traditions. God is not confined to our set order and habits of worship. The church that Christ built was uninhibited and free, as the Sprit moved and so shoukd we.

Written By: Dr. Ronald Sanders PhD
© By the Library of Congress 2006

BUILD MY CHURCH

This study will endeavor to show how the spiritual makeup of a church should be. Anyone can build a building and set up rules but many falls short in the spiritual guidelines God desires for his house.

Matthew 16:
15 He saith unto them, But whom say ye that I am?
16 And Simon Peter answered and said, Thou art the Christ, the Son of the living God.
17 And Jesus answered and said unto him, Blessed art thou, Simon Barjona: for flesh and blood hath not revealed *it* unto thee, but my Father which is in heaven.
18 And I say also unto thee, That thou art Peter, and **upon this rock I will build my church; and the gates of hell shall not prevail against it.**
19 And **I will give unto thee the keys of the kingdom of heaven:** and whatsoever thou shalt bind on earth shall be bound in heaven: and whatsoever thou shalt loose on earth shall be loosed in heaven.

Jesus was not referring to the name of Peter but of the revelation of who he was as being revealed by God. Peter the rock is how solid the revelation knowledge of God really is. If we will learn to trust, then we too can be as solid in faith and revelation knowledge of Christ.

II Corinthians 3: 6,
6 Who also hath made us able ministers of the New Testament; not of the letter, but of the spirit: for the letter killeth, but the spirit giveth life.

We get so used to God moving a certain way with a certain song or message. Where is the Spirit in all this? If we are sensitive to the spirit of God, then we can flow from the planned to the supernatural planning of God.

I Corinthians 2: 10- 12

10 But God hath revealed *them* unto us by his Spirit: for the Spirit searcheth all things, yea, the deep things of God.

11 For what man knoweth the things of a man, save the spirit of man which is in him? even so the things of God knoweth no man, but the Spirit of God.

12 Now we have received, not the spirit of the world, but the spirit which is of God; that we might know the things that are freely given to us of God.

I love this scripture because it explains a problem in the church. We have too long just read the word and said ok. But not sought for depth of the word. Many churches operate off the same level of knowledge as the world's view of the word. It is high time to cry out for deeper understanding of his marvelous word. As in a love letter from your mate, you can read between the lines because you were there. Well, we know we weren't living when the bible was wrote, however, we know the one who was and by knowing his heart we also can read the message of God's heart. It's not a message of do's and don'ts, but a message of alignment so that we may escape the natural realm and flow in the miraculous realm of Christ. A good example would be; it is against the laws of nature and scientific fact to walk on water, but Jesus did and he said we could too. Unless we align ourselves with the word, it will never happen to us.

Psalm 42:

7 Deep calleth unto deep at the noise of thy waterspouts: all thy waves and thy billows are gone over me.

8 Yet the LORD will command his lovingkindness in the daytime, and in the night his song shall be with me, and my prayer unto the God of my life.

There is a longing in every Spirit filled individual to understand the deep things of God. Revelation knowledge will cause you to walk in a place with God that even in the night while you sleep; you will hear songs sung unto you.

Job 35: 10,
10 But none saith, Where is God my maker, who giveth **songs** in the **night;**

If you go around telling people that the Lord caused you to hear music and singing in while you sleep, they will surely say you have lost your mind. It's all about revelation knowledge and expecting it to manifest in your life.

Acts 5: 15- 16,
15 Insomuch that they brought forth the sick into the streets, and laid *them* on beds and couches, that at the least the shadow of Peter passing by might overshadow some of them. {into...: or, in every street}
16 There came also a multitude *out* of the cities round about unto Jerusalem, bringing sick folks, and them which were vexed with unclean spirits: and they were healed every one.

What a service we would have if we were in the place of God to have this on a consistent basis in our own churches. What type of faith realm are we really talking about here?

Acts 8: 39
39 And when they were come up out of the water, the Spirit of the Lord caught away Philip, that the eunuch saw him no more: and he went on his way rejoicing.

Oh, this kind of faith. What is stopping us from having this same type of visitation and move of God? Are our churches so conformed to tradition that the very thought of being translated to another location is frowned upon and snickered at?

I Corinthians 2: 4- 5,

4 And my speech and my preaching *was* not with enticing words of man's wisdom, but in demonstration of the Spirit and of power: {enticing: or, persuasible}

5 That your faith should not stand in the wisdom of men, but in the power of God.

Step number one. We must first have the mindset that it's not about what I can do to bring in the Spirit of God. It's the realization that his Spirit is here and he desires to move so let me move out of the way and just be obedient. Many think the right song or right message with correct exaltation will surely move God and the people. If we can, then where's God?

Acts 12: 5

5 Peter therefore was kept in prison: but prayer was made without ceasing of the church unto God for him. {prayer...: or, instant and earnest prayer was made}

How often do we have earnest prayer? If we do our part in praying and seeking the Father, then the Father will seek us. The right kind of service is all about allowing the God of heaven empowering his children on earth.

Acts 4: 31- 33,

31 And when they had prayed, the place was shaken where they were assembled together; and they were all filled with the Holy Ghost, and they spake the word of God with boldness.

32 And the multitude of them that believed were of one heart and of one soul: neither said any *of them* that ought of the things which he possessed was his own; but they had all things common.

33 And with great power gave the apostles witness of the resurrection of the Lord Jesus: and great grace was upon them all.

Watch what happens when the power truly falls, not just a "Sample pack" hits us. You receive a fresh infilling and a greater anointing rests on you. New boldness of God explodes from within. You as a congregation become one. You lose interest in the worldly possessions because greater has overtaken the less. The drive to witness will be undeniable!

Acts 16: 25
25 And at midnight Paul and Silas prayed, and sang praises unto God: and the prisoners heard them.

These men beaten, worn and nigh death; yet that greater overtook the less. The spiritual overtook the natural. See, praises comes from the inside out not the other way around. When we learn to tap into the spirit realm then conditions and circumstances have nothing to do with your praise.

I Corinthians 14: 15
15 What is it then? I will pray with the spirit, and I will pray with the understanding also: I will sing with the spirit, and I will sing with the understanding also.

If a church would grasp the concept of how to just let go and praise the most high, our singing would become love songs to our God. We would flow from our English dialect right into the Holy Spirit dialect. We spent too much time pumping up and not plugging in.

Psalm 149: 3- 4
3 Let them praise his name in the dance: let them sing praises unto him with the timbrel and harp. {in...: or, with the pipe}
4 For the LORD taketh pleasure in his people: he will beautify the meek with salvation.

The more in tune with God you become the more your countenance will glow from his presence. If the last five chapters of psalms is about praising God with everything you have, then how important is praise? Priority one; when we enter this realm of praises our dance before the Lord will be instinctive and not commandment. We exhort so strongly to worship and praise the Lord that people do not want to respond because of commandment. If the prayer is made before service, and the praise is brought into the sanctuary then the response will be instinctive.

Acts 16: 26

26 And suddenly there was a great earthquake, so that the foundations of the prison were shaken: and immediately all the doors were opened, and every one's bands were loosed.

Watch this. Not only were the bands of the righteous loosed but also the unrighteous. We have difficulty getting the lost to the alter, but if we entered into his realm the lost would just simply follow you into his presence and be changed by reason of hunger for some of what you're enjoying. You will see the lost saved, the sick healed, the demon possessed delivered just by entering into the presence of the Lord for yourself. Wow!

Acts 12: 7

7 And, behold, the angel of the Lord came upon *him*, and a light shined in the prison: and he smote Peter on the side, and raised him up, saying, Arise up quickly. And his chains fell off from *his* hands.

Can you imagine being in such a peace of God that your death sentence hanging over your head can't even keep from the sweet sleep God said you would have? Most people would have never needed awaking, because you wouldn't be able to sleep. Oh yea, and never would have had an angel there to awake you because of your fear! Faith and peace breeds miracles.

Proverbs 3:

21 My son, let not them depart from thine eyes: keep sound wisdom and discretion:
22 So shall they be life unto thy soul, and grace to thy neck.
23 Then shalt thou walk in thy way safely, and thy foot shall not stumble.
24 When thou liest down, thou shalt not be afraid: yea, thou shalt lie down, and thy sleep shall be sweet.
25 Be not afraid of sudden fear, neither of the desolation of the wicked, when it cometh.

26 For the LORD shall be thy confidence, and shall keep thy foot from being taken.

Wisdom is seeing your circumstances thru God's eyes and not yours. Unless we seek for wisdom, we will not find it. Those whom lack wisdom talk a whole lot about common sense. If I have a choice and I do, to view things from feeling of being trapped by my circumstances verses being free because of who God is in my life, I'll take freedom every time.

Psalm 127:
2 It is vain for you to rise up early, to sit up late, to eat the bread of sorrows: for so he giveth his beloved **sleep.**

The world will tell you that to worry is natural. To lie in bed at night and contemplate tomorrow is ok. If that were so, then these two scriptures would not be accurate then would they?

II Chronicles 5: 13- 14
13 It came even to pass, as the trumpeters and singers *were* as one, to make one sound to be heard in praising and thanking the LORD; and when they lifted up *their* voice with the trumpets and cymbals and instruments of musick, and praised the LORD, *saying,* For *he* is good; for his mercy *endureth* for ever: that *then* the house was filled with a cloud, *even* the house of the LORD;
14 So that the priests could not stand to minister by reason of the cloud: for the glory of the LORD had filled the house of God.

The priest got drunk from the anointing because the singers and musicians entered into a place of praise for themselves. When we try to get everyone else into the presence of the Lord, we are too busy pushing others and we can't get there ourselves. Forget the congregation; let them enter as they will. You get into the presence of the Lord and they will follow!

II Chronicles 7: 1- 3,

Now when Solomon had made an end of praying, the fire came down from heaven, and consumed the burnt offering and the sacrifices; and the glory of the LORD filled the house. 2 And the priests could not enter into the house of the LORD, because the glory of the LORD had filled the LORD'S house. 3 And when all the children of Israel saw how the fire came down, and the glory of the LORD upon the house, they bowed themselves with their faces to the ground upon the pavement, and worshipped, and praised the LORD, saying, For he is good; for his mercy *endureth* for ever.

Too often when God has such a marvelous move, we find it hard to enter the same place again and again yet we see here that these did. It wasn't because they sung the exact same songs the exact same way or preached the exact sermon. It's not about semantics; it's about desire. That is, you're desire to be engulfed and hidden in his presence. That alone will cause the presence of the Lord to sweep thru the place like a wave of glory.

II Chronicles 7: 14- 16,

14 If my people, which are called by my name, shall humble themselves, and pray, and seek my face, and turn from their wicked ways; then will I hear from heaven, and will forgive their sin, and will heal their land.
15 Now mine eyes shall be open, and mine ears attent unto the prayer *that is made* in this place. {unto...: Heb. to the prayer of this place}
16 For now have I chosen and sanctified this house, that my name may be there for ever: and mine eyes and mine heart shall be there perpetually.
Here is one of the sweetest scriptures I know. God is emphasizing the importance of his house. Not the spiritual house of our souls but a literal place to gather. 7 steps to total explosion: 1) humble, 2) pray, 3) seek, 4) repent, then 5) he hears, 6) he forgives, and 7) he heals all. God then goes on to make covenant with this place and with us in that covenant. 1)

His eyes will be opening, 2) and his ears will hear when in 3) this place you pray. If that's not considered holy ground then we are just not seeing the same thing?

I Corinthians 3: 1-3
1 And I, brethren, could not speak unto you as unto spiritual, but as unto carnal, *even* as unto babes in Christ.
2 I have fed you with milk, and not with meat: for hitherto ye were not able *to bear it*, neither yet now are ye able.
3 For ye are yet carnal: for whereas *there is* among you envying, and strife, and divisions, are ye not carnal, and walk as men? {divisions: or, factions} {as men: Gr. according to man?}

Until we teach and learn how to enter into the sanctuary of the Most High, then we will minister to nothing but babes who are superficial and not supernatural. We as Christians have formulas of how to enter into his presence, but at best it is just a little tickle. Too often when the Spirit begins to move we slow down the pace so as to control the influx of the anointing; as if you can get too much of his presence. The fact still remains; we get afraid when we are not in control. The whole point of this study is to help you lose control!

Hebrews 5: 12- 14,
12 For when for the time ye ought to be teachers, ye have need that one teach you again which be the first principles of the oracles of God; and are become such as have need of milk, and not of strong meat.
13 For every one that useth milk is unskilful in the word of righteousness: for he is a babe. {is skillful: Gr. hath no experience}
14 But strong meat belongeth to them that are of full age, even those who by reason of use have their senses exercised to discern both good and evil. {Of full age: or, perfect} {Use: Or, a habit or, perfection}

See in the presence of the Lord, he begins to give you visions, words of prophecy, words of knowledge and his visitation. If you remember the scripture in I Corinthians 2: when Paul speaks of demonstration of the spirit and of power. How much power can you handle? Don't' control the Spirit. Allow the Spirit to control and saturate you. It's ok if you don't know what to do next. You have prayed, fasted, made preparation for the service and here God goes and changes everything. I say thank you God. My plans are always subject to change. It doesn't stop me from doing my part in being instant and ready. God doesn't fly by the seat of his pants and neither can we. Laziness in hopes of a move of God is ill prepared and displeasing to God.

Galatians 6: 1- 2,
Brethren, if a man be overtaken in a fault, ye which are spiritual, restore such an one in the spirit of meekness; considering thyself, lest thou also be tempted. {If: or, although}
2 Bear ye one another's burdens, and so fulfil the law of Christ.

When we are in the presence of the Almighty, then we'll be in the spirit of meekness. Then we can minister to someone else who has fallen. How can we restore if we aren't walking in the same place of restoration. How can you bring that person unto restoration? It's hard to describe the features of a Cadillac when you have only test drove one. When you own one, then you know how to entice others into desiring one. In the same aspect, we can't restore a brother until God has restored us. This is why we see so many getting healed today and find another sickness tomorrow. We have brought them out of their situation, but we haven't restored them into the fullness of God.

Matthew 12:
43 When the **unclean spirit** is **gone** out of a man, he walketh through dry places, seeking rest, and findeth none.
44 Then he saith, I will return into my house from whence I came out; and when he is come, he findeth *it* empty, swept, and garnished.
45 Then goeth he, and taketh with himself seven other spirits more wicked than himself, and they enter in and dwell there:

and the last *state* of that man is worse than the first. Even so shall it be also unto this wicked generation.

We brought them out of their infirmities yet have not restored back unto them something greater. The only way the healed can stay healed is to refill with the Spirit of the Most High. The Holy Spirit of God is intoxicating, engulfing, overwhelming, and uncontrollable. You loose your personality and identity and you could care less. This is the type of anointing that has to fill your being?

Galatians. 6: 6, 9- 10,
6 Let him that is taught in the word communicate unto him that teacheth in all good things.
9 And let us not be weary in well doing: for in due season we shall reap, if we faint not.
10 As we have therefore opportunity, let us do good unto all *men*, especially unto them who are of the household of faith.

I know this type of teaching probably isn't popular in our charismatic society. We are so used to floating along, getting a little good feel, maybe get slain in the Spirit, and yet not changed. The end time revival everyone is so adamant about seeing, is not going to ride in on a wind of charismatic, superficial and self-pleasing encounters. It will come when II Chronicles 5: and 7: come to pass in our churches. This is what we need to instill in our people.

Hebrews 10: 24- 25,
24 And let us consider one another to provoke unto love and to good works:
25 Not forsaking the assembling of ourselves together, as the manner of some *is*; but exhorting *one another*. and so much the more, as ye see the day approaching.

I've noticed that a drunk wants everyone to be as drunk as he is. He will give you of his drink. 42 times in the bible you will find the word "Provoke" yet this is the only time God encourages us to provoke someone. We are to incite people to love God.

That means give them a reason to love him. Then keep them excited about being in love.

Colossians. 1: 9- 10,
9 For this cause we also, since the day we heard *it*, do not cease to pray for you, and to desire that ye might be filled with the knowledge of his will in all wisdom and spiritual understanding;
10 That ye might walk worthy of the Lord unto all pleasing, being fruitful in every good work, and increasing in the knowledge of God;

Teaching is key to understanding. When we teach people to desire the spiritual things of God, then they can get there by themselves. Building a church on imparting wisdom and spiritual understanding is opening up a powder keg that will unhinge your church. In most cases in the New Testament, the church ended up in the street preaching, praying, dancing and ministering unto anyone who would stand still long enough to be enticed by the Spirit of God. The walls of your church aren't strong enough to keep the Spirit restrained in it. You will instinctively go into the streets with this power to demonstrate to the world just how big your God is and that's all the world really wants to see from your church, is a real God!

Romans 1: 11- 12,
11 For I long to see you, that I may impart unto you some spiritual gift, to the end ye may be established;
12 That is, that I may be comforted together with you by the mutual faith both of you and me.

I am embarrassed to invite people into my home when it is nasty and smelly. Let me get my house in order and I'll invite the president himself in to eat with me. When we have something to offer we won't mind sharing it. We are actually excited to share it. Just the thought that I have something that someone else desires. I've got skills baby!

Acts 2: 46,

46 And they, continuing daily with one accord in the temple, and breaking bread from house to house, did eat their meat with gladness and singleness of heart,

The churches of that day started in homes. They were not refined to just one home, but many. Yet in as many homes as the word was going forth, it was indeed the same word being preached in every home. We today are too afraid of home prayer meeting because of what may happen behind our backs. The fact of putting out fires of division is not desirous. When the fire of God burns brightly then we can rest in the fact that God is mediating those home prayer meetings. Starting a church in homes is not bad, if it's with the right spirit.

Acts 10: 24, 44

24 And the morrow after they entered into Caesarea. And Cornelius waited for them, and had called together his kinsmen and near friends.
44 While Peter yet spake these words, the Holy Ghost fell on all them which heard the word.

This home prayer meeting at Cornelius' house was a landmark in the ministry to the gentiles. Peter was the first to evangelize the gentiles. From this home, the rest of the known world would hear of Jesus and his saving grace. Disciplining others to minister in our stead is probably one of our largest downfalls. We have to have control of the situation for it to be God, or so we lead others to believe. The fact is, we aren't the only ones that God reveals him to.

I Thessalonians 5: 12,

12 And we beseech you, brethren, to know them which labour among you, and are over you in the Lord, and admonish you;

We have to know those over us in the Lord lest we be led astray. We have the tendency to surrender totally to those in leadership over us. Search their spirit and know their vision, then follow.

James 1: 27,
27 Pure religion and undefiled before God and the Father is this, To visit the fatherless and widows in their affliction, *and* to keep himself unspotted from the world.

Outreach is key to building a strong church. If we reach out to them who can't help themselves, then we literally become a Saviour to them. A Saviour is one who rescues another. Jesus rescued us so we must rescue others. In this scripture we can see the true motives of a ministry. If we are outreaching to our flock, ministering to their needs, you will see fertile fruits that you can enjoy.

Luke 14: 23,
23 And the lord said unto the servant, Go out into the highways and hedges, and compel *them* to come in, that my house may be filled.

With what kind of people? You mean those who are broke, and don't have a lot to offer?

Luke 7:
47 Wherefore I say unto thee, Her sins, which are many, are **forgiven**; for she loved **much**: but to whom little is forgiven, the same loveth little.
48 And he said unto her, Thy sins are forgiven.

The further down in the mire of sin you are, the clearer you can see the forgiving grace of our Saviour. Once they are washed and made pure, they will stick by you no matter what may come. You can watch God as he begins to bless and enlarge their garments. They may become your next millionaires.

Luke 10: 2,
2 Therefore said he unto them, The harvest truly *is* great, but the labourers *are* few: pray ye therefore the Lord of the harvest, that he would send forth labourers into his harvest.

Jesus went into the fisherman's villages to find disciples that would evangelize the world. There is no reason that any church in America should have less than a thousand people in attendance. We just haven't opened the doors to go out and get them. How large of a harvest do you want?

Luke 10: 17,
17 And the seventy returned again with joy, saying, Lord, even the devils are subject unto us through thy name.

How do you know the power of God in your lives except you test it out? These evangelists that Jesus ordained to go with him saw the fruits of their labour. If you want to explode your church, get them into the neighborhoods and allow them to operate in the fruits and gifts of the Spirit. As the old folks would say, "Then hold on to your hats, it's going to be a wild ride".

Matthew 10: 7- 8,

7 And as ye go, preach, saying, The kingdom of heaven is at hand.

8 Heal the sick, cleanse the lepers, raise the dead, cast out devils: freely ye have received, freely give.

He says as you're witnessing, perform miracles for them that need it. This isn't talking about the Christians, this is seeing sinners healed and prophesied to. When we minister it should never be with the intentions that I'm getting paid. Too many will charge you for ministering to your church. According to this scripture this is wrong. If they will receive an offering or just a gift from the church, then allow them to minister. We are not allowed to charge for what we cannot give! The spirit of God is not ours to merchandise. We should be blessed in our efforts, but it should never be a set amount charged. This is the reason Jesus ran the merchants out of the temple. They led people to believe that God wouldn't accept their sacrifice unless you bought it from us. They were trying to control God and enslave the people of God.

Mark 16: 15- 18,

15 And he said unto them, Go ye into all the world, and preach the gospel to every creature.

16 He that believeth and is baptized shall be saved; but he that believeth not shall be damned.

17 And these signs shall follow them that believe; In my name shall they cast out devils; they shall speak with new tongues;

18 They shall take up serpents; and if they drink any deadly thing, it shall not hurt them; they shall lay hands on the sick, and they shall recover.

I love this scripture. We are looking at a chronological order of events. First he says to go and preach. Second, he says baptize them that get saved. Third, he says signs will follow you who are saved in faith. Fourth, you will cast out devils. Fifth, you will speak with new tongues (Holy Ghost). Sixth, take up serpents and demons. Seventh, nothing can hurt you. Eight, you will lay hands on people and they shall be healed. Many stop at number four. They won't speak with new tongues, it's just too weird. Yet if they stop short of the Holy Ghost, then they still should be casting out devils! Hummm, interesting?

Acts 1: 8,
8 But ye shall receive power, after that the Holy Ghost is come upon you: and ye shall be witnesses unto me both in Jerusalem, and in all Judaea, and in Samaria, and unto the uttermost part of the earth.

Power to witness. So many are witnessing without this power and winning souls. How much more will they do if they have the Holy Ghost?

Acts 4: 29,
29 And now, Lord, behold their threatenings: and grant unto thy servants, that with all boldness they may speak thy word,

When the pressure's on, what will you do? Suggestion; call on the Holy Ghost. He will grant unto you more boldness than you could imagine.

Matthew 10: 16,
16 Behold, I send you forth as sheep in the midst of wolves: be ye therefore wise as serpents, and harmless as doves. {harmless: or, simple}

Learning the word is essential in soul winning. Teaching breads boldness and confidence. We are not to argue our views or even the bible. Arguments accomplish nothing and only prove you know nothing.

II Timothy 2:
13 If we believe not, *yet* he abideth faithful: he cannot deny himself.
14 Of these things put them in remembrance, **charging *them* before the Lord that they strive not about words to no profit, *but* to the subverting of the hearers.**

15 Study to shew thyself approved unto God, **a workman that needeth not to be ashamed, rightly dividing the word of truth.**

16 But **shun profane *and* vain babblings: for they will increase unto more unGodliness**.

17 And their word will eat as doth a canker: of whom is Hymenaeus and Philetus; {canker: or, gangrene}

18 Who concerning the truth have erred, saying that the resurrection is past already; and overthrow the faith of some.

19 Nevertheless **the foundation of God standeth sure, having this seal**, The Lord knoweth them that are his. And, **Let every one that nameth the name of Christ depart from iniquity**. {sure: or, steady}

We are not to argue. The truth is the truth whether or not you believe it. Your opinion won't change the facts of his word. You rightly divide the word of truth and the truth will not depart out of the heart of those who hear whether they agree or not. Confidence breed's truth and truth brings conviction. If they argue it's because of conviction. You've already won when you don't argue. Too many churches are built on the premises that unless you believe like us, then you're going to hell.

John 4: 34- 38,

34 Jesus saith unto them, My meat is to do the will of him that sent me, and to finish his work.

35 Say not ye, There are yet four months, and *then* cometh harvest? behold, I say unto you, Lift up your eyes, and look on the fields; for they are white already to harvest.

36 And he that reapeth receiveth wages, and gathereth fruit unto life eternal: that both he that soweth and he that reapeth may rejoice together.

37 And herein is that saying true, One soweth, and another reapeth.

38 I sent you to reap that whereon ye bestowed no labour: other men laboured, and ye are entered into their labours.

The first thing a church has to do is find the will of God for your ministry. Not all churches are destined to be nationwide on TV. God will give you a vision for your ministry. You will know to whom you are sent. A vision does not consist of how large your building is going to be or how must accumulation of wealth you have. It's about souls. There is a specific harvest field God has called you to. It's just a matter of hearing from God.

Habakkuk 2:
1 I will stand upon my watch, and set me upon the tower, and will watch to see what he will say unto me, and what I shall answer when I am reproved. {Tower: Heb. fenced place} {Unto me: or, in me} {When...: or, when I am argued with: Heb. upon my reproof, or, arguing}
2 And the LORD answered me, and said, Write the vision, and make it plain upon tables, that he may run that readeth it.
3 For the **vision** is yet for an **appointed time**, but at the end it shall speak, and not lie: though it tarry, wait for it; because it will surely come, it will not tarry.
4 Behold, his soul *which* is lifted up is not upright in him: but the just shall live by his faith.

Patience is an ingredient that many lack and thus missing the full potential of God. Importance of writing the vision is vital. When things don't seem to be falling in place, your vision will strengthen you.

I Samuel 30:
5 And David's two wives were taken captives, Ahinoam the Jezreelitess, and Abigail the wife of Nabal the Carmelite.
6 And David was greatly distressed; for the people spake of stoning him, because the soul of all the people was grieved, every man for his sons and for his daughters: but David encouraged himself in the LORD his God. {grieved: Heb. bitter}

If you're looking for everything just to happen on a schedule, you need to step away from the ministry while you can. As Habakkuk said, though you think the vision tarries, wait for it for it shall surely come. I like the next part when he said it will not tarry. Seems like a contradiction but it's not; our time and the time of fulfillment of the vision is on two entirely different schedules. God is on time, we are ahead of time.

I Corinthians 14: 33, 40,
33 For God is not *the author* of confusion, but of peace, as in all churches of the saints.
40 Let all things be done decently and in order.

Finding the place of peace and walking in it is crucial for success. You have to get your mind and spirit to a place of peace before you can stay there. Vision is all about patience. When we pray about circumstances and we feel uneasy or in a state of confusion, according to this scripture, who isn't the author of this situation. Tuck your britches legs and run like Elijah. God's way is always a way of peace.

I Corinthians 14: 30 –31,
30 If *any thing* be revealed to another that sitteth by, let the first hold his peace.
31 For ye may all prophesy one by one, that all may learn, and all may be comforted.

We have to allow God to move in whomsoever he will. We have to instruct our people that just because God has given you a word, that timing and order is of God. Two can't prophesy at once lest no one understand what is being prophesied. God's won't interrupt the preaching while the anointing is flowing to prophesy. If God has a word then, then God will allow the minister to pause until God gives him more word to preach thus giving an opportunity to yield to the Holy Ghost. God is not the author of a mess, but of the blessed.

Matthew 18: 15- 17,
15 Moreover if thy brother shall trespass against thee, go and tell him his fault between thee and him alone: if he shall hear thee, thou hast gained thy brother.

16 But if he will not hear *thee, then* take with thee one or two more, that in the mouth of two or three witnesses every word may be established.

17 And if he shall neglect to hear them, tell it unto the church: but if he neglect to hear the church, let him be unto thee as an heathen man and a publican.

18 Verily I say unto you, Whatsoever ye shall bind on earth shall be bound in heaven: and whatsoever ye shall loose on earth shall be loosed in heaven.

This is the three-fold stage of restoration between brethren. If the one who has no hard feeling approaches the one who does and tries sincerely to make amends and restore fellowship and there is no fellowship restored, then you have to go before two or three witnesses who have no influence in the situation. If this measure fails, then it has to come before the pastor or board to resolve. The understanding must be that whatever judgement is given by these men and women of God, it is final. When Godly council is sought after, it must be adhered to.

Matthew 5: 23- 24,
23 Therefore if thou bring thy gift to the altar, and there rememberest that thy brother hath ought against thee;
24 Leave there thy gift before the altar, and go thy way; first be reconciled to thy brother, and then come and offer thy gift.

Here it is in plain English. It is your responsibility to go to the person who is angry, hurt or bitter. The reason you go is because you have no feelings or emotion tied to that event. You are not to go for an argument or to prove your point. The only point is to get forgiveness for the wounds you inflicted. You can apologize for the hurt you caused and yet still retain the dignity that you may not have been wrong about the issue. You are not arguing the issue but seeking forgiveness for the wound that was inflicted.

Matthew 6: 14- 15,

14 For if ye forgive men their trespasses, your heavenly Father will also forgive you:

15 But if ye forgive not men their trespasses, neither will your Father forgive your trespasses.

This scripture must be applied to that situation for the person to release the hurt. If they don't, then their sorrow will turn inward and destroy the relationship they have with God.

I Timothy 5: 17- 20,

17 Let the elders that rule well be counted worthy of double honour, especially they who labour in the word and doctrine.

18 For the scripture saith, Thou shalt not muzzle the ox that treadeth out the corn. And, The labourer is worthy of his reward.

19 Against an elder receive not an accusation, but before two or three witnesses. {before: or, Under}

20 Them that sin rebuke before all, that others also may fear. To go along with the Godly council, we have to give honor and respect those in authority over us. The problem with respect in the house of God is that the ministers don't teach it. We are afraid that people will think that all we want is their money. With that mentality it shows when we teach or preach on tithing and giving. Honor comes because the people are taught to give honor. It's not just about money, but we know that money is a motivating factor.

I Peter 4: 15- 17,

15 But let none of you suffer *as* a murderer, or *as* a thief, or as an evildoer, or as a busybody in other men's matters.

16 Yet if *any man suffer* as a Christian, let him not be ashamed; but let him glorify God on this behalf.

17 For the time *is come* that judgment must begin at the house of God: and if *it* first *begin* at us, what shall the end *be* of them that obey not the gospel of God?

When things happen in the church, don't be too quick to freak out. God may be sending judgement to save your ministry. Many times God wants your church to reach a greater place in him but he can't because of stuff. When God convicts, people will repent and glory will be restored. Stuff happens in church and yet it's the place it should. If you're going to have a heart attack, where is the best place to have it? At the hospital, it's where you can get immediate attention and healing. Judgement is just judgement. Don't be ashamed when judgement comes, whether in you or in the members, its purification and perfection. Take it joyfully, move on into the glory!

LUKE 17: 1- 3,
1 Then said he unto the disciples, It is impossible but that offences will come: but woe *unto him*, through whom they come!
2 It were better for him that a millstone were hanged about his neck, and he cast into the sea, than that he should offend one of these little ones.
3 Take heed to yourselves: If thy brother trespass against thee, rebuke him; and if he repent, forgive him.

Watch this. Have you got your seat belts on? What is the one thing that most sinners complain about in the house of God? Isn't it hypocrites? I know they are a pain in every area of your body. They weary you, aggravate you, and so on. When the rapture of the church takes place, which will be left sitting on your pews? That's right, the hypocrites. They know the word, they know how to live for Christ, to know how to operate the church and they can do your job better than you, right? Watch this next scripture and you'll understand where I am headed with this train of thought.

Revelation. 7:
9 After this I beheld, and, lo, **a great multitude, which no man could number, of all nations, and kindreds, and people, and tongues, stood before the throne, and before**

the Lamb, clothed with white robes, and palms in their hands;

10 And cried with a loud voice, saying, Salvation to our God which sitteth upon the throne, and unto the Lamb.

11 And all the angels stood round about the throne, and *about* the elders and the four beasts, and fell before the throne on their faces, and worshipped God,

12 Saying, Amen: Blessing, and glory, and wisdom, and thanksgiving, and honour, and power, and might, *be* unto our God for ever and ever. Amen.

13 And one of the elders answered, saying unto me, What are these which are arrayed in white robes? and whence came they?

14 And I said unto him, Sir, thou knowest. And he said to me, These are they which came out of great tribulation, and have washed their robes, and made them white in the blood of the Lamb.

15 Therefore are they before the throne of God, and serve him day and night in his temple: and he that sitteth on the throne shall dwell among them.

16 They shall hunger no more, neither thirst any more; neither shall the sun light on them, nor any heat.

17 For the Lamb which is in the midst of the throne shall feed them, and shall lead them unto living fountains of waters: and God shall wipe away all tears from their eyes.

The hypocrites in your church will lead a number of souls to Christ during the tribulation that no man can number! Everyone is crying out about the great outpouring of God and an end time revival. They are right but they are wrong about the timing. It will happen in the tribulation period; a time of revival unknown to man. Those who are pushing this phenomenal outpouring of God are sitting on your pews right now irritating and aggravating the fire out of you. You got it, the hypocrites. You are actually grooming and discipline them. If they don't get it right before the rapture they will after you are delivered from them by the rapture. They will carry on the ministry without you and with more fire and determination than you.

Their very lives will be at risk thus pressure makes greater diamonds. Notice that in heaven they have died and they made their robes white in the blood of Jesus. Salvation wasn't the instrument of redemption but the word being manifest in their hearts did. They did whatever it took to be saved. More than I can say for our church today. It's like pulling eye teeth to get them to church and almost a miracle from heaven to get them to support the church in their giving. So, be of good cheer second shift is getting ready to go to work!

James 3: 14- 16,
14 But if ye have bitter envying and strife in your hearts, glory not, and lie not against the truth.
15 This wisdom descendeth not from above, but *is* earthly, sensual, devilish. {sensual: or, natural}
16 For where envying and strife *is*, there *is* confusion and every evil work. {confusion: Gr. tumult, unquietness}

Seems like when you have a group of people coming together in one place, you have little sparks of James 3: 14- 16 manifesting themselves. Religious jealousy is a viper that will not die. Someone thinks they can do your job better than you and is more qualified than you. Oh yea, and just as anointed as you. The fact is, if they were, God would have already placed them in that position. It's ok, you can laugh now, then sigh a breath of relief.

II Timothy 3: 16- 17,
16 All scripture *is* given by inspiration of God, and *is* profitable for doctrine, for reproof, for correction, for instruction in righteousness:
17 That the man of God may be perfect, throughly furnished unto all good works. {throughly...: or, perfected}

One of the hardest things for a true pastor or minister to do is fulfill this scripture. We can give the word with wondrous presentation. Yet when we have to use that same word to correct, reprove and as a father would to refocus their attention on Christ, it hurts. The last thing we want to do is to reprimand our sheep. If we want our sheep to be perfect in righteousness, thoroughly equipped for every blessing of God, then we have to correct. Do it with gentle tender love as not to bruise or wound their spirit.

II Timothy 4: 2,

2 Preach the word; be instant in season, out of season; reprove, rebuke, exhort with all longsuffering and doctrine.

We must be skilled in the word of righteousness and able to head off disaster at every turn. We are to be instant, or ever ready. Our job is the same as the Holy Ghost's.

I Corinthians 14:

But he that prophesieth speaketh unto men *to* edification, and exhortation, and comfort.

We are to edify and lift up the people of God. Take special notice of the things they are doing for God and encourage them to more of the same. We are to exhort which means to challenge them through the word to do greater exploits for God than ever before. When we see that God is moving in a direction in their lives, we are to nudge them in that direction. We have to comfort them when they are down or do not think they are accomplishing anything for God. We are there to hear from God for them and to confirm what God has dealt with them about so that they may not be afraid to launch out into deeper waters. Always remember for your sakes and theirs is this scripture.

Hebrews. 6:

9 But, beloved, we are persuaded better things of you, and things that accompany salvation, though we thus speak.
10 For God *is* not unrighteous to forget your work and labour of love, which ye have shewed toward his name, in that ye have ministered to the saints, and do minister.

God did not say he would reward you for the successful job done. He said he would reward you for the faithfulness in doing what he placed in your hands to do. It is not about success or failure; it is about trusting God and trying. You will be amazed at the rewards in heaven from what you feel was unsuccessful attempts at ministries.

Chapter XIV

LEARNING TO PRAY

I know after reading this study this comment may sound funny. "We are going to unlock the mysteries of successful prayer life." If you want to know how to pray, then hang on.

Written By: Dr. Ronald Sanders PhD
© By the Library of Congress
2006

Learning To Pray

I. Why Pray?   3/25/97

James 5: 16,
16 Confess *your* faults one to another, and pray one for another, that ye may be healed. The effectual fervent prayer of a righteous man availeth much.

The Old Catholic saying, "Confession is good for the soul." is not all entirely what this scripture is saying. There is a certain amount of privacy that we need to exercise, but when we have a need and need to bind together with someone to build faith, then we need to confide in someone that is a prayer warrior, not a gossiper. When we overcome difficulties in our lives, it is a tremendous faith builder in others that are experiencing the same thing you are going through, when they know that you came through it with God's help! You have experience in knowing how to pray for them and bind with them to help them to overcome just as you did. We have to learn from each other.

Romans 14: 7,
7 For none of us liveth to himself, and no man dieth to himself.

First thing we need to learn, is that we don't serve God alone. An example is:

I Kings 19: 14, 18,
14 And he said, I have been very jealous for the LORD God of hosts: because the children of Israel have forsaken thy covenant, thrown down thine altars, and slain thy prophets with the sword; and I, even I only, am left; and they seek my life, to take it away.
18 Yet I have left *me* seven thousand in Israel, all the knees which have not bowed unto Baal, and every mouth which hath not kissed him. {I have...: or, I will leave}
Elijah thought he was the only one serving God. He was at the point of giving up, and hiding out for the rest of his life,

all because of one mouthy woman. The most amazing thing about this story is, not about Elijah, but that the fact that God knew exactly how many there were left in Israel that were still there fighting against those who would take their lives. Here, Elijah was, sitting in safety, grumbling and complaining, while the seven thousand were still waging war against Baal. Those in church who do the most complaining are those who are not in the midst of the battle for souls, but bystanders, who are watching while you are fighting the battles. Have you ever noticed that they don't mind you fighting the battles alone, so long as they can set back and complain about every fault you have. Guess what? When you are in heaven rejoicing and partying with Jesus, they will still be sitting on that same pew collecting splinters. So, keep on fighting and getting the victory while the upright dead die on the pews. God will put you with other prayer warriors like yourself that you will draw strength from. This is why you are in the church that you are!

Ecclesiastes 4: 9- 12,
9 Two *are* better than one; because they have a good reward for their labour.
10 For if they fall, the one will lift up his fellow: but woe to him *that* is alone when he falleth; for *he hath* not another to help him up.
11 Again, if two lie together, then they have heat: but how can one be warm *alone?*
12 And if one prevail against him, two shall withstand him; and a threefold cord is not quickly broken.

God did not intend for us to try to serve God alone. He never did. Strength comes with a group. One will bear up another. God gives this command;

Hebrews 10:24- 25,
24 And let us consider one another to provoke unto love and to good works:
25 Not forsaking the assembling of ourselves together, as the manner of some *is*; but exhorting *one another*. and so much the more, as ye see the day approaching.
We are to draw from one another. If going to church was not a command, Jesus would not have spent so much time addressing it in the first three chapters of Revelation, would he?

I Timothy. 2: 8,
I will therefore that men pray every where, lifting up holy hands, without wrath and doubting.

If we are lifting up our hands in prayer to our love, Jesus, then we will not have time to be given to wrath toward others and ourselves. Building faith is simple. More time in prayer, more faith in God!

Philippians 4: 6,
6 Be careful for nothing; but in every thing by prayer and supplication with thanksgiving let your requests be made known unto God.

God commands that we pray, not once a day, but continually. A preacher made the statement that we do not need to pray about everything, he stayed at that church less than a year, before they asked him to leave. That preacher must not have read this scripture. "in everything by prayer", we can not grow in God, unless we spend time in prayer!!

1/ note the following in the book of acts:
    A. Chapter 2- the Spirit is poured out on a prayer meeting.
    B. Chapter 3- a cripple is healed while on the way to a prayer meeting.
    C. Chapter 4- multitudes are added to the church daily as earnest prayer results in a re-filling.

D. Chapter 5- the disciples go to the temple daily for prayer and many miracles occur, in the midst of the church being purged.

E. Chapter 6- the preachers commit to continuous prayer and deacons are selected.

F. Chapters 7& 9- Stephen (deacon) dies while praying, and Saul is converted.

Why Does God Desire Us To Pray?

Mark 11: 24,
24 Therefore I say unto you, What things soever ye desire, when ye pray, believe that ye receive *them*, and ye shall have *them*.

Isaiah 1: 18,
18 Come now, and let us reason together, saith the LORD: though your sins be as scarlet, they shall be as white as snow; though they be red like crimson, they shall be as wool.

God wants to commune with us. He created us in the beginning that he may fellowship with us. The word reason shows his desire to discuss with us. The word reason in the Hebrew means: to be right, to argue, chasten, convince, correction, dispute, reason.
Wow! God desires to discuss each situation together, even salvation! How often do we sit sown with daddy and discuss our lives with him? That is exactly what he wants us to do. God even said it was all right to argue or not to agree on everything. Because when we do, God will reveal to us his inner most desires for us. Therefore, we can talk to God as our daddy.

James 5: 14-15,
14 Is any sick among you? let him call for the elders of the church; and let them pray over him, anointing him with oil in the name of the Lord:
15 And the prayer of faith shall save the sick, and the Lord shall raise him up; and if he have committed sins, they shall be forgiven him.

God desires us to walk in divine healing. If your faith is not strong enough, then combine your faith with that of the church.

Galatians 6: 1- 2,
1 Brethren, if a man be overtaken in a fault, ye which are spiritual, restore such an one in the spirit of meekness; considering thyself, lest thou also be tempted. {If: or, although}

FOR THE PERFECTING OF THE SAINTS

2 Bear ye one another's burdens, and so fulfil the law of Christ.

Prayer is the most powerful method of bringing people together. When you are constant in prayer for others, a bond of God forms for them, thus making us more sensitive to their needs.

Hebrews 13: 15,
15 By him therefore let us offer the sacrifice of praise to God continually, that is, the fruit of *our* lips giving thanks to his name. {giving...: Gr. confessing to}

God likes to hear us give him praise. God delights in our praise.

Proverbs 15: 8, 29,
8 The sacrifice of the wickcd *is* an abomination to the LORD: but the prayer of the upright *is* his delight.
29 The LORD *is* far from the wicked: but he heareth the prayer of the righteous.

Our prayers are a delight to the very ears of God, and exceeding joy to his heart. God goes on to say;

Psalm 34: 15, 18- 19,
15 The eyes of the LORD *are* upon the righteous, and his ears *are open* unto their cry. 18 The LORD *is* nigh unto them that are of a broken heart; and saveth such as be of a contrite spirit. {unto...: Heb. to the broken of heart} {of a contrite...: Heb. contrite of spirit}
19 Many *are* the afflictions of the righteous: but the LORD delivereth him out of them all.
Why?

Psalm 34: 1- 3,
1 <*A Psalm* of David, when he changed his behaviour before Abimelech; who drove him away, and he departed.> I will bless the LORD at all times: his praise *shall* continually be in my mouth. {Abimelech: or, Achish}

2 My soul shall make her boast in the LORD: the humble shall hear *thereof*, and be glad.
3 O magnify the LORD with me, and let us exalt his name together.
And;

Psalm 34: 8,
8 O taste and see that the LORD *is* good: blessed is the man *that* trusteth in him.

The result of praising and bringing honor to his name is impartation of his wonderful nature and Spirit. We have the opportunity to know that God's eyes and ears are watching and waiting to bless his people because we bring delight to his name. The Lord wants us to try God, and sample of his goodness. Know his wondrous mercies and his bountiful fellowship. People don't hear the voice of God because, they are afraid to hear, don't want to hear, or haven't learned to hear. God has already said that he wants to reason together with us. That is not a one way conversation, but a dialogue, a two way conversation.

II. How Do I Know That God Hears Me?

I John 5: 14- 15
14 And this is the confidence that we have in him, that, if we ask any thing according to his will, he heareth us: {in: or, concerning}
15 And if we know that he hear us, whatsoever we ask, we know that we have the petitions that we desired of him.
First, we must have confidence that he can answer our prayers, second that he desires to and thirdly, that we are willing to wait and receive his answer.

I John 3: 19, 22,
19 And hereby we know that we are of the truth, and shall assure our hearts before him.

22 And whatsoever we ask, we receive of him, because we keep his commandments, and do those things that are pleasing in his sight.

How do we know he desires to answer our prayers? Simple, because we keep his commandments, and try to please him in all things. Thus, God desires to please us.
He heard a dying man convicted of thievery.

Luke 23: 39- 43,
39 And one of the malefactors which were hanged railed on him, saying, If thou be Christ, save thyself and us.
40 But the other answering rebuked him, saying, Dost not thou fear God, seeing thou art in the same condemnation?
41 And we indeed justly; for we receive the due reward of our deeds: but this man hath done nothing amiss.
42 And he said unto Jesus, Lord, remember me when thou comest into thy kingdom.
43 And Jesus said unto him, Verily I say unto thee, To day shalt thou be with me in paradise.

Notice that this thief had no time to neither ask the legal system for forgiveness nor give back that, which was stolen. He was not even baptized or get the Holy Ghost. Jesus did tell him that this day he would be with him in paradise. There were only two things this thief did that would get him into heaven. Let us look at these two and take heed.

1. He confessed Jesus as Lord, and the Christ. He desired forgiveness for his sins, of which Christ forgave.
I John 1: 9,
9 If we confess our sins, he is faithful and just to forgive us our sins, and to cleanse us from all unrighteousness.

2. He witnessed to the other thief on the cross. Seeing that the thief had a repentant heart, he witnessed to the other thief out of a sincere heart. The second thief realized that he was receiving a just reward for their deeds in the flesh. He was much like the woman caught in adultery. Caught in her sins,

not trying to hide them from Christ, revealed all to him with a repentant heart. Two things we will do before we can go to heaven.

Ask for forgiveness and witness about Jesus.

Mark 8: 38,

38 Whosoever therefore shall be ashamed of me and of my words in this adulterous and sinful generation; of him also shall the Son of man be ashamed, when he cometh in the glory of his Father with the holy angels.

Fact, if you are ashamed of Christ, then Christ will have no part with you. The thief on the cross, ashamed of his deeds, did not let his past keep him from accepting Christ into his heart. If Christ was not ashamed to have him, then why should he be ashamed to acknowledge Christ as Saviour of his life? Probably for the first time in his life, someone accepted him for who he was, and not just a thief on a cross.

Matthew 7: 11,

11 If ye then, being evil, know how to give good gifts unto your children, how much more shall your Father which is in heaven give good things to them that ask him?

God is our father, and desires to be treated as our father. He desires to give unto us, not because we deserve it, but for the simple fact that he is, our father and we are a part of him. He gave birth to us, both in the natural realm and in the spirit. Besides, Jesus gave his life that we may have the privilege of knowing our heavenly father. We were like children, taken from our father's arms at birth, and only after many years, finding our way back to him. He just simply loves us. The things that seem so great to us, are just simple things that God desires to bless us with. Do you remember when you were a child, and you asked for a dollar? To us, that dollar was the entire world's wealth, but to our parents, it was about 15 minutes worth of work on their jobs. It all depends which perspective we are looking at, ours, or God's.

God Promised That:

Matthew 7: 8- 10,

8 For every one that asketh receiveth; and he that seeketh findeth; and to him that knocketh it shall be opened.

9 Or what man is there of you, whom if his son ask bread, will he give him a stone?

10 Or if he ask a fish, will he give him a serpent?

Excellent promise; Ask, and you will receive. Seek the will of God or his word, and he promised to show us and reveal his desire to you.

Luke 11: 5- 10,

5 And he said unto them, Which of you shall have a friend, and shall go unto him at midnight, and say unto him, Friend, lend me three loaves;

6 For a friend of mine in his journey is come to me, and I have nothing to set before him? {in...: or, out of his way}

7 And he from within shall answer and say, Trouble me not: the door is now shut, and my children are with me in bed; I cannot rise and give thee.

8 I say unto you, Though he will not rise and give him, because he is his friend, yet because of his importunity he will rise and give him as many as he needeth.

9 And I say unto you, Ask, and it shall be given you; seek, and ye shall find; knock, and it shall be opened unto you.

10 For every one that asketh receiveth; and he that seeketh findeth; and to him that knocketh it shall be opened.

Before this story unfolds in God's word, we see the example Jesus gave his disciples of how to pray.

Jesus likens God to the friend at home already in bed. God will rise and give to us because we need his help. God will never leave you without, and in need, if we learn to ask.

If we learn to ask God, faith is as simple as this:

John 16: 23- 27,

23 And in that day ye shall ask me nothing. Verily, verily, I say unto you, Whatsoever ye shall ask the Father in my name, he will give it you.

24 Hitherto have ye asked nothing in my name: ask, and ye shall receive, that your joy may be full.

25 These things have I spoken unto you in proverbs: but the time cometh, when I shall no more speak unto you in proverbs, but I shall shew you plainly of the Father. {proverbs: or, parables}

26 At that day ye shall ask in my name: and I say not unto you, that I will pray the Father for you:

27 For the Father himself loveth you, because ye have loved me, and have believed that I came out from God.

God simply will do for us, and bless us just because we love Jesus, and believe that he is the son of God.

We limit God, simply because we do not see him. That should make no difference, that makes him no less God! It just makes us less of a child of God.

I Peter 1: 8,

8 Whom having not seen, ye love; in whom, though now ye see *him* not, yet believing, ye rejoice with joy unspeakable and full of glory:

Simply believing that he is, and loving him, creates great joy in us.

Without faith, we are not going to receive anything of the Lord.

Hebrews 11: 6,

6 But without faith *it is* impossible to please *him*: for he that cometh to God must believe *that* he is, and that he is a rewarder of them that diligently seek him.

What is faith? How do you have faith?

When you ask God, expect an answer, and results, this is the start of faith.

James 2: 17- 18,

17 Even so faith, if it hath not works, is dead, being alone. {alone: Gr. by itself}

18 Yea, a man may say, Thou hast faith, and I have works: shew me thy faith without thy works, and I will shew thee my faith by my works. {without: some copies read, by}

Faith is only hope, if there is no action put forth with it. Acting as if it has already been done, causes faith to manifest itself. It is the acting on faith that will cause it to happen. Some will say; what if I believe God and it does not happen? Two answers.

Romans 10; 11,

11 For the scripture saith, Whosoever believeth on him shall not be ashamed.

When operating in faith, you will not be ashamed that you did.

Hebrews 6: 10,

10 For God is not unrighteous to forget your work and labour of love, which ye have shewed toward his name, in that ye have ministered to the saints, and do minister.

From this one scripture alone, we find that nothing we ever do for Christ, because we love him, will ever go unnoticed before God. That brings us to number two.

James 4: 2- 3,

2 Ye lust, and have not: ye kill, and desire to have, and cannot obtain: ye fight and war, yet ye have not, because ye ask not.

3 Ye ask, and receive not, because ye ask amiss, that ye may consume *it* upon your lusts. {lusts: or, pleasures}

Secondly, we ask to get gain for ourselves to show the world that we are better than they are. Have you ever known anyone who has to tell you all the things they possess that they might make you feel badly or embarrassed? These ones did not receive it from the Lord. Those that are continually trying to condemn you are the ones not being blessed by God. There are two other ways they are being blessed; one, their own works obtained it, or Satan blessed them with it to destroy their relationship with God. A good example would be in Matthew 4: 1- 8 where Satan would have given back to Jesus his control over the world. This was given to Satan in Genesis 3: This would have been a blessing of Satan, but would have dethroned Christ as the son of God, and have put Christ under subjection to Satan even though it might of sounded good for Christ, if he did not know the motive behind Satan.

John 10: 10- 11,

10 The thief cometh not, but for to steal, and to kill, and to destroy: I am come that they might have life, and that they might have *it* more abundantly.

11 I am the good shepherd: the good shepherd giveth his life for the sheep.

Then how can I tell the difference?

James 3: 14- 18,

14 But if ye have bitter envying and strife in your hearts, glory not, and lie not against the truth.

15 This wisdom descendeth not from above, but *is* earthly, sensual, devilish. {sensual: or, natural}

16 For where envying and strife *is*, there *is* confusion and every evil work. {confusion: Gr. tumult, unquietness}

17 But the wisdom that is from above is first pure, then peaceable, gentle, *and* easy to be intreated, full of mercy and good fruits, without partiality, and without hypocrisy. {partiality: or, wrangling}

18 And the fruit of righteousness is sown in peace of them that make peace.

The one who blessed you with it, did they ever throw it up in your face or remind you of the favour or blessing? Have you felt uneasy about it since the blessing? Was there strings attached to the blessing? Did the blessing cause you more harm than good? These are blessings of the flesh or satanic blessings. When God brings a blessing, his glorious peace will be in the midst of the blessing. It will bring joy to your heart, and will become a wonderful memory of your Lord who loves you. When a blessing comes your way, you will feel a peace about receiving it. If you do not feel a peace about this blessing, do not receive it!!!! It is better to hurt their feelings then, than to live in torment for days, months, etc. to come, because of getting the wrong kind of blessing. The knowledge, of which direction the blessing came, comes from experience of knowing God. Because:

Romans 11: 29,
29 For the gifts and calling of God *are* without repentance.

I have always thought that this scripture should have an "!" point after it. You will not repent that the blessing came your way! Anything God has, whether a gift of God, or the call on your life, you will not be brought into bondage over it!
Do we ever have doubt? Of course, as long as we are spiritual beings, living in a fleshly body, subject to emotions, then there is room for doubt. Let us look at some who have had doubt, and see what Christ did about it.

Matthew 3: 13- 17,
13 Then cometh Jesus from Galilee to Jordan unto John, to be baptized of him.
14 But John forbad him, saying, I have need to be baptized of thee, and comest thou to me?
15 And Jesus answering said unto him, Suffer *it to be so* now: for thus it becometh us to fulfil all righteousness. Then he suffered him.
16 And Jesus, when he was baptized, went up straightway out of the water: and, lo, the heavens were opened unto him, and he saw the Spirit of God descending like a dove, and lighting upon him:
17 And lo a voice from heaven, saying, This is my beloved Son, in whom I am well pleased.

Here, we see Jesus being baptized by John the Baptist in Jordan river. John sees Jesus, knows he is the Son of God, hears a voice from heaven, sees the Holy Ghost descending, and preaching of Jesus the son of God, but in the next scripture, we see that John just wanted to make sure that Jesus was the one. Is it all right to doubt or question? Let us see.

Matthew 11:1- 4,
1 And it came to pass, when Jesus had made an end of commanding his twelve disciples, he departed thence to teach and to preach in their cities.
2 Now when John had heard in the prison the works of Christ, he sent two of his disciples,
3 And said unto him, Art thou he that should come, or do we look for another?
4 Jesus answered and said unto them, Go and shew John again those things which ye do hear and see:

John, just wanted to make sure this was who he thought him to be. John knew his life on earth was ending, and wanted to be sure of that which he believed. Jesus just strengthened John's faith by the works of God seen. Therefore, John the greatest of prophets and the last of the Old Testament prophets had doubts, but one simple answer of God calmed any doubts he had. This was another instance of doubt that Jesus calmed.

Mark 9: 23- 24, 26,
23 Jesus said unto him, If thou canst believe, all things *are* possible to him that believeth.
24 And straightway the father of the child cried out, and said with tears, Lord, I believe; help thou mine unbelief.
26 And the spirit cried, and rent him sore, and came out of him: and he was as one dead; insomuch that many said, He is dead.

This father wanted his son healed, but was afraid. He believed that Jesus could, but would he? Jesus assured him that all things are possible to him that believeth. It was not a matter of if it was God's will, but if he wanted God to deliver his son. He did, and Jesus did. Many times in God's words, men and women of God had reservations about the will of God to do, but when they released their faith, God performed mighty miracles. Questioning God is not a sin, but excepting God is a must! As we said before, falling in love with God makes trusting him easier.

Jude 20- 21,
20 But ye, beloved, building up yourselves on your most holy faith, praying in the Holy Ghost,
21 Keep yourselves in the love of God, looking for the mercy of our Lord Jesus Christ unto eternal life.
Keeping you "In the love of God." Isn't that romantic? There is a song, "I keep falling in love with him, over and over again. He gets sweeter and sweeter as the days go by, oh what a love between my Lord and I, I keep falling in love with him, over and over again."
That is the way I feel, and you should too. If you want to grow in God, then you will constantly do those things in your life that will cause you to love him more and more. Some of these things are:

Reading and studying God's word
Praying
Fasting
Witnessing
Loving those in Christ

When Should I Pray?

Psalm 63: 1,
1 <A Psalm of David, when he was in the wilderness of Judah.> O God, thou art my God; **early will I seek thee**: my soul thirsteth for thee, my flesh longeth for thee in a dry and thirsty land, where no water is; {thirsty: Heb. weary} {where...: without water}

Psalm 27: 4,
4 One thing have **I desired of the LORD, that will I seek after; that I may dwell in the house of the LORD all the days of my life,** to behold the beauty of the LORD, and to enquire in his temple. {the beauty: or, the delight}

Psalm 34: 1- 4,
1 <A Psalm of David, when he changed his behaviour before Abimelech; who drove him away, and he departed.> **I will bless the LORD at all times: his praise *shall* continually *be* in my mouth.** {Abimelech: or, Achish}
2 **My soul shall make her boast in the LORD**: the humble shall hear *thereof*, and be glad.
3 O **magnify the LORD with me, and let us exalt his name together.**
4 I sought the LORD, and he heard me, and delivered me from all my fears.

Acts 2: 46- 47,
46 And they, **continuing daily with one accord in the temple**, and breaking bread from house to house, did eat their meat with gladness and singleness of heart, {from...: or, at home}
47 Praising God, and having favour with all the people. And the Lord added to the church daily such as should be saved.

Let's face it, the more we pray and give thanks unto God, the better our day will be. Can you imagine continually being in the presence of God? Feeling that overwhelming joy and peace continually? Some old deadhead Christians say that you cannot stay in that awesome presence all the time, but what do the dead know of the living. We cannot always stay on our knees all day, but we can always be in prayer under our breath, and have our mind in a state of worship all day long. Then we can watch God send others to us for us to minister to them. Think of the miracles you can see God do each day, just by keeping our minds on God!

Prayer is one of the easiest things you will ever do as a Christian. Why, because there is no set way of talking to God; talk to him out of your heart. Tell him how your day is going, whether great or not so great. You hear people in church pray all these pretty prayers, but it is not necessary to get God's attention, it just sounds good to the crowd listening. We can get ideas from the Lord's Prayer, but we are not to confine ourselves to just this one prayer. Below is some prayers written in God's word. Remember, just talk to God as you would your closest friend.

Matthew 6: 7- 13,
7 But when ye pray, **use not vain repetitions**, as the heathen do: for they think that they shall be heard for their much speaking.
8 Be not ye therefore like unto them: for **your Father knoweth what things ye have need of, before ye ask him.**
9 After this manner therefore pray ye: Our Father which art in heaven, **Hallowed be thy name.**
10 **Thy kingdom** come. **Thy will** be done **in earth**, as it *is* **inheaven.**
11 **Give us** this day our daily bread.
12 And **forgive us** our debts, as we forgive our debtors.
13 And **lead us** not into temptation, but **deliver us** from evil: For **thine is** the kingdom, and the power, and the glory, for ever. Amen.

Here we see the model prayer. Notice the highlights of this prayer. Rehearsed prayers sound rehearsed, and boring. I know God knows my need before I ask. I ask so that I can communicate with my creator and friend. I want to bless his name and tell him how much I love him. I pray for his guidance and divine appointments each day. I pray for protection each day. I pray my spirit will be open to his leading that I may be a blessing to others as he has been in my life. Meet my needs that arise this day, whether bills, food, gas, or shelter. Save my loved ones. Forgive my hardness of heart and keep me tender before you that I may not desire to sin. Help me to forgive others who have been a stumbling block to me. I will purpose in my heart to forgive those whom I have animosity against. Let me hear your voice and not the voice of Satan that I may steer clear of temptations. Those who plot to destroy my credibility and harm my family or myself, let me know in advance that I may not fall into their traps. Your son Jesus, let him so shine in my life that the world may know there is a God in heaven. All power is your and my faith is steadfast in you, I will not fail this day, in Jesus' name, amen.

This is the summery of what the Lord's Prayer is for us. As you read this prayer, you will get more revelations than I did.

Acts 4: 24- 31,

24 And when they heard that, they **lifted up their voice to God with one accord**, and said, Lord, thou art God, which hast made heaven, and earth, and the sea, and all that in them is:

25 Who by the mouth of thy servant David hast said, **Why did the heathen rage**, and the people imagine vain things?

26 The kings of the earth stood up, and the rulers were gathered together against the Lord, and against his Christ.

27 For of a truth against thy holy child Jesus, whom thou hast anointed, both Herod, and Pontius Pilate, with the Gentiles, and the people of Israel, were gathered together,

28 For **to do whatsoever thy hand and thy counsel determined before to be done**.

29 And now, Lord, behold their threatenings: and **grant unto thy servants, that with all boldness they may speak thy word,**

30 By **stretching forth thine hand to heal; and that signs and wonders may be done by the name of thy holy child Jesus.**

31 And **when they had prayed, the place was shaken** where they were assembled together; and they were all filled with the Holy Ghost, and **they spake the word of God with boldness.**

In this prayer, their petition was simple. Give me more power than the enemy that rises above me. Let my words be sure and my heart steadfast. Let me walk in your will and operate in the gifts and callings of God, that you have purposed for my life. We have always heard that we should not question God, but Peter does. Why do the heathens rage? If you need to know something, who else can give the answer any better than the creator of the earth can? We need to expect God to shake us when we pray. Shake us loose from our expectations and opinions.

Acts 7: 58- 60,

58 And cast *him* out of the city, and stoned *him*: and the witnesses laid down their clothes at a young man's feet, whose name was Saul.

59 And they stoned Stephen, calling upon God, and saying, Lord Jesus, receive my spirit.

60 And he kneeled down, and cried with a loud voice, Lord, lay not this sin to their charge. And when he had said this, he fell asleep.

An absolute prayer of power. Stephen prayed for God's forgiveness of their sins. These were his enemies who are killing him. When we walk in a love of God that all we can see is Jesus, then we will have the anointing we so desperately crave. If we have a prayer lift, we too can fall asleep. Stephen's sleep was a little more permanent than ours was now. Just to know that there is nothing between your God and you, is worth letting go of anything that would hinder your prayers. In Stephen's last minutes the glory was so evident that the comment was made by his murderers that his face shown like an angel. When we spend quality time with Jesus our faces will shine like Stephens.

Acts 9: 10- 16,

10 And there was a certain disciple at Damascus, named Ananias; and to him said the Lord in a vision, Ananias. And he said, Behold, I *am here*, Lord.

11 And the Lord *said* unto him, Arise, and go into the street which is called Straight, and enquire in the house of Judas for one called Saul, of Tarsus: for, behold, he prayeth,

12 And hath seen in a vision a man named Ananias coming in, and putting *his* hand on him, that he might receive his sight.

13 Then Ananias answered, Lord, I have heard by many of this man, how much evil he hath done to thy saints at Jerusalem:

14 And here he hath authority from the chief priests to bind all that call on thy name.

15 But the Lord said unto him, Go thy way: for he is a chosen vessel unto me, to bear my name before the Gentiles, and kings, and the children of Israel:

16 For I will shew him how great things he must suffer for my name's sake.

This is the prayer life that God desires for every Christian that knows him. He can give such detailed instructions as to what the person is doing and even saying. This was no doubt a two-way conversation between God and Ananias. You know I heard a funny thing. Some preacher said that not all these folks that claim to hear God's voice is true. God does not speak to us. Well, Mr. Preacher here is your sign, if he spoke to Ananias who was unknown until this time, and then he can speak to you, that is if you get the lead out and unstop your ears. Assumption is the devil's play toys. We assume God is not the same today as he was two thousand years ago, but we all know the scripture that says he is the same, yesterday, today and forever. Do you reckon these preachers do not want the responsibility that comes from hearing the voice of God? That is something to think about?

Acts 10: 3- 7,

3 He saw in a vision evidently about the ninth hour of the day an angel of God coming in to him, and saying unto him, Cornelius.

4 And when he looked on him, he was afraid, and said, What is it, Lord? And he said unto him, Thy prayers and thine alms are come up for a memorial before God.

5 And now send men to Joppa, and call for *one* Simon, whose surname is Peter:

6 He lodgeth with one Simon a tanner, whose house is by the sea side: he shall tell thee what thou oughtest to do.

7 And when the angel which spake unto Cornelius was departed, he called two of his household servants, and a devout soldier of them that waited on him continually;

It was 3:00 pm when Peter had this conversation with God. The angel had instructed Cornelius to send men to Joppa, even as Peter was praying. This angel desires that Cornelius receives all that God has in store for him. That came with getting someone else to teach him how to simply receive. I recently in say the last eight years realized that not everyone has heard the voice of God or seen angels. That still blows my mind. When you look at the New Testament verses the Old Testament, there are more angel visitations in the 27 books of the New Testament than combined in all the Old. Wow! Do you think God is trying to tell us something? I believe that since the Holy Spirit is now residing in our hearts after salvation, that there is no more veils dividing us from the supernatural realm, only our faith and fears.

Acts 16: 25- 26,
25 And at midnight Paul and Silas prayed, and sang praises unto God: and the prisoners heard them.
26 And suddenly there was a great earthquake, so that the foundations of the prison were shaken: and immediately all the doors were opened, and every one's bands were loosed.

The greater the pain, the sweeter the prayer. When we learn to divert our attention from the things we see to the things we know, and then we too can sing in jail. Prayer is the key to your answer. Push past your feeling, push past your fear of pier pressure, pushing past your insecurities, and just have fun in the presence of the Lord.

1 Kings 18: 36- 38,
36 And it came to pass at the time of the offering of the evening sacrifice, that Elijah the prophet came near, and said, LORD God of Abraham, Isaac, and of Israel, let it be known this day that thou art God in Israel, and that I am thy servant, and that I have done all these things at thy word.
37 Hear me, O LORD, **hear me, that this people may know** that thou art the LORD God, and that thou hast turned their heart back again.
38 Then the fire of the LORD fell, and consumed the burnt sacrifice, and the wood, and the stones, and the dust, and licked up the water that was in the trench.

If you are trying to get fire to fall from heaven, would this be your prayer? It was Elijah's. He just simply asked God to show off and prove himself. He says he has been obedient to the word of the lord, and he expected God to send fire down our of the sky. Wow! What would happen if we had the same expectation from God? How many souls would you lead to the Lord? Elijah did not even need a prayer to get fire to fall. He prayed to make a point to all that heard him. See; when you have a prayer life, you do not have to spend 30 minutes to pray over the food. They should have went to the alter and prayed through so they did not have to while we were waiting to eat. If you have a prayer life, it does not take all day to get an answer. In fact, if Elijah had not prayed, fire still would have fallen from heaven. It is what he doe behind the alter that is obvious in front of it.

1 Kings 19: 9- 18,

9 And he came thither unto a cave, and lodged there; and, behold, the word of the LORD *came* to him, and he said unto him, What doest thou here, Elijah?

10 And he said, I have been very jealous for the LORD God of hosts: for the children of Israel have forsaken thy covenant, thrown down thine altars, and slain thy prophets with the sword; and I, *even* I only, am left; and they seek my life, to take it away.

11 And he said, Go forth, and stand upon the mount before the LORD. And, behold, the LORD passed by, and a great and strong wind rent the mountains, and brake in pieces the rocks before the LORD; *but* the LORD *was* not in the wind: and after the wind an earthquake; *but* the LORD *was* not in the earthquake:

12 And after the earthquake a fire; *but* the LORD *was* not in the fire: and after the fire a still small voice.

13 And it was so, when Elijah heard it, that he wrapped his face in his mantle, and went out, and stood in the entering in of the cave. And, behold, *there came* a voice unto him, and said, What doest thou here, Elijah?

14 And he said, I have been very jealous for the LORD God of hosts: because the children of Israel have forsaken thy covenant, thrown down thine altars, and slain thy prophets with the sword; and I, *even* I only, am left; and they seek my life, to take it away.

15 And the LORD said unto him, Go, return on thy way to the wilderness of Damascus: and when thou comest, anoint Hazael *to be* king over Syria:

16 And Jehu the son of Nimshi shalt thou anoint to be king over Israel: and Elisha the son of Shaphat of Abelmeholah shalt thou anoint to be prophet in thy room. {Elisha: Gr. Eliseus}

17 And it shall come to pass, *that* him that escapeth the sword of Hazael shall Jehu slay: and him that escapeth from the sword of Jehu shall Elisha slay.

18 Yet I have left *me* seven thousand in Israel, all the knees which have not bowed unto Baal, and every mouth which hath not kissed him. {I have...: or, I will leave}

Notice the first thing God asked Elijah? What is you doing way out here in the middle of nowhere? Who are you afraid of. The first thing we must do in prayer is get rid of our stinking thinking and cancel the pity party, because God is not coming to it. The second thing God told Elijah to do is get up. Our prayer life has to have enough power to get us back on our feet when we have been knocked down flat. Any other kind of prayer is somewhat redundant, isn't it?

II Kings 6: 15- 19,

15 And when the servant of the man of God was risen early, and gone forth, behold, an host compassed the city both with horses and chariots. And his servant said unto him, Alas, my master! how shall we do? {the servant: or, the minister}

16 And he answered, Fear not: for they that be with us *are* more than they that *be* with them.

17 And Elisha prayed, and said, LORD, I pray thee, open his eyes, that he may see. And the LORD opened the eyes of the young man; and he saw: and, behold, the mountain was full of horses and chariots of fire round about Elisha.

18 And when they came down to him, Elisha prayed unto the LORD, and said, Smite this people, I pray thee, with blindness. And he smote them with blindness according to the word of Elisha.

19 And Elisha said unto them, This is not the way, neither *is* this the city: follow me, and I will bring you to the man whom ye seek. But he led them to Samaria. {follow...: Heb. come ye after me}

If our prayer life is always concentrated on what we see instead of what we know, then how will we ever be able to believe for things we cannot control? Elisha walked by what he knew, not by what he saw. He knew that God was with him and that there were more for him than against him. This comes by knowledge and not observation. Prayer is a confidence builder. It is our way of being super human. Prayer is about forgetting what is in front of you and seeing what is over you. His anointing covers you like a cloud yet we spend so much time worrying about so many trivial things, we cannot even look up. Your circumstances will change when you absolutely refuse to have the answer that is obvious. We have to have concrete faith, sheer determined faith. He wants us to have the kind of faith that dares the devil to step across your line, refusing to accept defeat and a negative report.

Psalm 51: 1- 19, (Prayer That The Jewish Nation Prays Every Day.)

1 <To the chief Musician, A Psalm of David, when Nathan the prophet came unto him, after he had gone in to Bathsheba.> **Have mercy** upon me, O God, according to thy lovingkindness: according unto the multitude of thy tender mercies blot out my transgressions.

2 **Wash me throughly** from mine iniquity, and **cleanse me** from my sin.

3 For **I acknowledge my transgressions**: and my sin is ever before me.

4 Against thee, thee only, have I sinned, and done *this* evil in thy sight: that thou mightest be justified when thou speakest, *and* be clear when thou judgest.

5 Behold, I was shapen in iniquity; and in sin did my mother conceive me. {conceive...: Heb. warm me}

6 Behold, thou desirest truth in the inward parts: and in the hidden *part* thou shalt make me to know wisdom.

7 **Purge me** with hyssop, and I shall be clean: wash me, and I shall be whiter than snow.

8 Make me to hear joy and gladness; that the bones which thou hast broken may rejoice.

9 Hide thy face from my sins, and blot out all mine iniquities.

10 Create in me a clean heart, O God; and **renew a right spirit** within me. {right: or, constant}

11 Cast me not away from thy presence; and **take not thy holy spirit** from me.

12 **Restore unto me the joy of thy salvation**; and uphold me *with thy* free spirit.

13 *Then* **will I teach transgressors** thy ways; and **sinners shall be converted** unto thee.

14 **Deliver me** from bloodguiltiness, O God, thou God of my salvation: and my tongue shall sing aloud of thy righteousness. {bloodguiltiness: Heb. bloods}

15 O Lord, open thou my lips; and my mouth shall shew forth thy praise.

16 For thou desirest not sacrifice; else would I give *it*: thou delightest not in burnt offering. {else...: or, that I should}

17 The sacrifices of God *are* a **broken spirit: a broken and a contrite heart**, O God, thou wilt not despise.

18 Do good in thy good pleasure unto Zion: build thou the walls of Jerusalem.

19 Then shalt thou be pleased with the sacrifices of righteousness, with burnt offering and whole burnt offering: then shall they offer bullocks upon thine altar.

We could easily call this an in-depth sinners' prayer. Watch this, when you forgive my sins, I will teach those who are sinning your ways, and I will convert sinners. Once we pray, then we have to act. Prayer is just the warm-up. The workout is beginning to start. To keep fellowship with God, we must take what he has done in us to the streets and convert the lost. We must disciple others, and give sound instruction. I will sing aloud. I will not hold my tongue. I will change my world and them around me. Prayer is a tool to the supernatural. The supernatural lies within you waiting to be released by prayer, so free it.

Chapter XV

WHAT HAPPENS WHEN I DIE?

This qustion has been asked for thousands of years, and we always receive the same answer. "You go to heaven sweethears." How factual is that statement? When do we go to heaven and why? There are instances in the Bible that tell us what happens after death. Let us discuss this issue and see what God has to say about it.

Written By: Dr. Ronald Sanders PhD
© By the Library of Congress 2006

I. What Happens When I Die?

This question is asked thousands of times each year. Many wonder what will happen after death. In this study, we will endeavor to uncover a mystery that is of vital concern to all.

The Jehovah's Witnesses have a simple solution to death. They believe that when you die, it is final. We are as any other animal, there is no after life. Death is final, just as the Sadducees in biblical days also believed.

How does the Lord feel about the death of his people?

Psalm 116: 15,
15 Precious in the sight of the LORD *is* the death of his saints.

Matthew 28: 20,
20 Teaching them to observe all things whatsoever I have commanded you: and, lo, I am with you alway, even unto the end of the world. Amen.

God said he was there, even to the end of the world. Whether in death or here on earth, we will never again be without the Lord's presence. The Lord sees us as precious in his sight, even in death.

I Corinthians 15: 26, 55- 56,
26 The last enemy *that* shall be destroyed *is* death.
55 O death, where *is* thy sting? O grave, where *is* thy victory? {grave: or, hell}
56 The sting of death *is* sin; and the strength of sin *is* the law.

To the saint, there is no sting of death. Seventeen times in the New Testament death is referred to as sleep. When death is mentioned in the New Testament, more times than not, it is referred to as sleep. Sleep is a rest of peacefulness, awaking to a newness of life.
I Corinthians. 15: 16- 23,
16 For if the dead rise not, then is not Christ raised:

17 And if Christ be not raised, your faith *is* vain; ye are yet in your sins.

18 Then they also which are fallen asleep in Christ are perished.

19 If in this life only we have hope in Christ, we are of all men most miserable.

20 But now is Christ risen from the dead, *and* become the firstfruits of them that slept.

21 For since by man *came* death, by man *came* also the resurrection of the dead.

22 For as in Adam all die, even so in Christ shall all be made alive.

23 But every man in his own order: Christ the firstfruits; afterward they that are Christ's at his coming.

The only hope that we have is in Christ. We know he rose from the grave because we feel him in our heart, and is in charge of our lives. This is our assurance that what he said is true.

I Corinthians 15: 51- 54,

51 Behold, I shew you a mystery; We shall not all sleep, but we shall all be changed,

52 In a moment, in the twinkling of an eye, at the last trump: for the trumpet shall sound, and the dead shall be raised incorruptible, and we shall be changed.

53 For this corruptible must put on incorruption, and this mortal *must* put on immortality.

54 So when this corruptible shall have put on incorruption, and this mortal shall have put on immortality, then shall be brought to pass the saying that is written, Death is swallowed up in victory.

We know that Jesus shall come back to earth to rapture the church out, that if we are dead in Christ, then we shall rise first, to meet Jesus in the air. What a glorious moment that will be!

My question and yours is what happens until then?

Luke 16: 19- 26,

19 There was a certain rich man, which was clothed in purple and fine linen, and fared sumptuously every day:

20 And there was a certain beggar named Lazarus, which was laid at his gate, full of sores,

21 And desiring to be fed with the crumbs which fell from the rich man's table: moreover the dogs came and licked his sores.

22 And it came to pass, that the beggar died, and was carried by the angels into Abraham's bosom: the rich man also died, and was buried;

23 And in hell he lift up his eyes, being in torments, and seeth Abraham afar off, and Lazarus in his bosom.

24 And he cried and said, Father Abraham, have mercy on me, and send Lazarus, that he may dip the tip of his finger in water, and cool my tongue; for I am tormented in this flame.

25 But Abraham said, Son, remember that thou in thy lifetime receivedst thy good things, and likewise Lazarus evil things: but now he is comforted, and thou art tormented.

26 And beside all this, between us and you there is a great gulf fixed: so that they which would pass from hence to you cannot; neither can they pass to us, that *would come* from thence.

Here, we see the only actual account of what happens after death. "There was a certain rich man." "This was not a story or parable. This is an actual account of events. There is life after death. The rich man awoke in hell. There was not great judgment, but at death, the first judgment is instantaneous. We know according to Revelation 20: 10-15, that this is the second death. Thus, hell is just a holding facility until the white throne judgment.

Revelation 20: 10 -15,

10 And the devil that deceived them was cast into the lake of fire and brimstone, where the beast and the false prophet *are*, and shall be tormented day and night for ever and ever.

11 And I saw a great white throne, and him that sat on it, from whose face the earth and the heaven fled away; and there was found no place for them.

12 And I saw the dead, small and great, stand before God; and the books were opened: and another book was opened, which is *the book* of life: and the dead were judged out of those things which were written in the books, according to their works.

13 And the sea gave up the dead which were in it; and death and hell delivered up the dead which were in them: and they were judged every man according to their works. {hell: or, the grave}

14 And death and hell were cast into the lake of fire. This is the second death.

15 And whosoever was not found written in the book of life was cast into the lake of fire.

We have seen the events of the White Throne judgment. Now let us examine what God just said, that we may come to understand the word of God written unto us.

Revelation 1: 18,

18 I *am* he that liveth, and was dead; and, behold, I am alive for evermore, Amen; and have the keys of hell and of death.

Jesus descended into hell, by way if death, and took authority over them. What good does it do us?

Daniel 12: 1- 2,

1 And at that time shall Michael stand up, the great prince which standeth for the children of thy people: and there shall be a time of trouble, such as never was since there was a nation *even* to that same time: and at that time thy people shall be delivered, every one that shall be found written in the book.

2 And many of them that sleep in the dust of the earth shall awake, some to everlasting life, and some to shame *and* everlasting contempt.

This is a description of a period just before the great tribulation. We call it the rapture of the church. Here, Daniel says that we shall awake, from the earth. If the account of events in the life of Lazarus is true, then we shall rest in Abraham's bosom. Jesus made us a promise that he would always be with us.

Matthew 28: 20,
20 Teaching them to observe all things whatsoever I have commanded you: and, lo, I am with you alway, *even* unto the end of the world. Amen.

Jesus will not leave us in death. The most special part of the story of Lazarus is that angels called him to Abraham's bosom, a place of peace and rest. He was not left in the earth; he was carried and looked after with great care. The word comforted in Luke 16: means to be "Called near," Lazarus was "Invited". "Invoked (By imploration, exhortation or consolation)", and was of "Good comfort."
Remember the Lord said, that precious in his sight is the death of his saints.

We find two things as fact.
1. There is a hell, and all those who are not Christians will go there.

Hebrews 9: 27,
27 And as it is appointed unto men once to die, but after this the judgment:

The first judgment comes at death. The righteous enter into rest, and the unrighteous enter into hell.
2. we await Jesus' coming to go with him to heaven.

I Thessalonians 4: 13- 18,
13 But I would not have you to be ignorant, brethren, concerning them which are asleep, that ye sorrow not, even as others which have no hope.
14 For if we believe that Jesus died and rose again, even so them also which sleep in Jesus will God bring with him.

15 For this we say unto you by the word of the Lord, that we which are alive *and* remain unto the coming of the Lord shall not prevent them which are asleep. {prevent: or, come before, or, anticipate, or, precede}

16 For the Lord himself shall descend from heaven with a shout, with the voice of the archangel, and with the trump of God: and the dead in Christ shall rise first:

17 Then we which are alive *and* remain shall be caught up together with them in the clouds, to meet the Lord in the air: and so shall we ever be with the Lord.

18 Wherefore comfort one another with these words. {comfort: or, exhort}

We do not automatically go to heaven when we die. We are carried to a place of rest in Abraham's bosom, awaiting the voice of Jesus to arise as he did. Seeing he has the keys to death and hell, we are only subject to the grave, which is once.

Now let us see what happens to those who are not Christians. God desires that all men come to repentance.

II Peter 3: 9,

9 The Lord is not slack concerning his promise, as some men count slackness; but is longsuffering to us-ward, not willing that any should perish, but that all should come to repentance.

Thus, those who do not except Christ:

Luke 13: 3,

3 I tell you, Nay: but, except ye repent, ye shall all likewise perish.

John 8: 24,

24 I said therefore unto you, that ye shall die in your sins: for if ye believe not that I am *he*, ye shall die in your sins.

Isaiah 5: 14,

14 Therefore hell hath enlarged herself, and opened her mouth without measure: and their glory, and their multitude, and their pomp, and he that rejoiceth, shall descend into it.

Hell has to enlarge herself, so that it can contain one more soul. Hell is only large enough for those there. Hell has to make room for you. God does not desire you to go to hell, but seeing this is the sentence carried out upon Satan and his angels, when we follow him, we are given the same sentence of eternal dying. Where is hell?

Isaiah 14: 9,
9 Hell from beneath is moved for *thee* to meet thee at thy coming: it stirreth up the dead for thee, *even* all the chief ones of the earth; it hath raised up from their thrones all the kings of the nations. {Hell: or, The grave} {chief...: Heb. leaders, or, great goats}

Ezekiel 31: 16- 17,
16 I made the nations to shake at the sound of his fall, when I cast him down to hell with them that descend into the pit: and all the trees of Eden, the choice and best of Lebanon, all that drink water, shall be comforted in the nether parts of the earth. 17 They also went down into hell with him unto *them* that be slain with the sword; and *they that were* his arm, *that* dwelt under his shadow in the midst of the heathen.

We find that hell is in the heart of the earth, the same place as the molten lava is found. Between hell and the grave is a great gulf fixed, and by this gulf is Abraham's bosom. Below is a diagram of what is in the earth.

_____OUTERCRUST_____
_____GRAVE_____
___ABRAHAM'SBOSOM(PARADISE,UPPERSHEOL,INTHEGREEK)
#############GREAT   GULF##############################
###
~~~HELL (SHEOL, IN THE GREEK, PURGATORY, HEART EARTH)~~~
~~~~~~

We know that hell is not the ultimate destination of sinners. The lake of fire is.

II Peter 3: 10- 11,
10 But the day of the Lord will come as a thief in the night; in the which the heavens shall pass away with a great noise, and the elements shall melt with fervent heat, the earth also and the works that are therein shall be burned up.
11 *Seeing* then *that* all these things shall be dissolved, what manner *of persons* ought ye to be in all holy conversation and Godliness.

Revelation 20: 14- 15,
14 And death and hell were cast into the lake of fire. This is the second death.
15 And whosoever was not found written in the book of life was cast into the lake of fire.

What is hell like?

Matthew 8: 12,
12 But the children of the kingdom shall be cast out into outer darkness: there shall be weeping and gnashing of teeth.

Matthew 25: 46,
46 And these shall go away into everlasting punishment: but the righteous into life eternal.

Mark 9: 46,
46 Where their worm dieth not, and the fire is not quenched.

Luke 16: 25,
25 But Abraham said, Son, remember that thou in thy lifetime receivedst thy good things, and likewise Lazarus evil things: but now he is comforted, and thou art tormented.

Weeping, grinding of teeth. There are cries and screams of torment, fire and brimstone, worms, and maggots. The worst part of hell is seeing those in Abraham's bosom, at peace and rest, enjoying God's presence, and knowing that you can never see that place of rest again. Every person that has ever told you about Jesus, you will recall their words every moment in hell. The torment of hearing words of warning and cries of help for you will be replayed day and night in hell.

I Peter 3: 18- 22, Christ preached in Abraham's bosom.
18 For Christ also hath once suffered for sins, the just for the unjust, that he might bring us to God, being put to death in the flesh, but quickened by the Spirit:
19 By which also **he went and preached unto the spirits in prison;**
20 Which sometime were disobedient, when once the longsuffering of God waited in the days of Noah, while the ark was a preparing, wherein few, that is, eight souls were saved by water.
21 The like figure whereunto *even* baptism doth also now save us (not the putting away of the filth of the flesh, but the answer of a good conscience toward God,) by the resurrection of Jesus Christ:
22 **Who is gone into heaven,** and is on the right hand of God; angels and authorities and powers being made subject unto him.

From this scripture comes the custom that we also who were dead went to heaven. It is plain who went to heaven, it was Jesus. He made a pit stop on the earth for 40 days to prove he was the Son of God, and then proceeded to heaven. We are still waiting in paradise for Jesus' marvelous return. Paradise is where the souls of the saints are, without the limitations of the flesh. Now, if we know this is true, and the whole place is redeemed, then what is left to hinder the very presence of God to be there, seeing he is omni-present? Nothing, his presence is felt there greater there than even our minds can comprehend, seeing God can't pour out his glory on sin, and Paradise is a place of no sin, there is no limit to God there. Jesus can walk with us there as he did with Adam and eve in the cool of the garden. The only difference between heaven and paradise is location.

-Other scriptures on hell, & death.
Isaiah 14: 9, 15 Hell From Beneath...
Ezekiel 32: 21 Speak Out Of Hell
Ephesians 4: 9- 10, Christ Descended Into The Lower Parts Earth
Matthew 12: 40, Jesus In Earth 3 Days
Romans 8: 38, Life Nor Death Separate Us From God
Revelation 20: 13, Death And Hell Delivered Dead, White Throne Judgement
Hebrews 11: 5, Should Not See Death
Romans 6: 23, Gift God Eternal Life
Romans 6: 9, Death No More Dominion
Philippians 1: 21, Die Is Gain
Ecclesiastes 7: 17, Why Die Before Your Time
Job 14: 14, Will Live Again

II. Will Suicide Carry Me To Hell, & Why?

Let us find out what the dictionary says is suicide.
Suicide (Latin suicidium, from sui caedere, to **kill oneself**) is the act of intentionally terminating one's own life, although in many dictionaries it connotes "willful destruction of one's self-interest," not necessarily physical death . ...

The act of killing oneself intentionally. Ruin of interest of one's interests through one's own actions.

The next question is, when is suicide a sin? In addition, when does the sin begin?

Proverbs 23: 7,
7 For as he thinketh in his heart, so *is* he: Eat and drink, saith he to thee; but his heart *is* not with thee.

Here, we find a result of what we are thinking as who we are.

Matthew 12: 34,
34 O generation of vipers, how can ye, being evil, speak good things? for out of the abundance of the heart the mouth speaketh.

Faith begins in the heart. Our bodies bring to pass our faith. We react according to our faith. Thus, sin begins in the heart.

Matthew 5: 28,
28 But I say unto you, That whosoever looketh on a woman to lust after her hath committed adultery with her already in his heart.

Sin is committed in the heart first, and then we fulfill our sin in the flesh. The lusting of the thought is the first sin, and carrying out our lust is a second sin.

Mark 10: 19,
19 Thou knowest the commandments, Do not commit adultery, Do not kill, Do not steal, Do not bear false witness, Defraud not, Honour thy father and mother.

Do not kill. When are we guilty of killing? When we think it in our hearts, though, at that time, we can repent of it, and go on. If we listen to our hearts, and kill ourselves, then there is no time for repentance.

James 1: 14- 15,
14 But every man is tempted, when he is drawn away of his own lust, and enticed.
15 Then when lust hath conceived, it bringeth forth sin: and sin, when it is finished, bringeth forth death.

Conception starts on the inside of the heart. Next result of conception is birth of sin. The result of all sin is death, whether spiritual or physical.
There is one grey area in suicide. According to James 1:, death is a result of sin. We know that sin becomes judgeable when it is conceived in the heart. Once is goes past the temptation stage, it starts a process of death and sin. Now, if a person tries to commit suicide, and they live, they can repent of this evil. That is, if they are truly repentant!

John 8: 22- 24,
22 Then said the Jews, Will he kill himself? because he saith, Whither I go, ye cannot come.
23 And he said unto them, Ye are from beneath; I am from above: ye are of this world; I am not of this world.
24 I said therefore unto you, that ye shall die in your sins: for if ye believe not that I am *he*, ye shall die in your sins.

Accepting Jesus as Lord and Saviour is the only way to get forgiveness of sins.

Matthew 19: 23- 24,
23 Then said Jesus unto his disciples, Verily I say unto you, That a rich man shall hardly enter into the kingdom of heaven.
24 And again I say unto you, It is easier for a camel to go through the eye of a needle, than for a rich man to enter into the kingdom of God.

Luke 23: 39,
39 And one of the malefactors which were hanged railed on him, saying, If thou be Christ, save thyself and us.

What if a person tries to commit suicide and they do not die instantaneously? Is there room for repentance? Many bible theologians feel that the sin of breaking the commandment of, "Thou shalt not kill," is not final until death, thus making it impossible to repent, seeing you have not killed yourself yet, and only after you are dead is it sin. In this next scripture, we see that not excepting Jesus as Saviour is grounds for dying in your sins. I wonder, if a person who has seen the sin and the grave mistake they are committing, that while death is coming upon them, will God be merciful enough to forgive them before they die? To be honest, it would be a very hard place to be and find out. The odds of them being repentant in the first place of this act, is like unto the rich man entering the kingdom of heaven.

Here we see two examples of the word. In the first, Jesus shows the hardness of heart of a person. A rich man can go to heaven, but he must first be willing to make Christ first, be willing to obey God in all things. When a person makes up their mind to commit suicide, they become like the rich man, for them to repent and summit to Christ, is a very slim possibility. In the second illustration, we see a thief on a cross dying for his crimes, just as a person is dying for their crime of murder of one's self. The thief on the cross was not interested in repenting, but saving his own self. No doubt, if he had of been spared, he would have repeated his crimes again, and still ended up on a cross. The possibility of one seeing the error of their way is possible, but not likely.

Let us not forget the next verses, (Luke 23: 40 -43,), there was one thief that accepted Jesus as Lord. The possibility is there, but is a scary thought of waiting that long, and having the frame of mind for repentance. Let us not forget the previous scriptures that tell us that out of the abundance of the heart the mouth speaketh. Thus, when murder is premeditated, suicide will not be forgiven; a person has hardened their heart, and will not except forgiveness. An example of this hardness of heart;

Exodus 14: 17, 23- 26,
17 And I, behold, I will harden the hearts of the Egyptians, and they shall follow them: and I will get me honour upon Pharaoh, and upon all his host, upon his chariots, and upon his horsemen.
23 And the Egyptians pursued, and went in after them to the midst of the sea, *even* all Pharaoh's horses, his chariots, and his horsemen.
24 And it came to pass, that in the morning watch the LORD looked unto the host of the Egyptians through the pillar of fire and of the cloud, and troubled the host of the Egyptians,
25 And took off their chariot wheels, that they drave them heavily: so that the Egyptians said, Let us flee from the face of Israel; for the LORD fighteth for them against the Egyptians. {that they...: or, and made them to go heavily}
26 And the LORD said unto Moses, Stretch out thine hand over the sea, that the waters may come again upon the Egyptians, upon their chariots, and upon their horsemen.

We see the result of a long period of time God dealt with Egypt and the Pharaoh. We will show how that Pharaoh hardened his own heart until it was too late, then God would not let him repent. God had turned him over to a reprobate mind to believe a lie and be damned.
In **Exodus 7: 14, 22, 8: 15, 32,** Pharaoh hardened his heart against God, even after seeing two new creations, lice and flies. So in;
Exodus 9: 7, 12, 11: 9, 14: 4, 17, God hardened Pharaoh's heart, so that God could show that he was God. They had a space for repentance, but would not. Thus, when a person is contemplating suicide, they can repent as long as they have not hardened their heart. Thus, if a person plans their own murder, then they have usually reached a place that they have hardened their heart against God's continual gentle tugging to

repent of this sin, and allow him to change their lives, to give them something to live for.

If a person in despair, in torment, or a spirit of heaviness and despair has overwhelmed them; at a spur of a moment commits suicide or attempts, and immediately afterwards, realizes what they have done, may have a space to be forgiven. This is of course, if they are alive after their attempt, either permanently or shortly. There is no biblical basis or teaching on praying someone out of purgatory. This is a lie of the devil. Once you have made your decision, then no one else can change your choice or will! Even if forgiveness is granted, the individual must with all seriousness and sincerity asks God's forgiveness. As we said before, this is a grey area of the word. If possible, few have ever found repentance for this sin.

Jeremiah 15:
6 Thou hast forsaken me, saith the LORD, thou art gone backward: therefore will I stretch out my hand against thee, and destroy thee; **I am weary with repenting**.
7 And I will fan them with a fan in the gates of the land; I will bereave them of children, I will destroy my people, *since* they return not from their ways. {children: or, whatsoever is dear}

There can come a time that God can say that he is tired of repenting over your life. At which point you won't have to worry about God convicting your life any longer. He will allow you to live in your sin and die. God is patient and his mercy ever lasting, yet there is a time that God tires of beckoning.

II Corinthians 5:
2 (For he saith, I have heard thee in a time accepted, and in the day of salvation have I succoured thee: behold, now is the accepted time; **behold, now is the day of salvation.**)

Succoured
997 bohqe,w boetheo {bo-ay-theh'-o}
Meaning: 1) to help, succour, bring aid

Behold is a strong statement. Stop, take notice and give heed to, is the emphasis on this word. Right now, is the time to be saved? When Satan is on your back because of events that have crushed you, it is time to stop hesitating, just get saved. God can then begin to drag you out of the hole you fell into, and rescue you. We must make the first step, because God is waiting.

Test Booklet

For The

"Perfecting Of the Saints"

Chapter I.
Is That You Lord?
Introduction

1) Many say that the age of miracles and visitations ended when the disciples died. According to Galatians. 1: 6- 8 how are we to answer these skeptics?

    A) Just because the disciples died doesn't mean he did?
    B) Let them be doomed to destruction?
    C) It's ok to believe your way as long as you don't condemn me for believing?

2) In Numbers 23: 19- 20 is a good answer to such skeptics and faithless persons. How should we explain this to them?

    A) Just because you can't hear God, doesn't mean he's not speaking?
    B) Once God imparts his blessings upon us he can't reverse it. It is left to us to receive or reject it.
    C) It is according to my faith as to whether God will speak to me.

3) According to I Thessalonians 5: 23 how do we know it's the voice of God we're hearing?

    A) By faith
    B) If we feel his peace is in us, his Spirit keeps us faultless.
    C) If I walk sanctified then his is the only voice I'll hear.

4) It is commonly said among those who refuse to accept the entirety of the bible, that there are errors and contradictions thus the bible is flawed. How do we counter this theory according to II Timothy 3: 14- 17?

    A) You can use the bible to support what you believe.
    B) It is inspired of God, written by man, and proofread by the Holy Ghost for perfection.
    C) It is circumstantial and may not apply.

Is that you Lord
I. The Word of God

1) II Timothy 3: 14- 17 tells us that the word of God is written by the inspiration of God. What is God's ultimate motive here?

  A) To make you perfect.
  B) That you may have good works.
  C) That you get gain.

2) In II Timothy 2: 14- 16 give us a second reason for the word of God. What is it?

  A) To persuade the hearers of your words.
  B) So you won't be made ashamed.
  C) That you make a profit.

3) In the same scripture we see the third thing the word is designed to do for us as believers. What is it?

  A) To accurately interpret the heart of God.
  B) Put to shame the vain babbling.
  C) To judge people with.

4) In Ephesians 4: 14- 15 we find a fourth reason for the word. What is it?

  A) Learning to speak lovingly and be established.
  B) To get to heaven by growing in God.
  C) To get understanding.

5) I Timothy 4: 14- 16 tells us of the fifth reason for the word. What is it?

  A) That you may look good to all who see you.
  B) That everyone will see me get profit.
  C) That I can rescue myself and those that will listen to me.

6) According to Ezekiel 18: 20 24 what is the danger of living a lukewarm Christian life?

A) You cannot enjoy the full pleasures of God.

B) If you die in sin your life as a Christian won't be remembered.

C) If you live in sin you'll die.

7) When you combine II Peter 1: 20- 21 and Habakkuk 1: 2- 4, what conclusion can we biblically make?

A) The bible is still being written by you and me.

B) The Holy Ghost is the giver of insight and direction for your life.

C) If God imparts it we are to write it.

8) When we read such great scriptures as Hebrews 4: 14- 16, why should we become excited?

A) We have a high priest (Jesus) who can't feel what we are going through.

B) We have a high priest (Jesus) who can feel our problems.

C) It doesn't matter whether he can feel what we are going through or not, just as long as we are able to pray.

Is That You Lord?
II. Small Still Voice

1) When reading I Kings 19: 9- 18 I want to be there on that mount with Elijah. With God being such an awesome God I find it hard to grasp how God desires to speak to us. What is so unusual about his voice?

A) He's terrifying.

B) His voice is loud and overpowering.

C) He speaks so softly we have to be attentive to hear him.

2) Matthew 11: 25- 30 explains why the word has to be so simple to understand yet when reading this right behind I Kings 19: 9- 18 we can understand something about the quality of God's voice. What is it?

A) Just like a child we don't listen so there's no point in God screaming at us.

B) Being meek and lowly in heart automatically makes you soft spoken and shy.

C) If God will reveal the word to even children then the only way they can receive it is with a soft calm voice.

3) Read Proverbs 15: 1 and Hebrews 12: 6- 15 then answer this question. If we are to be corrected by God in our errors then what significance does the tone of God's voice play with us?

A) If he doesn't say it boldly and sternly then we won't pay any attention.

B) Harsh words stir up anger and rebellion.

C) If we are always obedient to God it doesn't matter what tone he uses with us.

4) So many people in our society today say that God does not talk to people. When reading John 10: 26- 28 and John 14: 15- 21 what can we confidently say about such people?

A) They are the sheep of another fold Jesus once referred to.

B) If they can't hear it's because they are not Christians.

C) They have not learned to walk in the peace and comfort of God.

5) As you read John 14: 15- 21 we see an excellent reason why God does not have to shout when speaking to us. What is it?

A) If you read the word then he doesn't need to speak to you?

B) If you love God then you don't want him to shout at you.

C) If the Holy Ghost of God lives in you then you hear from the inside out not the outside in. He doesn't have to shout above the outside world's noises.

354

Is That You Lord?
III. Impressions

1) When reading John 14: 15- 18 we see who the Holy Ghost is and where he will dwell. When looking at this chapter of impressions, the question that comes to mind is this; what makes it easy for the Lord to deal with us with impressions?

  A) The Holy Ghost will come upon you.
  B) The Holy Ghost will give you signs to follow.
  C) The Holy Ghost lives in you thus he simply draws you.

2) When reading Acts 11: 12, we find an important ingredient in knowing when the Lord wants us to listen to his leading. What is it?

  A) The Lord sets hindrances in our path and troubles our spirit.
  B) If others follow me.
  C) Someone opens the door of opportunity to us.

3) In our religious society today we see so many with a haughty or Jezebel spirit. Many will use the scripture found in I John 2: 27 as a proof that they don't have to listen to anyone else. They will tell you that if God wants them to know then he will tell them himself. Which of the following answers is the right attitude?

  A) The anointing is never wrong and man is. If I just listen to God and don't receive instruction from my brethren then I'll always be right. I don't need anyone's help.
  B) The anointing brings to remembrance the scriptures to confirm what others are telling and teaching me. By This I know the Spirit of truth from the spirit of error.
  C) I am probably the most spiritual person among my piers so I have to get my knowledge straight from God.

Is That You Lord?
IV. Prophecy

1) There are only three things that New Testament prophecy will do. What are those three things?

  A) Judge, correct, and chastise.
  B) Condemn, expose, rebuke unrighteousness.
  C) Build up, encourage, confirm.

2) We know that prophecy is to build up the believer, but what effect does it have on the unbeliever who is sitting by according to I Corinthians 14: 24- 25?

A) They see us as kooks and crazy.
  B) They will call you a holy roller and run.
  C) They will realize God sees into their hearts and nothing is hid from God.

3) According to I Timothy 1: 18- 19, what one mind set can we have about the prophecies we have received?

  A) Confidence to fight spiritual warfare.
  B) You put away faith
  C) Just wait and see if they will come to pass.

Is That You Lord?
V. Audible Voice

1) If God speaks to you, where does this voice come from?

  A) From out of your heart.
  B) From heaven
  C) Doesn't matter.

2) When hearing an audible voice, can others hear what God is saying to you?

  A) I guess it all depends whether God wants anyone else to hear.

B) It's personal and not for public display.
C) He speaks from within so no one can hear

Is That You Lord?
VI. Visions

1) How many types of visions are there?

  A) One
  B) Two
  C) As many as God desire.

2) Who can have visions?

  A) Any believer
  B) Just old men.
  C) Just daughters

3) According to Acts 10: how much information can God give to us in a vision?

  A) Just what we need to know.
  B) As much as our faith will allow.
  C) Very little because we see through a glass darkly but then face to face.

4) What is a trance an example of?

  A) Dream
  B) Closed eye vision
  C) Spirit being absent from the body.

5) In a vision can the spirit actually leave the body?

  A) Of course if it's the Lord's will.
  B) No, a vision has to be seen through the natural eyes
  C) No, the spirit can never leave the body except in final death.

6) After reading the scripture and the caption after Matthew 14: 22- 32 answer this question. Who is our real enemy? Is it Satan?

A) Yes, he comes to steal kill and to destroy.
B) No, it is those whom Satan uses.
C) No, we are the real enemy.

Is That You Lord?
VII. Dreams

1) What are the two types of dreams given by God?

A) those unfolding immediately and those unfolding somewhere in the future.
B) awake and asleep
C) Godly and unGodly.

2) are dreams meant to be understood?

A) not always
B) yes, whether now or in the future.
C) some things we will understand in heaven.

Is That You Lord?
VIII. Revelations

1) Why would God close the understanding of his word to thesinner?

A) So they can't get saved.
B) So the world can see God in us.
C) So the world can't use the word to the destruction of their souls.

2) According to Romans 1: who is the creation?

A) Idols
B) Plants, animals and inanimate objects.
C) Mankind

3) In John 14: 16- 17, 26 we see the manifestation of the Holy Ghost in our lives. With this in mind, can the Holy Ghost teach every Holy Ghost filled Christian all things?

A) No, the revelation power of God comes by faith and some just don't have it.
B) Yes, if God dwells in you then you will automatically learn all things.
C) Yes, this is not conditional to our spiritual standing with God.

4) In the same scripture and adding Romans 12: 6 to the equation, what two things govern our ability to have revelation knowledge?

A) Length of time serving God and our ability to remember.
B) Our knowledge and our faith.
C) Our faith and our ability to act on what we hear..

5) After reading the scripture Daniel 3: 15- 21 and the comments, what one word could summarize the three Hebrew boys attitude?

A) Hope
B) Defiance
C) Confidence

Is That You Lord?
IX. Visitations

1) Read Daniel 10: 4- 19 and answer this question. What human emotion often occurs in the presence of an angel?

A) Pride, because I have had a visitation.
B) Humility and loss of all physical strength.
C) Honor and excitement at his arrival.

2) When reading Matthew 4: 10 –11, what two emotions might a human feel in the presence of Satan?

A) Anger and humility
B) Loss of all strength and great fear.
C) No changes in emotion. For I am blood bought.

3) Read three scriptures. Acts 5: 18- 26, Acts 12: 6- 9, 21- 24 and Acts 27: 22- 24. Then answer this question. What happens to us as Christians after an angel visitation?

A) Confusion
B) Confidence
C) New place in God.

4) Read II Corinthians 11: 4, 15; Philippians 4: 4- 8; Galatians 1: 6- 9 and I John 4: 1- 4. Now answer the next two questions. When we have had a visitation, our physical man will fail of strength. What emotion should we feel in our spirit?

A) Troubled
h
C) Confusion

5) Question two. When a demonic spirit reveals himself to us, what will we feel in our spirit?
A) Troubled
B) A peace
C) Confusion

6) As a Christian, what will be our last visitation on earth?

A) Our angels will carry us to paradise.
B) Judgment seat of Christ.
C) We won't have a visitation until we get to heaven.

Chapter II.
Angels Unawares!

1) In Luke 24: 13- 18, 29- 32, we see the story of Jesus' uncle Cleopas (John 19: 25) walking with another Christian. They were speaking of the recent events of Jesus. Why didn't Jesus' uncle recognize Jesus?

  A) Jesus' face and body had been so marred by his torture and crucifixion.
  B) They were so engrossed in their conversation they didn't pay attention.
  C) The eyes of their understanding was closed. To recognize Jesus is to know his Spirit just as we recognize each other by the Spirit of God in us.

2) According to the old testament, who was the only person that the honor of washing Jesus' feet?

  A) Adam
  B) Abraham
  C) Moses

3) When reading Genesis 19: 1- 2, 4- 5, 11, 29 what one characteristic can we observe about individuals who are possessed with demons?

  A) They'll go blind.
  B) Their thirst for sin is as great as their determination to commit it.
  C) Sin can't enter your home.

4) In the previous scripture and the other scriptures about angels, what one thing is always true about every appearance of angels in the bible?

  A) They are always male.
  B) They always have wings.
  C) They always carry a sword.

5) After reading Ephesians 1: 17- 19 answer this question. Why can't the sinner in the world understand the depth of the bible?

A) They won't spend the time trying to learn.
B) Revelation of the word is our inheritance as saints of God.
C) The world doesn't know how to pray for understanding.

6) We have always understood that angels are sent from God to minister unto us, but according to Hebrews 1: 13- 14 what other fact can we see?

A) The word "For" changes the meaning. They not only minister to us also for us.
B) Angels have a throne in heaven, just not on God's right side.
C) Angels have no enemies.

Chapter III.
The Ministry Of Great Love!

1) How can you tell that a person is not walking in God's perfect love?

  A) They have stress, fear or anxiety in their lives.
  B) They are grumpy.
  C) They are not forgiving.

2) Read Isaiah 55: 12- 13. What is so special about his scripture?

  A) If I plant something it will grow.
  B) It is the opposite of Genesis 3: 17- 19.
  C) When plants are fertile it is a sign of God.

3) What is one way that we know we have eternal life according to I John 5: 13- 15?

  A) He hears us and grants our prayers.
  B) He gives us confidence.
  C) We know his will.

4) We see so many conflicts in the house of God amongst brethren and we know it ought not to be. Is there a biblical explanation for this commotion?

  A) His suffering crushed Peter's faith.
  B) Peter realized he wasn't ready to die for Jesus.
  C) Jesus in all his suffering had such an anointing that one look would reveal sin and purge hearts.

5) In reading Ephesians 4: 1- 3, 11, 15 we see a mentality of true minister. Why do ministers find it so hard to portray these characteristics?

  A) Because a true minister is not there to be seen or exalted.
  B) These are just characteristics we are to strive at being, but never fully perfecting.
  C) Speaking the truth in love is almost impossible.

6) In Revelation 1: 18, how many and what keys did Jesus have?

  A) 3, death, hell and the grave.
  B) 2, death and hell.
  C) 4, death, hell, the grave and life.

7) To walk in such great love, what is one of the first things we have to come to grasp with?

  A) Love is conditional. The degree of love shown is varied by the receptiveness of the receiver.
  B) If you love, you will be hurt and wounded by others.
  C) When telling the truth, love is not a factor.

8) Fill in the blank. Perfect love gives_____?

  A) With common sense.
  B) At often times.
  C) All

9) In understanding how to have this great love, what is one thing you have to be willing to do?

  A) Be hurt
  B) Understand and care but not getting personally involved.
  C) Be strong, telling those to whom you minister the answer and not sparing their feelings.

10) When walking in this great love to what extreme are you willing to take?

  A) To lay down my life and desires.
  B) Turn my other cheek, knowing it will be the last time.
  C) To flow in this anointing when I am preaching and teaching.

FOR THE PERFECTING OF THE SAINTS

Insert For Ministry Of Great Love
Next Step Anointing!

1) Matthew 8: 28- 29 is a powerful scripture when understanding the anointing that God desires for our life. What makes this occurrence different from other occasions of demon possession?

  A) The demons came out to stop Jesus from entering into the city.
  B) They were terrified because of the power of love that Jesus flowed in.
  C) They came out to beat Jesus up.

2) In Acts 3: 4- 5 Peter asked this man to do only one thing, what was it?

  A) Give me your hand.
  B) Listen to me.
  C) Look at me.

3) In Luke 9: 49-50, 55- 56 we see a story that melts the heart of Jesus but how did it affect those around him?

  A) He spoke with such authority of love that not only did the parents believe but also they were comforted.
  B) They were afraid.
  C) They mocked him.

4) On page fifteen in Luke 22: 60- 64 we see a very familiar scripture about Jesus in his greatest hour of trial. How did Jesus affect Peter?

  A) His suffering crushed Peter's faith.
  B) Peter realized he wasn't ready to die for Jesus.
  C) Jesus in all his suffering had such an anointing that one look would reveal sin and purge hearts.

5) When Jesus went into the land of the Gadarenes, who was his welcoming party?

A) Pig herders
B) City council
C) Homeless man

6) What was the first emotion the demonic had?

A) Fear
B) Anger
C) Confusion

7) What is the result of true salvation?

A) Fear
B) Clothed
C) Anger

8) In Luke 9: 52- 56, why was calling fire down from heaven a problem?

A) They didn't have the power to call fire down.
B) They had the wrong spirit.
C) Fire from heaven was a little extreme.

9) According to Mark 5: 28- 33, why should we always be conscientious of God's presence in our lives?

A) So we don't sin
B) So we don't get into the flesh.
C) So the anointing can minister in our place.

Chapter IV.
Cuttings, Paintings And Piercing?

1) According to Leviticus 19: 26- 29, what word means the same as tattoos?

  A) Mar the corners of the beard.
  B) Printing marks
  C) Cuttings in your flesh.

2) Read Romans 1: 21- 31 then answer this question. What does homosexuals and those who cut themselves have in common?

  A) They are given to vile affections.
  B) They dishonor their bodies between themselves.
  C) Driven by the lust of their heart.

3) Read I Kings 18: 24- 29 then answer this question. The Old Testament gives history have the purposes and customs used in cutting the flesh. What is that custom?

  A) To get a pagan God's attention.
  B) To show their strength and endurance.
  C) To transmit fear to all who watch.

4) Romans 14: 16- 18 gives a scripture that is so widely used to prove a point. How does this scripture relate to the subject of tattoos, carving and piercing?

  A) The sight of tattoos and so on give the indication that an individual enjoys the torture of their body, which is just wrong.
  B) Since our spirit is all that enters heaven we are allowed to do whatever we desire to our bodies.
  C) If you enjoy cutting yourself and getting tattoos and piercing, there is no wrong or harm to my testimony of Christ.

5) If you are operating in the scripture Philippians 4: 4- 9, seeing you have peace of mind and joy in Christ, how will it affect your desires toward the body?

A) Your tattoos will be milder and sweeter.
B) Having peace and satisfaction will reflect in our respect for our bodies.
C) I don't know

Chapter V.
A Little Wager Never Hurt Anybody?

1) Romans 8: 13- 16 gives one of the first things that reflect a problem with gambling. What is it?

  A) Giving heed to the flesh and its desires.
  B) You receive a spirit of bondage into your life.
  C) We cease killing the lust of the flesh.

2) In I Timothy 6: 7- 10 we find one word that shows the real heart behind gambling. What is that one powerful driving word?

  A) Money
  B) Love
  C) Having

3) Proverbs 15: 26- 33 reflects truth. What is meant in the following phrase? "But he that hateth gifts shall live."

  A) Never accept gifts.
  B) Not expecting something for nothing.
  C) The next gift could kill you.

4) In Isaiah 56: 11- 12 we see the word calls these peoples greedy dogs, stupid shepherds and looking out just for number one. In this same scripture how do they intend on accomplishing this feat?

  A) Steal, kill and destroy.
  B) Tomorrow will be a better day.
  C) Let's get drunk and forget our troubles.

Chapter VI.
Promissory Notes, Interest And Lending

1) In Proverbs 6: 1- 5 we see the word surety. What does it mean?

  A) Co-signer
  B) Be dependable
  C) Bodyguard

2) Proverbs 11: 13- 15 uses the word smart. What does it mean?

  A) Educated
  B) Regret
  C) To stand up

3) In Proverbs 27: 13, what is he saying?

  A) If you sign for a loan make sure you get collateral.
  B) Make him swear that he will pay it back.
  C) If a man is borrowing for a woman, go ahead and take his clothes because when she is through with him, that's all he'll have left.

4) Deuteronomy 23: 19- 20 is very specific about usury. If you are of the household of faith, you are under no circumstances allowed to charge or receive usury. What is usury?

  A) Vows of repayment.
  B) Charging of interest or fees.
  C) Cannot lend anything that is used and not new.

5) If you are a Christian and lend money or anything else to a sinner, can you charge usury?

  A) Yes
  B) No
  C) Usury does not apply to sinners.

6) In Ezekiel 18: 12- 18 God speaks to the people of God on several subjects. One subject of course is usury. What two things is God saying to those who receive usury on anything lent to a Christian by a Christian?

A) It is an abomination and you will not have eternal life because you have sinned.
B) Its o.k. to charge usury as long as you do not collect the interest charged.
C) As long as the Christian agrees to the terms of the contract you may charge interest.

7) When using Exodus 34: 7 on this subject and we apply it to charging interest, how does our actions toward other Christians affect our homes and us?

A) God will withhold his hand of blessing from your family and your great-great grand children.
B) You will stand in judgment for your sins.
C) Charging Christians interest is not a sin so therefore God will not require anything at my hand or my family's.

8) Is it God's will for us to invest our money in the stock markets and investments of business and expect an increase?

A) Yes, this is not charging interest on lent money to individual Christians. This is building businesses and being a sower into business ventures.
B) No, you are expecting a return of more than you gave out.
C) Yes, as long as the investment is not to a Christian business.

9) after reading ex. 22: 14- 15, can we rent items to other Christians and get paid for it?

A) No, we are exacting funds from other Christians.
B) Yes, this is being paid a fair price for rental fees. If it is broken then we cannot charge them for the item broken.
C) Better not to rent than to rent and get it broke.

Chapter VII.

Tragedy To Triumph, The Book Of Ruth

1) In II Kings 2: 1- 14, how many times did Elijah ask Elisha to wait for him while he went alone?

   A) Once
   B) Twice
   C) Thrice

2) Each time that Elijah asked Elisha to tarry behind there was confirmation given to Elisha that Elijah's departure was at hand. How many times did God prophesy Elijah's departure to Elisha?

   A) Once
   B) Twice
   C) Thrice

3) In verses 12- 14 we see the scene of Elijah's departure. What a wonder it must have been? We know that Elijah and Elisha were there, but how many spectators does it say that watched as Elijah went up?

   A) Three
   B) Twenty-five
   C) fFfty

4) Read II Kings 2: 23- 24 and answer this question. How many children died at the spoken word of Elisha and why?

   A) It doesn't say. They were taunting Elisha.
   B) 42, because the prophets and parents did not teach them to respect God's anointed due to the fact they were guilty of mocking Elisha also.
   C) 24, because the sons of the prophets were jealous of Elisha and taught the children to disrespect him.

5) in Ruth 1: 15- 18 Ruth said she would not leave Naomi for any reason. In Matthew 8: 18- 22, we see others telling Jesus

their desire to follow him. The answer Jesus gave affected their attitude. How was Jesus' answer any different from Ruth's?

   A) It wasn't.
   B) Ruth knew she would have a place to sleep in Bethlehem-Judah.
   C) Naomi knew she had friends that would take her in.

6) Ruth 1: 15- 18, Ruth made a five-fold statement. Nine generations before another individual made the same kind of faith stand. Who was this person?

   A) Elijah
   B) Abraham
   C) Isaac

7) When you combine Naomi and Ruth's name from the Hebrew text, what definitions do you get?

   A) Mara or bitter friend
   B) Pleasant friend
   C) Friend of strangers

8) In chapter two we discuss the commands of God concerning crop planting and harvesting. What formation was the Jews commanded to plant and harvest?

   A) Plant to the four corners of the field and only harvest the inner circle of it once leaving a triangle in each corner untouched.
   B) Plant to the four corners of the field, and harvest the whole field only once.
   C) Plant to the four corners and harvest it all leaving nothing to waste. God commands thoroughness.

9) According to Genesis 19: 32- 38, from who were the descendants of Moab derived from?

   A) Abraham
   B) Lot
   C) Hagar

10) What was so wrong with the method in that the Moabites were created?

 A) They were the result of date rape and incest.
 B) They were the children born in Sodom.
 C) Their fathers were homosexuals from Sodom.

11) According to Deuteronomy 23: 1- 6, under what condition could the Moabites come into the tabernacle and worship?

 A) They had to first live amongst the Jews for ten generations.
 B) They had to first marry an Israelite and bear children to them.
 C) There was no condition set forth in that they could come into the congregation of the Lord. They were banded for eternity.

12) As Christians we realize that we have divine appointments set forth of God. According to verse three and four of chapter two how does this apply to Ruth?

 A) She wasn't paying attention to what she was doing.
 B) It doesn't apply to Ruth.
 C) Boaz came into his field to check on the welfare of his workers.

13) In the next verses, what impression did Ruth make on Boaz' servants?

 A) She was the daughter of an accursed nation.
 B) She required a lot of attention.
 C) She was a hard worker.

14) According to John 4: when we seek to do the will of God what unexpected results can we count on?

 A) Souls will be saved.
 B) We will receive 30, 60, or 100 fold return.
 C) We will reap in areas we did not labor.

15) Find and read I Corinthians 14: 3 then answer this question. According to Ruth 2: 15, what does I Corinthians 14: 3 have in common with this scripture?

A) When God speaks to us he won't embarrass or humiliate us.
B) Nothing because Ruth didn't have the Holy Ghost or the gift of prophesies.
C) Boaz was showing Godly love toward Ruth.

16) Hebrews 6: 9- 12 is a covenant promise from the Father to us. What three things can we determine as fact here?

A) Be positive, be not lazy, and God will reward.
B) Have faith, wait on God, and you will make it to the end.
C) Work hard; don't fail at what you start, then God will reward.

17) In Ruth chapter four, verses one thru seven, what does Boaz call his near kinsman?

A) A ho
B) Near kinsman
C) By name

18) In Proverbs 5: 15- 16, when it uses terms like "Drink waters, running waters, fountains, and rivers", to what is the bible referring?

A) Having your own well and source of water.
B) Giving to others
C) Sexual climaxes both male and female.

Chapter VIII.

Grasshoppers And Locust; The Mini Giants Of God!

1) The first three pages we are referred to as grasshoppers. We see how being a grasshopper can be a good or bad thing depending on how we see ourselves. In which way should we view this?

   A) God can take the base things that are despised to confound the things that are mighty.

   B) As a grasshopper, i can stay in the background and not get into anyone's way.

   C) As a grasshopper, my opinion really doesn't matter.

2) In Proverbs 30: 21- 33 God speaks of four seemingly insignificant creatures yet God had special things to say about each. What did God say about the locust?

   A) They break off into small bands or groups.

   B) They all fly and graze together in unity.

   C) They have stripes on their bodies.

3) Psalm 78: 45- 46 gives another characteristic of locust. What is it?

   A) Locust work hard.

   B) Locust hardly works.

   C) They reap where they bestowed any labor.

Chapter IX.
I Will Not Murmur Because The Ax Head Swims!

1) Exodus 16: 2- 3 records that complaint of the Israelites in the wilderness. The section that is highlighted, talks about their desire to die while sitting and eating like slaves in Egypt. Looking into their future, how does this comment reflect on their future?

A) We were happy as long as we have all the food we could eat.
B) They spoke their own deaths. God indeed let them die without seeing freedom.
C) God is a liar.

2) What is God saying the result of murmuring is?

A) It will kill you.
B) It delays his blessings.
C) How can you enjoy his blessings when you can't get past your past?

3) If Matthew 6: 30 is true, then how does I Corinthians 10: 9- 13 affect this scripture?

A) When we complain it's not our circumstances we are complaining about, it's God we're complaining about.
B) If we complain we have to make sure we're not tempting Christ.
C) If we murmur we will never see the way of escape.

Chapter X.
Shout!

1) When we see Joshua 6: we see what the real power is. When we use the same weapon what will happen for us?

  A) Nothing, it was just an instrument that God used that one time.

  B) Not yielding to what you see and having a victory shout will crumble the walls of opposition for you too.

  C) It was sound waves and the vibration of the army's marching that actually toppled the walls so unless we duplicate it exactly it won't work for us.

2) In Acts 4: 24, 31 we see a prayer of power. When trials hold you bound. How do you need to pray in these circumstances?

  A) With all sincerity.

  B) Raise your voice above the turmoil of your mind. We call it violent prayer.

  C) Pray until you have well covered the problem.

3) In Matthew 11: 12 we find a new error in faith. How do we take the kingdom of Satan by force?

  A) By doing as Jesus and picking up a sword.

  B) By crying out to God for help?

  C) By praying and taking authority over the situation.

4) In Genesis 49: 8- 12, Judah means praise. The crouching lion is indicative of wisdom and patience. This is all a product of what praise will do. Because of this heritage of praise where else will praise lead you?

  A) To the poorhouse.

  B) Keep you on the run from your enemies.

  C) You will end up in leadership.

Chapter XI.

A Time To Stand!

1) According to Judges 6: 11- 13; when the enemy looks stronger and more powerful than we are, why should we stand firm?

   A) When you're going to die, might as well look good doing it.
   B) If we run, we might have missed the opportunity to be a David.
   C) The enemy that is starring you in their face may not be your enemy but your ally.

2) In Psalm 35: 1- 4 we find a scripture that rejoices the heart and levitates the soul. He speaks to us to strengthen the weak hands and feeble knees. Those who are fearful we are to speak faith to them and strengthen then with hope. As ministers who's going to do this for us?

   A) No one
   B) Anyone that will
   C) We can do it to ourselves.

Chapter XII.
How Do I Handle Domestic Disturbances

1) In Matthew 5: 23-24, which of the following people are told to leave their gift at the altar?

  a) The person who has wronged another person
  b) The person who had not done wrong
  c) The person to whom someone has hard feelings against

2) What type of person does Proverbs 18:19 tell us is harder to be won than a strong city?

  a) A brother offended
  b) An angry man
  c) A lost sinner

3) In Genesis 43, the story of Joseph yearning with great love for his brothers, what important lesson does that teach us in today's church?

  a) The importance of family ties
  b) Ministry in foreign lands
  c) Love and restoration of our brothers and sisters in the church

4) According to Matthew 18:12-17, what is the procedure for dealing with a brother or sister in Christ who has wronged you?

  a) Take them to court
  b) Ignore the problem
  c) Talk to them alone, then with a witness if necessary, and finally if needed take it to the church

5) According to 1 Corinthians 12: 25-27, what should we do to prevent division in the body?

  a) Suffer with those who suffer, rejoice with those who rejoice
  b) Go to a different church if you disagree with someone
  c) Stay home when someone upsets you

6) Which of the following statements does 11 Thessalonians 3: 6 tell us how to handle troublemakers in the body?

a) Go to any length to make them happy
b) Stay away from them
c) Drag them to the altar for prayer

7) Sinners do by nature what is sin; a Christian does by nature what is righteousness; so if a leader in the church is walking in open sin, then we need to_____?

a) Try to win them back to Christ
b) Tell everyone you know about the problem
c) Just hope they will change

8) According to 1 Corinthians 16:22, "If any man love not the Lord Jesus Christ, let him be anathema maranatha." what does the phrase anathema maranatha mean?

a) Jesus is Lord
b) The anthem of the Lord
c) Cursed unto the coming of our Lord

9) According to 1 Timothy 5: 19- 20, how many witnesses are necessary to bring an accusation before an elder?

a) Five
b) Two or three
c) One

10) As a leader, we have to live closer, straighter, and stronger than the average person, what other important quality is needed in leaders?

a) Being transparent
b) Being in a hurry
c) Being happy all the time

11) What 3 things are we told in 1 Timothy 4: 9-16 to concentrate on?

a) Blood, water, and earth
b) Reading, exhortation and doctrine
c) Work, recreation and sleep

12) One of the greatest joys that a leader can hope for that makes it worth all the pain and effort involved is_____?

a) Souls being saved
b) Going to church
c) Prayer meeting

Chapter XIV.
Learning To Pray

1) We should confess our faults as commanded in James 5:11-16 to_____?

    a) One to another
    b) Prayer warriors
    c) The Pastor

2) According to 1 Timothy 2:8 and Philippians 4:6; God says we should pray_____and_____?

    a) Everywhere; about everything
    b) In church; during prayer
    c) At home; when in need

3) What is one of the primary advantages to praying together in a group?

    a) Love
    b) Strength
    c) To get together to talk

4.) According to 1 Timothy 2:8, what are we told to pray without

    a) Music
    b) Noise
    c) Erathand doubting

5) How often should we pray?

    a) Continually
    b) Once a day
    c) When we go to church

6) There are 6 very important events that took place in the book of Acts between the chapters 2 and 9. What one aspect of the Christian life made the most impact on these events?

    a) Reading the bible
    b) Prayer meeting
    c) Singing

7) Why does God desire us to pray?

  a) He created us to commune with him
  b) So that we seem religious
  c) So he knows what we want

8) According to James 5: 14-15, we should call for the elders of the church and have them anoint us with oil and the pray for healing. Why?

  a) To make them feel important
  b) Our faith is stronger when we combine it with others
  c) The oil heals us

9) What is one of the most wonderful results of praising and bringing honor to the name of Jesus?

  a) We partake of his wonderful nature and Spirit
  b) We never get sick
  c) We always get instant answers

10) Prayer is a_____.

  a) One way conversation
  b) Two way conversation
  c) Quiet conversation

11) What assurance do we have from God according to 1 John 5: 14-15, and Matthew 7:10 regarding prayer?

  a) We know that he hears us and desires to answer our prayer
  b) We need to pray with confidence that he hears us
  c) We know that he desires good things for us.
  d) All of the above

12) What is the most important thing we must possess to receive answers to our prayer?

  a) Love offerings
  b) Faith
  c) Courage

13) What is one of the greatest reasons for unanswered prayer?

    a) Asking with the wrong motives
    b) Not praying long enough
    c) Not praying loud enough

14) How can we be absolutely sure that a blessing has come from God and not the world or Satan?

    a) Blessings only come from God.
    b) It will come with peace, if it comes from God.
    c) It will come with some confusion

Chapter XV.
What Happens When I Die?

1) What religious group in the bible believed that death was final?

  a) Pharisees
  b) Sadducees
  c) Prophets

2) How does the Lord view the death of his saints according to Psalms 116: 15?

  a) Precious
  b) Sad
  c) Lonely

3) According to Matthew 28:20, which of the following statements is true?

  a) Believer's will never again be without the lord's presence, even in death
  b) We will be without the lord's presence until the resurrection
  c) Once we die, we are forever separated from the lord

4) To what is death referred to seventeen times in the New Testament?

  a) Torment
  b) Loneliness
  c) Sleep

5) Which statement best describes hell, according to Luke 16: 19-26?

  a) Hell is just a scare tactic
  b) Hell is only going to contain demons, no people
  c) Hell is a holding facility until the great White Throne Judgment

6) According to 1 Thessalonians 4: 13-18, do we go directly to heaven when we die?

  a) Yes
  b) No
  c) Only if we have never sinned

7) God did not create hell for man and does not desire any man to go to hell, so who will go to hell?

  a) Those that do not believe and accept Jesus as their Saviour
  b) Everyone goes there until Jesus comes again
  c) Those that do the worst sins

8) Where is the ultimate destination of unrepentant sinners according to Revelation 20: 7- 15?

  a) Hell
  b) Lake of fire
  c) Grave

9) According to Matthew 12:34 and 5:28, where does sin begin?

  a) In the heart
  b) In the mouth
  c) In our actions

10) Exodus 14: 17, 23-26 is a perfect example of what the end result of a hardened heart is?

  a) Running from God
  b) Being turned over to a reprobate mind to believe a lie and be damned
  c) Death

Answer Key

For

"For The Perfecting Of The Saints"

Chapter One
Is That You Lord?
Introduction

1) B) Let them be doomed to destruction?
2) B) Once God imparts his blessings upon us he can't reverse it. It is left to us to receive or reject it.
(All the other answers sound good, but this one is accurate.)
3) B) If we feel his peace is in us, his Spirit keeps us faultless.
4) B) It is inspired of God, written by man, and proofread by the Holy Ghost for perfection.

Is That You Lord?
I. The Word Of God.

1) A) To make you perfect.
2) B) So you won't be made ashamed.
3) A) To accurately interpret the heart of God.
4) A) Learning to speak lovingly and be established.
5) C) That i can rescue myself and those that will listen to me.
6) B) If you die in sin your life as a Christian won't be remembered.
7) A) The bible is still being written by you and me.
   B) The Holy Ghost is the giver of insight and direction for your life.
   C) if God imparts it we are to write it.
8) B) We have a high priest (Jesus) who can feel our problems.

Is That You Lord?
II. Small Still Voice

1) C) He speaks so softly we have to be attentive to hear him.
2) C) If God will reveal the word to even children then the only way they can receive it is with a soft calm voice.
3) B) Harsh words stir up anger and rebellion.
4) Both B) and C) are true. Jesus said if you were his then you would hear his voice.

B) If they can't hear it's because they are not Christians.

C)they have not learned to walk in the peace and comfort of God.

5) C) If the Holy Ghost of God lives in you then you hear from the inside out not the outside in. He doesn't have to shout above the outside world's noises.

Is That You Lord?
III. Impressions

1) C) The Holy Ghost lives in you thus he simply draws you.

2) A) The Lord sets hindrances in our path and troubles our spirit.

3) B) The anointing brings to remembrance the scriptures to confirm what others are telling and teaching me. By this I know the Spirit of truth from the spirit of error.

Is That You Lord?
IV. Prophecy

1) C) Build up, encourage, confirm.

2) C) They will realize God sees into their hearts and nothing is hid from God.

3) A) Confidence to fight spiritual warfare.

Is That You Lord?
V. Audible Voice

1) B) From heaven

2) A) I guess it all depends whether God wants anyone else to hear.

Is That You Lord?
VI. Visions

1) B) Two.

2) A) Any believer.

3) B) As much as our faith will allow.

4) B) Closed eye vision.

5) A) Of course if it's the Lord's will.
6) C) No, we are the real enemy.

Is That You Lord?
VII. Dreams

1) A) Those unfolding immediately and those unfolding somewhere in the future.
2) B) Yes, whether now or in the future.

Is That You Lord?
VIII. Revelations

1) C) So the world can't use the word to the destruction of their souls.
2) C) Mankind.
3) A) No, the revelation power of God comes by faith and some just don't have it. See James 2: 14- 26
4) C) Our faith and our ability to act on what we hear..
5) C) Confidence. See Isaiah 54: 17

Is That You Lord?
IX. Visitations

1) B) Humility and loss of all physical strength.
2) B) Loss of all strength and great fear. See II Timothy 1: 7
3) B) Confidence.
4) B) A peace.
5) A) troubled &
   C) confusion.
6) A) our angels will carry us to Paradise.

Chapter Two
Angels Unawares!

1) C) The eyes of their understanding was closed. To recognize Jesus is to know his spirit just as we recognize each other by the Spirit of God in us. We can see someone who has backslidden and many times won't recognize them.
2) B) Abraham.

3) B) Their thirst for sin is as great as their determination to commit it.

4) A) They are always male.

5) B) Revelation of the word is our inheritance as saints of God.

6) A) The word "For" changes the meaning. They not only minister to us also for us.

Chapter Three
The Ministry Of Great Love!

1) A) They have stress, fear or anxiety in their lives.

2) B) It is the opposite of Genesis 3: 17- 19.

3) A) He hears us and grants our prayers.
   B) He gives us confidence.
   C) We know his will.

4) B) Yes in Proverbs 17: 17

5) A) Because a true minister is not there to be seen or exalted.

6) B) 2, death and hell.

7) B) If you love, you will be hurt and wounded by others.

8) c) all.

9) A) Be hurt.

10) A) To lay down my life and desires.

Insert For Ministry Of Great Anointing
Next Step Anointing!

1) B) They were terrified because of the power of love that Jesus flowed in.

2) C) Look at me.

3) A) He spoke with such authority of love that not only did the parents believe but also they were comforted.

4) A) His suffering crushed Peter's faith.
   B) Peter realized he wasn't ready to die for Jesus.
   C) Jesus in all his suffering had such an anointing that one look would reveal sin and purge hearts.

5) C) Homeless man.

6) A) Fear.

7) B) Clothed

8) B) They had the wrong spirit.

9) C) So the anointing can minister in our place.

Chapter Four
Cuttings, Paintings And Piercing?

1) B) Printing marks

2) A) They are given to vile affections.

    B) They dishonor their bodies between themselves.

    C) Driven by the lust of their heart.

3) A) To get a pagan God's attention.

4) A) The sight of tattoos and so on give the indication that an individual enjoys the torture of their body, which is just wrong.

5) B) Having peace and satisfaction will reflect in our respect for our bodies.

Chapter Five
A Little Wager Never Hurt Anybody?

1) A) Giving heed to the flesh and its desires.

    B) You receive a spirit of bondage into your life.

    C) We cease killing the lust of the flesh.

2) B) Love

3) B) Not expecting something for nothing.

4) C) Let's get drunk and forget our troubles.

Chapter Six
Promissory Notes, Interest And Lending

1) A) Co-signer.

2) B) Regret.

3) A) If you sign for a loan, make sure you get collateral.

4) B) Charging of interest or fees.

5) A) Yes.

6) A) It is an abomination and you will not have eternal life because you have sinned.

7) A) God will withhold his hand of blessing from your family and your great-great grand children.

8) A) yes, this is not charging interest on lent money to individual Christians. This is building businesses and being a sower into business ventures.

9) B) Yes, this is being paid a fair price for rental fees. If it is broken then we cannot charge them for the item broken.

Chapter Seven
Tragedy To Triumph, The Book Of Ruth

1) C) Thrice
2) B) Twice verses 3 & 5
3) C) Fifty verse 7
4) B) 42, because the prophets and parents did not teach them to respect God's anointed due to the fact they were guilty of mocking Elisha also.
5) A) It wasn't.
6) C) Isaac Genesis 22: 7- 18
7) B) Pleasant friend
8) A) Plant to the four corners of the field and only harvest the inner circle of it once leaving a triangle in each corner untouched.
9) B) Lot
10) A) They were the result of date rape and incest. The daughters got their father lot drunk and date raped him.
11) C) There was no condition set forth in that they could come into the congregation of the Lord. They were banded for eternity.
12) Both A) She wasn't paying attention to what she was doing.
  C) Boaz came into his field to check on the welfare of his workers.
13) C) She was a hard worker. See verse 7
14) C) We will reap in areas we did not labor. Verse 38
15) A) When God speaks to us he won't embarrass or humiliate us. See the definition of "Reproach her not."
16) A) Be positive, be not lazy, and God will reward.
Any questions about B), see James 2: 18- 19.
Any questions about C) read Romans 10: 11 & Hebrews 6: 10. Nothing about success or failure, just giving God your all in faith. Ecclesiastes 9: 10
17) A) A ho
(This is just a play on modern words, like calling him a whore)
18) C) Sexual climaxes both male and female.

Chapter Eight
Grasshoppers And Locust; The Mini Giants Of Gods!

1) A) God can take the base things that are despised to confound the things that are mighty.
2) B) They all fly and graze together in unity.
3) C) They reap where they bestowed any labor.

Chapter Nine
I Will Not Murmur Because The Axe Head Swims!

1) B) They spoke their own deaths. God indeed let them die without seeing freedom.
2) B) It delays his blessings.
3) A) When we complain it's not our circumstances we are complaining about, it's God we're complaining about.
   C) If we murmur we will never see the way of escape.

Chapter Ten
Shout!

1) B) Not yielding to what you see and having a victory shout will crumble the walls of opposition for you too.
2) B) Raise your voice above the turmoil of your mind. We call it violent prayer.
3) C) By praying and taking authority over the situation.
4) C) You will end up in leadership.

Chapter Eleven
A Time To Stand!

1) C) The enemy that is starring you in their face may not be your enemy but your ally.
2) C) We can do it to ourselves.

Chapter Twelve
How Do I Handle Domestic Disturbances

1) B) The person who had not done wrong
2) A) A brother offended
3) C) Love and restoration of our brothers and sisters in the church.

4) C) Talk to them alone, then with a witness if necessary, and finally if needed take it to the church
5) A) Suffer with those who suffer, rejoice with those who rejoice.
6) B) Stay away from them.
7) A) Try to win them back to Christ.
8) C) Cursed unto the coming of our Lord.
9) B) Two or three.
10) A) Being transparent.
11) B) Reading, exhortation and doctrine.
12) A) Souls being saved.

Chapter Fourteen
Learning To Pray

1) A) One to another.
2) A) Everywhere; about everything.
3) B) Strength.
4) C) Wrath and doubting.
5) A) Continually.
6) B) Prayer meeting.
7) A) He created us to commune with him.
8) B) Our faith is stronger when we combine it with others.
9) A) We partake of his wonderful nature and Spirit.
10) B) Two way conversation.
11) D) All of the above.
12) B) Faith.
13) A) Asking with the wrong motives
14) B) It will come with peace, if it comes from God.

Chapter Fifteen
What Happens When I Die?

1) B) Sadducees
2) A) Precious
3) A) Believer's will never again be without the Lord's presence, even in death
4) C) Sleep

5) C) Hell is a holding facility until the great White Throne Judgment
6) B) No
7) A) Those who do not believe and accept Jesus as their Saviour
8) B) Lake of Fire
9) A) In the heart
10) B) Being turned over to a reprobate mind to believe a lie and be damned

Note From The Author

This is one in a series of books by me, Rev. Ronald Sanders. Each of these books began as studies that have been taught or preached during the now 35 years of ministry (2010). I guess a good way to start explaining how these revelations of God arrived at your doorstep would be to explain the history behind writing them.

I was saved and Holy Ghost filled at age 5 in a Jacksonville, Florida Church Of God (Pastor Braddock) in 1964. God called me into a healing ministry at age 5. As a child I was able to pray for my Mother, Aunt to Dr. Charles Stanley, who was dying from a ruptured artery in her left temple from an automobile wreck. God so graciously stopped the bleeding and spared her life. My prayer was simple, "God stop the bleeding, don't let my mama die," and he did.

We moved to North Carolina at age 10. my mom Irene E. Stanley Sanders, (Aunt of Dr. Charles Stanley) was left to raise four children by faith. There were many days that someone from the South Rocky Mount Church Of God felt led of God to leave groceries on our door-step. This church was instrumental in my growth and longing for more of God as a youth. With such great mentors as Pastor A.E. Lewis, Pastor James Blackmon, Pastor Paul Tetter, Pastor E.L. Newton, Pastor Edger Rainer, James Pittman, Donald Melvin, Tommy Starling, Bro. B C Blanton and Sister Betty Blanton, Bill Benfield, Al Dunbar, Rev. Jerry Thomas, Pastor Tony and Wanda Bossolona, Rev. Arthur Manning, Wayne White, Rev. Sam Johnson, Grace Johnson, Helen Johnson and this list goes on. Mom was disabled for many years. She was a woman of great faith, always believing God to provide the necessities of life. Thank God, for those who were obedient to the voice of God, being a source of hope that helped our family to survive during the many years of hardship? I thank God for everyone in the church and owe you a debt of gratitude that I will never be able to repay. My books will carry this page of gratitude for these Christians that have influenced my life. South Rocky

Mount Church Of God at the age of 13 got me involved in the witnessing program, and at age 16, I was asked to teach Sunday School to the senior shut-ins who were not able to be in church because of health and age. Caressa Dunbar, Star Pope and the C.E. Department encouraged me to step into that calling. I consider myself so blessed to have all the influences that kept me in the house of God all these years. These have given me the foundation of the word that would catapult me into the next phase of the ministry.

In 1980, I was introduced to ten people that would transform my life as a minister of the gospel of Jesus Christ forever. These were Pastor Gerald & Stella Parker, Apostle Ann & Johnny Baines (My Spiritual Father and Mother), Pastor Jean & Winston Matthews, Pastor Kenneth Emanuel, Pastor Garreth Johnson and Apostle Wallace (Sonny) Heflin Jr. of Calvary Pentecostal Campground in Ashland Virginia. I saw by example how to flow in the Spirit and allow God to use me through these ten. They were the guides into what the ministry would become and is today. I gained an understood of the anointing of God and how to be obedient that the miraculous would become a part of this ministry. I launched into new avenues of ministry through these men and women of God. I began to preach because of the anointing that was imparted from them. I can truly say that God has directed my footsteps to create in me his heart's desire. I am so overwhelmed and honored to be used of God. As you can see through life, I had nothing, and expected little to happen, yet God would not allow all that these great men and women of God had instilled into my life fall to the ground fruitless. Thank God for his unmerited favor!

Pastors David and Ann Pridgen and I traveled on missionary journeys both at home and abroad seeing thousands saved, healed and set free by God's marvelous power. Pastor David and Ann Pridgen and I have street ministered from Rocky Mount to New Orleans, LA. Seeing many saved and healed. I have been in teaching ministry since 1975 and preaching the gospel of Christ since 1980. I live my life as not to embarrass all those who have been such a tremendous influence upon my life.

I have watched my biological dad in a drunken stupor try to kill my mom on several occasions but unsuccessfully. Once using a 22 cal. Remington pump rifle, this misfired 19 times. The horrors of watching him hang her by the neck yet he was unable to take what did not belong to him. She was blood bought, and heaven bound. I learned early in life "That no weapon formed against thee shall prosper." In August 1983, I was involved in a wreck that broke my neck and died. I watched my spirit leave my body. On the stretcher, the next day I watched the 2 sets of x-rays as God placed all the bones back in place. One year earlier, February 1982, I got shot through the head by an intruder breaking into my home on Villa St. in Rocky Mount, NC, and God instantly healed me. Having passed through death four times, I can testify that death to the saint is such sweet peace. These writings come from a long life of having to stand by faith, just to live and not die. Thus, our perspective of God's unfailing Word may seem a little more radical than normal.

In 2000, I was blessed with my gift from God, in marrying Lyn Sanders, known to all as "Babylove." God has truly blessed our life, and Lyn has been a soul mate to me. She is active in ministry with me and we look forward to God doing greater miracles in the days to come. Together we have founded Faith Builders International Conference in 2007. We have grown to over 341 churches and we are in four other countries. In 2015, we launched Faith Builders International Bible College. Teaching the revelations God has imparted into our lives to them who would receive. Never in our wildest imagination could I have dreamed of being where we are right now in ministry. May God richly bless you!

Your Servant in Christ Jesus
Rev. Ronald Sanders